Youth Justice

Youth Justice
Ideas, Policy, Practice

Roger S. Smith

WILLAN
PUBLISHING

Published by

Willan Publishing
Culmcott House
Mill Street, Uffculme
Cullompton, Devon
EX15 3AT, UK
Tel: +44(0)1884 840337
Fax: +44(0)1884 840251
e-mail: info@willanpublishing.co.uk
website: www.willanpublishing.co.uk

Published simultaneously in the USA and Canada by

Willan Publishing
c/o ISBS, 5824 N.E. Hassalo St,
Portland, Oregon 97213-3644, USA
Tel: +001(0)503 287 3093
Fax: +001(0)503 280 8832
e-mail: info@isbs.com
website: www.isbs.com

First published 2003

ISBN 1-84392-021-2 (paper)

British Library Cataloguing-in-Publication Data
A catalogue record for this book is available from the British Library

Project management by Deer Park Productions
Typeset by GCS, Leighton Buzzard, Beds
Printed and bound by T.J. International, Padstow, Cornwall

Contents

New starts, false dawns and lost opportunities

Motives

This book was born out of a profound sense of frustration at the state of the youth justice system in England and Wales. This frustration is epitomized by the depressing trend of the current era towards an ever greater reliance on the most punitive means of control available, which permeates the entire spectrum of youth justice practice from early interventions for minor misdemeanours to custodial sentencing for 'persistent young offenders'. In directly observable terms, the consequences have been damaging (Lyon *et al.*, 2000; Goldson, 2002) and, in some cases, tragic (Bright, 2002).

The machinery of youth justice seems to have developed a logic and a momentum of its own, producing ever more expensive, irrational and counter-productive outcomes. It is supposed to be about 'preventing youth crime', and yet it relies increasingly heavily on custodial solutions, which are known to be criminogenic. It is supposed to be 'evidence-based', promoting good practice on the basis of 'what works'; so why does it ignore the lessons of recent decades, which demonstrate the value of informal, problem-solving and inclusive solutions? It is supposed to be 'just'; so why does it persistently ignore the criticisms of international human-rights organizations that condemn its failure to meet accepted standards (United Nations Committee on the Rights of the Child, 2002)?

My present frustrations are compounded by my past experience as a practitioner and manager, working in a setting where many positive lessons were learned. From that context I have been able to draw the conclusion that a liberal and humane approach to delivering youth justice is both desirable and achievable; and it may even be acceptable to the community as a whole. We need not reach for 'the big stick' as a matter of course. However, much of the progress made during the 1980s has been lost, and I suppose that the motivation for writing this book lies in a wish to understand the reasons for these retrogressive trends, in order to begin to think again about a way forward. The appearance of conviction and inevitability about much of current practice might appear daunting, but it can surely be no more so than the prospects facing those working in what was then the 'juvenile justice' system under the Thatcher government at the beginning of the 1980s. Optimism is called for in order to begin to sketch out the renewed possibilities for progressive change in policy and practice in the present day.

The book itself is constructed in three parts, which effectively equate to past, present and future perspectives, although each is approached in a rather different way, as will become clear.

Changing Fashions?

The recent history of youth justice provides evidence of some remarkable contrasts, as well as some significant continuities (for example, the persistence of the 'tariff'), and it therefore provides a good basis for making sense of current experience.

The first chapter assesses the developments of the 1980s, when an ostensibly right-wing and authoritarian government presided over one of the most benign and liberal periods ever witnessed in the administration of youth justice. An emerging pattern of increased use of diversion (cautioning and informal action) was paralleled by a substantial decline in the use of custody and the emergence of a thriving body of 'alternative' community programmes. These tends can be accounted for in a number of ways, as the chapter demonstrates, including the creativity of practitioners, economic expediency and political good fortune. The important lessons to be taken from this era include the value of imaginative 'bottom up' initiatives, the evidence that a strategy based on 'minimum intervention' can be both effective and politically acceptable, and the erroneous nature of many assumptions about popular opinion.

By stark contrast, the 1990s saw the emergence of youth justice as a political football, with the result that it, and all those within its ambit, fell prey to populist gimmickry; a period of radical retrenchment ensued, characterized by the depressing and misleading slogan 'prison works'. That this assertion was unsupportable, but still became conventional wisdom, captures the essence of a decade characterized by a spirit of prejudice, ignorance and hostility towards the young. The consequences were dramatic, with a complete reversal of previous achievements and, even as crime rates were reported to be falling, a significant increase in the use of custody for young people. The professional skills of youth justice practitioners were neutered, and the principled 'systems management' of the 1980s was replaced by a technocratic managerialism with no principles or independent rationale.

In concluding this part, I shall seek to demonstrate that a change of government in 1997, and a much trumpeted reform programme, crystallized in the Crime and Disorder Act 1998, appear to have done no more than continue these trends, in some respects intensifying them, focusing on spurious questions of efficiency and effectiveness, while apparently overlooking the continuing injustices of discriminatory interventions and the unnecessary use of custody. The rhetoric of radical reform has created unrealistic expectations of dramatic short-term gains, in youth justice as in other areas, such as the health service. Of itself, this generates all sorts of systemic pressures, which appear to have resulted in a series of contrived outcomes to meet the political agenda. The logic of these demands results in an ever-increasing reliance on mechanisms of control, which are expected to produce immediate, tangible and predictable results. In concentrating on these superficial issues, however, more fundamental principles and key values are lost or compromised. The appearance of effectiveness becomes all that matters (Pratt, 2000).

The Machinery of Control

In the second part, I will move on to consider the implications of the New Labour reform programme in more detail, focusing on the three levels of policy, delivery systems and practice. One of the advantages in assessing the kind of intensive reform programme witnessed under the Labour government after 1997 is that it has generated a very substantial amount of policy documentation and other material. Thus, Chapter 4 is based on a detailed exploration of the initiatives put in place to deliver the reform programme. The National Standards for Youth Justice, promulgated by the Youth Justice Board (2000), are subjected to detailed scrutiny, as is the performance of the Board itself. In addition, the implications of the emergence of the new delivery mechanisms, the Youth Offending Teams, will be considered. The chapter concludes that these developments collectively represent a significant extension of 'corporatist' (Pratt, 1989) and 'managerialist' tendencies, but that these are not uniform in their impact. Contradictions between aims and principles are likely to lead to unpredictable and unplanned outcomes, while opportunities for the (re)development of progressive practice will still exist 'between the cracks'.

Chapter 5 moves from the level of strategy and structures to consider the implications of reform for youth justice practice on the ground. It relies, to a large extent, on a detailed examination of the extensive body of evaluative material generated in response to the reform programme heralded by the Crime and Disorder Act 1998. This material is character-ized by an emerging pattern of 'routinized control', which subsumes practitioners' professional skills and participants' distinctive interests under the demands of a highly prescriptive, centralized legislative agenda. Early claims of success for the reform programme have also been subjected to extensive and pointed criticism, it is noted, generating a highly charged and polarized debate about the merits of recent develop-ments. The chapter concludes that excessively tight prescription will, in time, prove to be unsustainable at the level of practice, leading to a process of adaptation, and potentially a renewed spirit of resistance and creativity.

At this point I turn to the task of assessing the 'state of play', subjecting the evidence presented of early success attributed to the 'new youth justice' (Goldson (ed.), 2000) to more detailed scrutiny. The measures of success put in place (such as a reduction in delays) are found to be largely superficial and unconvincing. Indeed, the chapter notes that, if anything, the trends identified represent no more than a continuation of the 'toughening up' of the youth justice system evident in the 1990s. More young people are seen to be drawn into the formal networks of control, at an earlier age, for more minor transgressions (Jennings, 2002). The predictable consequence of this is a progressively more punitive pattern of interventions, supported, as it is, by the legislative expansion of punish-ment options. The use of increasingly sophisticated forms of control and punishment permeates the entire system, with the inevitable upshot that more young people experience periods of custodial detention. By focusing, too, on the impact of the reforms on specific groups, such as young women and young Black people, the discriminatory and op-pressive nature of youth justice practices is further highlighted here.

Rethinking Youth Justice

The final part of the book sets out to develop an appraisal of developments in youth justice in order to establish the basis for a more progressive refocusing of policy and practice. In order to set the scene for this, Chapter 7 takes a step back to formulate a theoretical framework for understanding our preoccupation with the intertwined issues of youth and disorder. The problematic nature of 'youth' itself is taken as the starting point, with a brief discussion of the issues of socialization and control surrounding adolescent transitions. This is related to broader structural questions of power and legitimacy, and the roles of law and justice, in achieving popular support for specific control strategies. From this basis, it will be argued, it is possible to sketch out the potential for the development of a particular technology of control, which is manifested in the specific machinery and practices of the youth justice system (see, for example, Foucault, 1979). Youth justice is likely, as a result, to be characterized by a pattern of routinized techniques of identification, assessment and targeted interventions, which claim to be scientifically based, empirically justified, and are thus regarded as normal.

Chapter 8, by contrast, explores the experiences and aspirations of a number of 'stakeholder' groups, who may be said to have a legitimate concern in the delivery of youth justice, including victims, young people, and ethnic minorities. These groups are found to share a number of concerns about the limitations of what is on offer, which can be summarized in the commonly held view that the system simply 'doesn't work'. Not only is this conclusion generally shared, but there also appears to be substantial common ground for the development of effective alternatives, based on principles of negotiation, rights and social inclusion. Complex and multi-faceted social phenomena require sensitive, creative and flexible responses, it is clear.

Finally I will turn to the task of sketching out some ideas for future development. The problems of youth justice are restated, in order to provide a baseline from which possible alternatives can be charted. I set out a series of principles that should underpin an effective youth justice system, before offering a range of policy, organizational and practice initiatives that could help to achieve these aims. Overall, it is concluded, youth justice needs to be characterized by a commitment to social as well as criminal justice. Problem-solving, minimum intervention, rights and inclusiveness need to be prioritized, in preference to routinized surveillance, monitoring and control.

Chapter 1

The 1980s: Margaret Thatcher – soft on crime

A Good Starting Point?

The choice of a starting point for any historical account is always an arbitrary one. This is no less the case in the present context. It would be possible to specify other dates, with equal validity (key legislation relating to young offenders was passed in the years 1969, 1948, 1933 and 1908, for example), so there is perhaps a need to offer some form of justification for the decision to begin the story around 1980.

To begin with, there is a need to find some sort of balance between what may be seen as an unhelpful 'foreshortening' effect, on the one hand, and questions about the value of any kind of historical account, on the other. It may be argued, for example, that to concentrate on the past 20 years or so gives an over-emphasis to relatively ephemeral contemporary developments (such as the *relatively* small recent decline in officially recorded crime figures, set against their inexorable rise over a century or more; Home Office, 2001b, p. 19). On the other side of the argument, it could be argued that an extended historical account has little to offer by way of practical assistance to hard-pressed agencies and practitioners, who are more concerned with effective delivery than achieving a deeper understanding of distant debates about the antecedents of the modern youth justice system.

However, in addition to the pragmatic justifications for trying to balance different interests, there are other, rather more positive reasons for focusing on the 20(ish)-year period since 1980. Notably, it has been a time of substantial change in policy and practice in youth justice, with a number of major pieces of legislation, a keen continuing public interest, a variety of imaginative and potentially valuable practice developments, and perhaps a broader sense of upheaval associated with the late 20th century and the transition to the new millennium.

While these themes may be common to the whole 20-year period, there is another sense in which this is a useful timespan to consider for our purposes. This relates to the evident contrast which can be drawn between the experiences of the 1980s and those of the 1990s (and, so far, beyond) in juvenile/youth justice (even the essential terminology has changed!). From this perspective there is a broader question as to what lessons can be learned from these divergent experiences, for practitioners, providers (agencies), policy-makers and even for academic interests (see also Haines and Drakeford, 1998). With this proposed demarcation for comparative purposes, a number of other possible 'critical points' are being implicitly rejected here, notably the change of government in 1997 (which, I shall argue, merely heralded a frenetic period of 'radical repackaging').

Clearly, in the light of wider historical and social factors, it would be unwise to suggest an absolute break between the 1980s and 1990s; nevertheless, a comparative approach will provide a helpful framework for our attempts to understand just what has been going on in youth justice recently.

Into the 1980s: The Policy Context

In looking back, it is almost inevitable that we will be tempted to make some fairly simplistic assumptions about the Thatcher era, and the implications for youth justice of an explicitly radical right-wing government. This was a time when the choices appeared fairly stark, and the sense of 'us' against 'them' (whichever side you were on) was a continuing theme in the world of social policy. Much of the official rhetoric of the time was confrontational, and appeared directed towards dealing decisively with fundamental perceived threats to core social values. Thus we heard references to the need to deal with 'the enemy within' alongside calls to rebuild and reinforce key institutions such as the family. This was an essentially ideological project, and one which left no room, it seemed, for weakness, sentimentality, or compassion.

These examples of ideological rhetoric were also paralleled by a number of significant events that appeared to provide concrete evidence of the political and social project being undertaken. Thus, the Falklands War (1982), the response to the Miners' Strike (1984–85), and later, in a different context, the Community Charge (Poll Tax) and Child Support Act all bore the hallmarks of this radical restatement of 'traditional values'. The emphasis on the essential character of 'Britishness', the integrity of the family, economic independence, and personal responsibility seemed to add up to a coherent whole, with little room for acknowledging difference, taking account of disadvantage, or excusing wrongdoing (Gamble, 1988). Confrontation between the state and marginalized groups became almost an annual feature of the decade, with major outbreaks recorded in 1981 and 1985 in particular (Davies, 1986). The 'riots' and the response to them were also characterized by a sense of ethnic conflict and a perceived threat from young Black people. In this political and ideological context, then, the 1980s might not seem a fertile decade for the emergence of creative initiatives or a liberalization of the system for dealing with youth crime.

Legislative and Policy Change: Targeting Young Offenders

Not only was there a spirit of authoritarianism in the broader government agenda, but there was also evidence of a more punitive shift in the sphere of youth justice itself. On taking office in 1979, the Conservative government announced its intention to establish the 'short, sharp shock' regime in two detention centres for 14–17 year olds, an experiment that was extended to a number of other custodial establishments, and eventually to all detention centres (Pitts, 1988).

There was also a reflection of this mood in the legislative changes in youth justice heralded by the White Paper *Young Offenders* (Home Office, 1981). In the language of the time, this represented a victory for 'justice' over 'welfare' (in contrast to the 1970s: see Thorpe *et al.*, 1980), and a move towards reinforcing the notion of individual responsibility consistent with the prevailing ideological agenda. While many had been arguing for an end to the confusing pattern of welfare and justice disposals that characterized the system previously (under the Children and Young Persons Act 1969), there was nevertheless a real sense of apprehension as to the outcome of the measures signposted by *Young Offenders*, and made law by the Criminal Justice Act 1982.

Specific measures that amplified these concerns included the Night Restriction Order and the Supervised Activity Order, which both appeared to represent a closer measure of control over young offenders (and over their supervisors in the social work and probation services), heightening the punitive aspects of intervention. Alongside these measures, the 1982

Act introduced a new sentence of Youth Custody to replace the indeterminate Borstal regime, and the Residential Care Order to offer courts a measure of control over what was ostensibly a 'welfare' disposal. The overall intention of these reforms appears to have been to promote a shift from a rehabilitative or correctional agenda towards an emphasis on retributive sentencing deterrence, and just deserts. This is important because it set the tone for practice at all levels of the justice system over the ensuing years. One might anticipate subsequent arguments by suggesting that the challenge under this type of regime was to define at what point a particular type of disposal was merited, rather than to think in terms of 'tailoring' interventions to individual circumstances or correctional aims.

Alongside the measures introduced by the 1982 Act, however, the government introduced a measure that turned out to be at least as significant, if not more so. The incoming 1979 Conservative government had a clear agenda of reducing both state spending and state interference in everyday life, and this was reflected even in its approach to youth crime. *Young Offenders* showed a concern with the levels of custody for juvenile offenders; and in the introduction of the Bill that became the Criminal Justice Act 1982, the Home Secretary (William Whitelaw) spoke of 'broadening and strengthening existing non-custodial provisions [to] assist the courts to avoid a custodial sentence except where one is absolutely necessary' (Nacro, 1987, p. 11). It has been suggested that the government agenda was driven, at least in part, by a concern to reduce the cost of imprisonment (Pitts, 1988); but whatever the motivation, in 1983 the Department of Health and Social Security launched its intensive Intermediate Treatment initiative (DHSS, 1983), and provided a sum of £15 million over three years to develop alternatives to custody under this scheme. The aim was to create an additional 4,500 places in the community for serious young offenders. As Hudson (1987) puts it, the era of 'net-widening' was to be succeeded by a period of 'net-strengthening', where community sentences would be expected to compete with their custodial equivalents to demonstrate similar levels of toughness and control over young people's behaviour.

Further evidence that government was seeking to balance cost savings with punitive interventions is offered by subsequent policy initiatives, including, notably, the influential Home Office Circular on 'cautioning' (Home Office, 1985), which promoted an increase in the use of options short of prosecution, including cautions and informal action by the police. Once again, this development was presaged by *Young Offenders*, which argued that 'juvenile offenders who can be diverted from the criminal justice system at an early stage in their offending are less likely to re-offend than those who become involved in judicial proceedings' (quoted in

9

Nacro, 1987, p. 15). The 1985 Circular strengthened this message and encouraged the use of a variety of options by which offenders could make amends for their wrongdoing, including involvement in local youth activities, making an apology, direct or indirect reparation or voluntary supervision. Indeed, the Circular took the principle of diversion one stage further, by encouraging the use of informal disposals to deal with offences, in order to avoid the 'net-widening' potential of indiscriminate use of formal cautions.

The combined effect of these policy initiatives, stemming from the same roots in the 1980 White Paper, has been described as one of 'bifurcation' (see, for example, Pickford, 2000), whereby governments can get 'tough and soft simultaneously'. The redefinition of a relatively small group of offenders as 'dangerous and threatening' enables a distinction to be made between them and the great majority of offenders who may be wayward, misguided or 'easily led'. By taking this approach, the government was able to maintain its reputation as tough on crime, while at the same time keeping costs down and relieving pressures on the system.

By the second half of the decade, the government felt able to extend this policy strategy further with the publication of a Green Paper, *Punishment, Custody and the Community* (Home Office, 1988), which reiterated a twin-track approach to dealing with crime in its first paragraph. Stating that a custodial sentence was the right decision for many offenders, and emphasizing the government's commitment to crack down on violent crimes and lenient sentences, the paper also observed that

> for other, less serious offenders, a spell in custody is not the most effective punishment. Imprisonment restricts offenders' liberty, but it also reduces their responsibility; they are not required to face up to what they have done or to make any recompense to the victim or the public. (Home Office, 1988, p. 1)

The phrase 'punishment in the community' was introduced to allay concerns that offenders might be getting off lightly, while emphasis was also placed on the correctional and restorative aspects of the proposed strategy. In this way the government sought to extend to offenders of all ages the lessons learned, in previous years, from dealing with young offenders.

This commitment was underlined in the ensuing White Paper, *Crime, Justice and Protecting the Public* (Home Office, 1990b), which laid the foundations for the Criminal Justice Act 1991. In this respect, the policy trends of the 1980s extended beyond the end of the decade, and it was a year or two yet before signs of a reversal emerged. It has been argued, for example, that the 1991 Act represented the epitome of the 'due process' approach to dealing with youth crime (Haines and Drakeford, 1998). Provisions such as unit fines, compensation orders and the de-emphasizing of previous convictions in sentencing were examples of a philosophy that sought to introduce a greater degree of equity into the system, and at the same time maintained a focus on the offence rather than the offender. Interestingly, this sort of perspective is consistent with an emphasis on offence resolution and expiation, as much as deterrence or retribution.

The Changing Face of Practice: New Paradigms?

The relationship between policy and practice is never straightforward, and there is no reason to assume that the kind of changes outlined above had any kind of direct influence on the conduct of youth justice in the 1980s. Indeed, it is just as likely that policy follows practice rather than vice versa; and there are many examples of policy change which have no real influence on practical outcomes. However, there is evidence of a series of practice developments during the 1980s that were effective and influential, including the emergence of diversion, and the refocusing of IT (Intermediate Treatment). As we shall see, despite their rather different points of intervention, these initiatives shared a number of key characteristics, including a commitment to 'minimum intervention', a 'systems management' perspective and an orientation towards dealing with 'offences' rather than 'offenders'.

Diversion in practice

Cautioning as a way of dealing with relatively minor offences by young people had been part of the portfolio available to justice agencies (particularly the police) since the 1960s, and an expansion in its use was encouraged as early as 1968 by the White Paper *Children in Trouble* (Home Office, 1968). Following an initial increase in cautioning rates, however, usage remained fairly static until the early 1980s, when, largely as a result of practice developments, further rises were to be observed (Nacro, 1987).

Much of the growth in cautioning, and other pre-prosecution disposals, can be linked with developments initiated by agencies and youth justice practitioners, led by areas such as Hampshire and Northamptonshire (Nacro, 1987). The development of diversion in Northamptonshire, in particular, has been identified as a major achievement in youth justice, and it may be helpful here to consider this in more detail.

The first Juvenile Liaison Bureaux (JLBx) were established in Wellingborough and Corby in 1981. A further Bureau was set up in

Northampton in 1984, and eventually the scheme was extended to cover the whole county. The initiative was the result of a collaboration between senior members of the police and social services who were aware that existing processes for dealing with youth crime were inefficient and ineffective. The agreed aims underpinning the JLBx were:

1. To divert young people, wherever possible, away from the penal and welfare systems into informal networks of control, support and care.
2. To avoid the imposition of those forms of penalties and welfare intervention which tend to aggravate the very problem they seek to reduce.
3. To enable the agencies to respond to delinquent behaviour in ways which will reduce re-offending and enable young people to become responsible adults.
4. To encourage the normal institutions of society to respond constructively to adolescent behaviour.

(Hinks and Sloper, 1984)

As the vehicles for achieving these aims, the JLBx were established as arms-length multi-agency teams (police, social services, education, probation and youth service) with a responsibility for responding to police reports of alleged young offenders by offering alternatives to prosecution.

The consequences, in statistical terms at least, were fairly dramatic. The Wellingborough JLB, for example, saw an immediate halving of the local prosecution rate for young offenders, from 40% to 19% (Thorpe, 1984), and similar changes were subsequently observed elsewhere in the county (Stevens and Crook, 1986). In 1992, the JLBx received 2,399 reports from the police (relating to 1,389 young people), and only 9% of those referred were prosecuted (Bell et al., 1999). As a consequence, custodial sentences also declined significantly, and agencies were able to focus their resources on those more serious cases giving rise to real concern. Not only was there a demonstrable reduction in the use of punitive sanctions, and a corresponding increase in efficiency, but also the recorded crime rates for young people declined over this period (Home Affairs Committee, 1993).

Not only did the JLBx have a demonstrable impact in terms of headline figures, they also represented a significant change in practice, in terms of the ways in which the offences of young people were dealt with. In essence, this represented a shift in focus from the offender to the offence. At the time this could be seen as an attempt to move away from the rather sterile contemporary arguments about 'welfare versus justice' and to develop a new paradigm (Kuhn, 1970), represented by the term 'diversion' (Smith, R., 1987). This paved the way for a more informal, less pro-grammed, and more pragmatic approach to dealing with the problems that individual offences appeared to represent. The JLBx quickly built up a repertoire of interventions, for use as appropriate. These included, for example, promotion of youth work programmes for those whose offences might have been related to the lack of anything to do; liaison with, and reintegration of young people into, schools; the establishment of groups that attempted to help young people control their behaviour; and a range of interventions that focused on making amends for offences. This latter category included face-to-face meetings with victims, indirect apologies (usually by letter), meetings with managers of victimized shops and businesses, and indirect reparation (for example, work on a local nature conservation scheme). For example, in Corby:

> A number of young people became involved in burglaries of shops, clubs and other premises in a particular area of town. The sums involved, of damage and stolen property, put thoughts of com-pensation out of the question. As an alternative they were invited to contribute to a mural being painted at the under 5's centre in the neighbourhood. This work was carried out to everyone's satisfaction and under no compulsion. The offenders were not prosecuted. (Smith, R., 1987)

Interventions of this kind were based on a set of agreed principles:

- the reasons for intervention must be clear, explicit and have positive consequences for the offender or injured party;

- intervention should be directed towards resolving offences informally and treating the offender as a 'normal' adolescent;

- minimum appropriate intervention should be used;

- intervention should aim to increase the amount of community involvement and create a greater tolerance and understanding of the problem of juvenile crime;

- concern should be shown for the injured party as well as the offender. (Bell *et al.*, 1999)

The JLBx, then, developed over a number of years a form of 'negotiated justice' (Abel, 1982), which appeared to meet the needs of the community, the statutory agencies, and young offenders, in a way that was broadly beneficial to all concerned.

Of course, sometimes the intervention proposed did not work. Sometimes, satisfactory negotiated outcomes could not be agreed, some compensation arrangements were not kept to by young people, and some offenders reoffended, just as any other form of intervention to deal with youth crime has its failures. (Sadly, for example, the JLB staff in Corby were unable to satisfy the demand of the elderly victim of one offence that the young person concerned should: 'fuck off, and live somewhere else'). Despite these occasional failures, by most conventional measures the JLBx were successful. Reoffending rates were low, with only 30% of those reported by the police reoffending, and only 10% offending more than 3 times, according to an evaluation of offending patterns carried out in 1990 (Bell *et al.*, 1999). In addition, evaluations of 'user satisfaction' (Dignan, 1992) suggested that, for the most part, offence victims were not being exploited, and were happy with the outcomes of young people's efforts to make amends.

In addition to the various measures of success developed for evaluative purposes, the JLBx were also extensively researched (Thorpe, 1984; Cheetham, 1985; Reynolds, 1985; Blagg *et al.*, 1986; Davis *et al.*, 1989; Smith, R., 1989; Dignan, 1992). It is fair to say that the results of these studies were not uniformly positive, with particular concern focusing on two areas: the emergence of 'administrative justice', and the interests of offence victims. It was argued, for instance, that in some instances questions of guilt and innocence might be 'fudged' to the disadvantage of those alleged to have committed crimes. In other words, young people might be encouraged to admit offences in exchange for a caution, rather than contest the case.

At the same time, it was suggested that victims might be engaged in reparation schemes that would be unhelpful to them, either because of the additional stress caused, or because their rights to compensation might be compromised (Davis *et al.*, 1988; 1989). While there were undoubtedly risks of this kind associated with the JLBx, the evidence did not suggest that they were fatally flawed. As already noted, Dignan (1992), for example, found that victims' interests were generally respected, and were not subordinated to those of offenders; and the reductions in prosecutions and custodial sentences associated with the JLBx suggested that there was little evidence of 'net-widening' (Blagg, 1985).

Intensive Intermediate Treatment

The other area of youth justice practice to see major developments in the 1980s was Intermediate Treatment and its refocusing. Its earlier characteristics as a preventive programme available to a broad range of children and young people were largely superseded by the changes instigated by the Department of Health and Social Security's 1983 investment (Smith, D., 1999). The government's intention was that the new, intensified programmes proposed would meet the requirements of the Supervised Activity Order introduced in 1982.

In ideological terms, the practice developments that this gave rise to were supported by the arguments that 'justice' interventions should not be confused with 'welfare' objectives (Thorpe *et al.*, 1980), and that the proper focus for work with offenders should be their offending behaviour. Imposing intervention on any other grounds would, in effect, be to punish young people inappropriately, and would be likely to draw them into the penal system unfairly. Practitioners also believed that maintaining this explicit focus for IT would enhance its credibility and contribute to achieving the aim of establishing it as a genuine alternative to custody.

As Hudson puts it, the corollary of this was that intermediate programmes would have to exercise a sufficiently demanding regime to justify a degree of equivalence with locking children up: 'to be seen by sentencers as suitable ... community corrections have to incorporate appropriate degrees of control, and offer the promise of effectiveness in stopping the delinquent behaviour' (Hudson, 1987, p. 153). Programmes that stood as alternatives to detention centre or youth custody therefore would be likely to include requirements for regular (perhaps daily) attendance, elements of surveillance ('tracking'), behaviour-management courses, and possibly community work of some kind. Associated with this approach, too, was a commitment to 'breach' and returning to court young people who failed to comply with programme requirements. These programmes thus stood in stark contrast to the kind of preventive IT which had previously incorporated befriending programmes, youth activities and adventure holidays (such as mentoring) or even developments such as Youth Inclusion and Summer Splash in the early 2000s!). The £15 million investment by the Department of Health and Social Security enabled 110 projects to be established through partnerships with voluntary organizations, of which 95 survived beyond the initial 3-year funding period (Smith, D., 1999).

Critics have argued that the strategy adopted by practitioners of developing IT strictly as a custodial alternative was flawed for a number of reasons. Pitts (1988), for example, suggested that its proponents were, in effect, endorsing an increasingly authoritarian tendency within the justice system, while Hudson (1987) argued that Intensive IT projects had 'blurred the boundaries' with custody, and that the experiences of the two regimes had become increasingly similar. In her view, the strategy of trying to reduce the use of custody by mimicking its characteristics would not succeed, purely because custodial places would still remain available and would therefore be filled. Haines and Drakeford (1998) argue that the 'new orthodoxy' that characterized IT, and other forms of supervision of offenders in the 1980s, tended to focus very narrowly on offending behaviour, to the exclusion of other legitimate areas of concern, such as 'social, family or material circumstances'. They suggest that youth justice practice in the 1980s was characterized by:

> Offence confrontation work – reinforcing the unacceptability of offending;
>
> Developing a victim perspective – educating young people into the impact of their offending on victims;
>
> The offending curriculum – teaching young people how to avoid situations where offending can occur.
> (Haines and Drakeford, 1998, p. 66)

D. Smith (1999), on the other hand, suggests that the 'justice model' associated with the emerging alternatives to custody became associated with a kind of nihilism on the part of practitioners, and a rejection of the possibility of any kind of effective preventive or developmental inter-vention. As he also points out, the absence of any kind of principled objection to 'controlling' interventions reduces the ability of practitioners (and others) to advance objections to increasingly repressive regimes on the basis of clear and explicit anti-oppressive values.

However, set against these concerns are the arguments, seasoned with a degree of pragmatism, that such interventions could be judged a 'success' (Goldson, 1997). Individual programmes were held to be successful in reducing both the use of custody and offending rates (Children's Society, 1988). Smith attributes this success to the fact that:

> … youth justice workers in the 1980s developed methods of face-to-face work with young people in trouble which were broadly in line with what subsequent research and analysis have suggested is likely to be most effective in reducing offending. This is in a sense paradoxical, since many of these practitioners were strongly influenced by the view that had prevailed since the mid-1970s that 'nothing worked' (Smith, D., 1999, p. 153).

Haines and Drakeford (1998), too, argue that when programmes are devised and delivered in a way that is genuinely 'community-based', they are effective in reducing offending. Others, however, have taken a rather more equivocal view of the levels of success achieved, at least in reducing the levels of re-offending among young people undertaking IT programmes (Bottoms *et al.*, 1990; Bottoms, 1995).

Patterns of Change: Offending and Outcomes in the 1980s

We have identified changes in policy and practice associated with the 1980s (and early 1990s). It is important to set these in the context of the general pattern of offending, interventions and outcomes observed over the course of this decade.

Many commentators have argued that this was a very distinctive period in terms of the way in which the youth justice system operated (Smith, R., 1995, Goldson, 1997, Haines and Drakeford, 1998), and it is argued that this is reflected in the figures available from official sources – although we should always be conscious of the need to treat such figures with caution. According to The Children's Society (1993), the 1980s saw parallel declines in the number of known juvenile offenders, the use of prosecutions, and the custody rate. In one of those categories, known young offenders, the period 1977–1991 saw a dramatic decline as follows:

Table 1.1 Number of young people cautioned or found guilty of indictable offences per 100,000 population

Category		1977	1986	1991
Male	10–13	3,468	2,257	1,817
Male	14–17	7,456	7,048	6,378
Female	10–13	1,029	761	535
Female	14–17	1,553	1,706	1,973

Source: *Criminal Statistics England and Wales 1991* (Home Office, 1992)

With the exception of 14–17 year-old girls or young women, the official figures show a clear reduction in the number of young people being formally processed by the justice system over this period. While part of the reason for the fall in known juvenile offenders was demographic, the rate of known juvenile offenders per 100,000 of the population could also be seen to be falling, with the period 1980–90 showing a 16% decline. In addition, the proportion of all detected offences attributed to juveniles fell, from 32% in 1980 to 20% in 1991 (Children's Society, 1993).

However, it was also noted that, within this overall pattern of decline, some offences, such as car-related thefts – commonly associated with young offenders – were on the increase. Significant geographical variations in offending rates were also to be observed, reflecting a clear north–south divide, with higher rates associated with the less affluent northern police areas (Children's Society, 1993).

The risks involved in drawing any strong conclusions from known offending rates are further amplified by the recognition that a very small proportion of crime is even recorded by the police, and an even smaller proportion is detected and leads to offenders being processed. In its evidence to the Home Affairs Committee's inquiry into Juvenile Crime (Home Affairs Committee, 1993), the Association of Chief Police Officers argued that far from a decrease, there had actually been an increase in the number of offences committed by young people in the period 1980 to 1990. This was partly masked, in their view, by the increased use of informal disposals and diversionary measures, which meant that offences were being 'cleared up' but offenders were not being formally processed. In other words, the very success of diversionary strategies might have led to an apparent reduction in the numbers of 'known offenders'. In the Association's view, this was largely an illusion, arising primarily from the growth in the use of informal means of processing offences.

Explanations of the apparently differing trajectory of offending patterns for young women aged 14–17 have been fairly tentative, but might reflect an increasing 'awareness' of 'criminal girls' by the justice system (Worrall, 1999). In the same way that both behaviour and expectations appear to have shifted and affected the gender balance in educational outcomes, a parallel process might be evident in the criminal justice sphere.

Despite the lack of certainty about the meaning of the figures relating to young people's participation in crime, the trends they suggest were paralleled by developments in the treatment of young offenders over the course of the 1980s. According to The Children's Society (1993), cautioning rates increased in response to government policy at the same time as overall numbers processed by the justice system declined.

Thus, in the space of just over a decade, the ratio between these outcomes had changed dramatically for young offenders across the board. Whereas in 1977, prosecutions were brought and young people found guilty in 48% of cases, this proportion had declined to just 21% found guilty by 1991. While prosecution was clearly the preferred outcome for older young offenders (identified as 14–16 year olds before the Criminal Justice Act 1991) at the start of this period, this was clearly not the case by the beginning of the 1990s, with the group most likely to be prosecuted

Table 1.2 Changes in the numbers of young people cautioned or found guilty of indictable offences 1977–91 ('000s)

Found guilty		1977	1986	1991
Males	10–13	19.2	6.1	2.3
Males	14–16	59.8	37.7	17.2
Females 10–13		2.4	0.5	0.2
Females 14–16		7.6	3.7	2.2
Total		89.0	48.0	21.9

Cautioned		1977	1986	1991
Males	10–13	39.4	26.3	21.0
Males	14–16	31.3	43.6	41.0
Females 10–13		14.0	8.7	6.3
Females 14–16		10.5	14.9	14.8
Total		95.2	93.5	83.1

Source: *Criminal Statistics England and Wales 1991* (Home Office, 1992)

(14–16 year-old boys) being cautioned in 70% of cases. For girls and young women, despite the apparent change in patterns of offending, the likelihood of being prosecuted was even more remote.

While there has, for some time, been evidence of racial discrimination within the justice system, it is only comparatively recently that official statistics have been collected in a way that enables this to be identified. Although there was previously evidence of racial bias in decision-making structures, even in the context of cautions and informal disposals (Landau and Nathan, 1983, for example), official records shed little light on this issue until the 1990s, when Section 95 of the Criminal Justice Act 1991 imposed a requirement on criminal justice agencies to take matters of race into account when reporting on their activities.

Nevertheless, progressively fewer young people were being brought before the courts, both proportionally and in absolute terms, over this period. In addition, at the point of sentencing, courts were noted to be passing an increasing number of supervision orders, in line with the policy of promoting intensive community programmes (Children's Society,

1993). According to Haines and Drakeford (1998), the use of community-based supervision increased from 15% to 20% of all court disposals between 1980 and 1990. This was not a uniform pattern, with the proportion of custodial sentences remaining relatively stable over the earlier part of the decade; but the net effect appears to have been a displacement of custody by community alternatives.

The evidence of changing patterns in the processing of young offenders appears therefore to have had a consequential impact on the numbers being locked up, with the 1980s again seeing a significant fall in the use of custodial sentences.

Table 1.3 Numbers of young people aged 14–16 processed and sentenced to custody 1981–91 ('000s)

Date	Cautioned/found guilty (A)	Sentenced to custody (B)	(B) as a proportion of (A)
1981	113.7	7.7	6.8%
1986	99.8	4.4	4.4%
1991	75.2	1.4	1.8%

Source: *Criminal Statistics England and Wales 1991* (Home Office, 1982)

At the apex of the justice system, then, the use of custody declined by around 82% in this 10-year period. On the basis of this dramatic evidence alone, it might be reasonable to conclude that Margaret Thatcher was, indeed, 'soft on crime' (Smith, R., 1995). At each key decision point, changes in policy and practice appeared to have combined to refocus youth justice in a dramatic and unexpected manner: (1) fewer young people were being made subject to formal action by the police; (2) more 14–16 year olds were being cautioned; (3) fewer young people were being prosecuted; (4) more young people were being made the subject of community-based supervision; (5) fewer young people were being sentenced to custody. The cumulative effect of these changes is thus intensified. As Haines and Drakeford put it:

> ... if more and more minor and younger offenders are being diverted from formal prosecution then it is increasingly the older and more serious offenders who appear in court ... If there were no changes to courts' sentencing behaviour, then an increase in diversion would be

likely to lead to a proportionate increase in more severe sentences. But this did not happen in the 1980s ... Juvenile justice practitioners were not just successful in reducing the custody rate, they were even more successful in reducing this rate for a relatively older and more serious cohort of offenders. (Haines and Drakeford, 1998, p. 60)

Despite the appearance of dramatic achievements, we should be careful about the foreshortening effects of potentially arbitrary choices when considering statistical evidence. As D. Smith (1999) observes, for example, the use of custody in 1996 proved to be lower than 10 years previously. To characterize the 1980s simply as the 'decade of diversion' would be to over-simplify. It would also obscure the importance of considering trends and inconsistencies in patterns of disposals, rather than focusing on 'snapshots', or exceptional figures. Despite this observation, a clear pattern emerges of a shift away from the use of formal sanctions, a move towards the use of community-based supervision, and a parallel reduction in the use of custody for young people.

The Meaning of 'Success'

The important task here for those concerned with delivering a fair and effective youth justice system is first to unravel the possible reasons for the achievements of the 1980s, and subsequently to draw out lessons for policy, management and practice.

Perhaps we should start by clarifying our understanding of what is meant by 'success'. As we have noted, the headline figures suggest that a parallel reduction in offending rates and the use of custodial disposals was secured over this period. However, evidence of success in wider terms is rather less dramatic. Evaluations of specific interventions such as the Cambridge IT study (Bottoms, 1995) have found evidence of a small influence on reoffending rates for some types of intensive programmes (see also Audit Commission, 1996). These findings are supported by other, more localized studies (Children's Society, 1993), which appear to demonstrate that carefully targeted programmes can reduce offending rates at the individual level. This chimes with the experience of many practitioners who feel that their own interventions have led to successful outcomes in particular cases where they feel that they have been able to 'make a difference' (Smith, R., 2002).

Despite these observations, the overall impact of such programmes on offending rates appears limited (Haines and Drakeford, 1998). In addition, other indicators of 'success' in the context of youth justice are even less favourable. During the 1980s, and at least up until the latter half of the 1990s, crime rates continued to increase, from the perspective of victims (Mirrlees-Black *et al.*, 1998). At the same time, police clear-up rates remained low (Audit Commission, 1996). This provided little support for the argument that diversionary strategies would free police time for the investigation of more challenging cases.

Equally, public perceptions of risk and danger from young people continued to remain high (Home Affairs Committee, 1993). Pearson (1983) suggests that the fear of the young is endemic to society, and demonstrates that an over-dramatized sense of threat remains close to the surface of public and media consciousness. This, it has been noted, is an issue of particular concern because of the associated risks of stereotyping and discriminating against particular groups of young people, such as young African–Caribbean men (Haines and Drakeford, 1998; Goldson and Chigwada-Bailey, 1999). The 'successes' of the 1980s were not associated with an equivalent achievement in reducing the over-representation of this group in the youth justice system at all levels, including most significantly, custody (Gordon, 1983; Pitts, 1988), despite the evidence that they are no more likely to be involved in crime (Graham and Bowling, 1995).

So, in seeking to explain the successes of the 1980s, we must be a little circumspect. In a number of key respects, the significance of the achievements documented may have appeared greater to those working within the system than to outside interests. An apparent over-concentration on one measure of success (the reduction in the use of custody) may have obscured the need to consider wider constituencies (Haines and Drakeford, 1998), whose priorities are likely to be different. This may be a mundane observation, but it may help us to understand the relative fragility of what was achieved in this one specific time period.

Explaining 'Success'

Despite these cautionary notes, it is worth considering in more detail possible explanations for the outcomes observed. It is probably best to think in terms of a constellation of factors, which combined to create a favourable climate for the liberalization of youth justice during the 1980s. Thus, contextual factors such as the political mood, enabling factors such as policy shifts, and delivery factors such as practitioner initiatives should all be seen as contributing to the momentum for change that developed over time.

Political influences

As already observed, the 1980s was typified by a right–wing Conservative government which had little time for liberal sentiments. Despite this, a number of political factors proved favourable to a progressive agenda in youth justice. To begin with, the government's concern to cut state spending encouraged the reduction in the use of expensive custodial options. As Rutherford (1992) observes, one example of this was the decline in provision of secure accommodation from 1981 onwards.

In addition to this cost-cutting agenda, other political influences came into play. Whether it was coincidental or not, most of the Thatcher years' Home Secretaries were relatively liberal, despite their obligatory declamatory performances at Party conferences. Ministers did not seem uncomfortable with rational arguments for the reduction in the use of custody. John Patten, Minister of State at the Home Office, for example, stated: 'I think there is now a fairly wide consensus about what the response to juvenile offending should be … formal intervention should be kept to the minimum consistent with the circumstances and seriousness of each case' (Patten, 1988). There was also a sense in which these concerns with saving money and minimal intervention fitted with another central tenet of Thatcherism which was the concept of 'laissez-faire' (Fox Harding, 1997), whereby the state should resist intervening in civil society unless absolutely necessary. This principle, in turn, was consistent with the notion of 'bifurcation', as applied to the justice system (Bottoms, 1977). Thus, state intervention in relatively minor cases should be avoided, while the use of coercive measures should be reserved for extreme cases where an authoritarian response would carry greater weight, both substantively and symbolically. A more cynical interpretation of this 'rolling back' of the state might be that the Conservative government was relatively dis-interested in those working-class areas where particular types of antisocial behaviour and crime had the most damaging effects. This was certainly a view expressed by some Labour politicians (Straw and Michael, 1996), and is consistent with the arguments of the 'Left realists', reflecting on the impact of crime on particular groups and neighbourhoods: 'responsibility for "trivial" or "secondary" crime is hived off from the police, and, in effect, thrown back upon those sectors of society who have the greatest need for responsive and effective policing' (Kinsey et al., 1986).

Policy factors

Unusually, youth justice policy throughout the 1980s demonstrated a high degree of consistency. Thus, the principles of minimum intervention, proportionality, and punitive sanctions which informed the White Paper

Young Offenders (Home Office, 1980) at the start of the decade, were to be found in much the same combination in its counterpart *Crime, Justice and Protecting the Public* (Home Office, 1990), 10 years later.

These principles could be seen to flow from the dominant political themes, and were reflected in specific measures that supported particular types of practice development. For instance, the restrictive criteria incorporated into the Criminal Justice Act 1982, which inhibited the use of custody, could be seen as a 'trade off' with the emphasis on more intensive forms of supervision in the community. In this sense, 'bifurcation' received explicit recognition as an appropriate youth justice strategy. Pitts (1988) draws attention to the irony by which the intensive IT initiative launched by the government in 1983 (DHSS, 1983) was planned to provide exactly the same number of community places (4,500) as the initial Home Office projections for the increase in the use of custody following implementation of the 1982 Act. In fact, of course, the increase in demand for custodial provision did not materialize. Again, this might partly be to do with the increasingly explicit demarcation between minor and less experienced offenders on the one hand, and those whose offending careers were more entrenched on the other. As a consequence, the 'short, sharp shock' regime offered by detention centres lost its rationale for existence. Compounded by the publication of a critical evaluation (Thornton *et al.*, 1984), their use declined rapidly, leading to their abolition as a consequence of the Criminal Justice Act 1988.

Clearly, other policy developments, such as the official endorsement of cautioning in 1985 (Home Office, 1985), were consistent with the broader thrust towards minimum intervention and the targeting of resources at the 'heavy end' of youth offending. The Home Office argued that prosecution should not be the norm for young offenders, but should be used only where the 'public interest' required it (Home Office, 1984). Indeed, so consistent were the messages emerging from a range of policy pronouncements, that it led to suggestions from some quarters that this represented 'the end of the argument' about youth justice policy (Smith, R., 1989).

Practitioner initiatives

The 'permissions' offered by the policy developments of the early and mid-1980s were eagerly seized on by practitioners in a wide range of geographical areas, and at different strategic points in the justice system (see, for example, Smith, R., 1989; Rutherford, 1992; Children's Society, 1993; Haines and Drakeford, 1998; Smith, D., 1999; Goldson, 2000). While the favourable political climate is an important factor, the achievements of the 1980s owe a lot to the energy and commitment of a large band of practitioners and managers who made good use of the opportunities presented. This is an important point, which needs to be strongly emphasized, because it provides a safeguard against the mood of paralysis and pessimism (Eadie and Canton, 2002) which might otherwise infuse youth justice when the going gets tough. Examples include the establishment of a 'custody-free zone' in Hampshire (Rutherford, 1992), the rapid ascent of Northamptonshire from the bottom to the top of the 'diversion' league table (Stevens and Crook, 1986), and the reductions in re-offending and the use of custody achieved by voluntary sector IT projects (Children's Society, 1988).

While these initiatives tended to originate and develop independently, they came to share a number of characteristics. To begin with, they tended to operate fairly strict 'gate-keeping' criteria, in order to target inter-ventions only at those young people whose behaviour merited them. This principle was clearly derived from the academic evidence, which sug-gested that confusing welfare and justice objectives tended to suck in young people whose behaviour alone did not merit formal action (Morris et al., 1980; Thorpe et al., 1980). In addition, youth justice work became established as a distinct area of practice, with a degree of distance being established between such schemes and conventional social work or probation functions (Haines and Drakeford, 1998). Thus a distinctive structural and operational identity emerged for this body of work, even though much of it was based on inter-agency or cross-sector partnerships. Indeed, some have argued that this 'blurring' of agency roles was a deliberate part of the emerging strategy (Smith, R., 1999). As a result of these developments, interventions became increasingly offence-focused, and have been seen by some to exclude important welfare considerations (see Haines and Drakeford, 1998).

Nevertheless, the fact that youth justice initiatives shared such distinctive characteristics also contributed to another important feature of their success, namely 'system management'. The establishment of specialist teams with discrete areas of responsibility coincidentally enabled the development of a measure of control over the youth justice system by creating, for example, a unified knowledge base, and by providing a single locus for decisions about intervention and resource allocation. This development, in turn, made it easier to deliver a coherent system-wide strategy directed towards the reduction of punitive inter-ventions. Those areas with a coherent approach to system management appear to have been able to deliver more consistent and dramatic results, which led to the observation that what was, in fact, being delivered was 'justice by geography' (Children's Society, 1988).

Messages from the 1980s

While it is clear that current youth justice practices are influenced by a different climate and a new political agenda, it is still of value to consider what lessons might be drawn from the experience of the 1980s to inform policy and practice.

The evidence of positive achievements from that decade is strong and compelling, but we should be careful to season any simplistic conclusions with an acknowledgement of some of the possible shortcomings which can be observed, too. For example, the strategy which informed youth justice practice in the 1980s was simply too narrowly-based for some: 'the 1980s juvenile justice new orthodoxy was essentially based on an anti-custody philosophy ... In other words, it was the avoidance of custody for young people that justified and gave meaning to the actions of juvenile justice workers.' (Haines and Drakeford, 1988, p. 74). This objective, combined with increasingly sophisticated systems management strategies, rendered youth justice practice rather sterile and restrictive, according to this argument. As Smith puts it, the associated belief that intervention of any kind would at best be ineffective, and at worst destructive, possibly led to a rather tokenistic view of direct work with young people: 'their conviction that nothing worked meant that some workers came to believe that it did not matter what they did, as long as they did little of it' (Smith, D., 1999, p. 153). Where these criticisms held some validity, real difficulties could be anticipated when the requirements of youth justice policy changed, and 'system management' offered little by way of principled argument against the new demands imposed (Smith, D., 1999). It is difficult to defend a form of intervention that is essentially self-deprecating, and attributes no value to the skills and practices of those engaged in it.

However, the 'anti-custody orthodoxy' did not hold sway to quite the extent suggested by its critics. Within the wide range of initiatives developed during the 1980s there was substantial variation in practice, and new models of active intervention were also emerging. For example, as already noted, the aims of diversion projects such as the Northampton-shire JLBx were not restricted to reducing the number of prosecutions, and their objectives incorporated both the prevention of further offending and reparation. These objectives were reflected in practice, and a portfolio of what would now be seen as 'restorative' interventions was established.

Examples of innovative practice could also be observed in the Intermediate Treatment projects developed as alternatives to custody, which offered a range of 'active and participatory' programmes, and helped young people to 'develop their problem-solving skills', among other things (Smith, D., 1999).

Characterizations of 1980s' practice as a dominant and uniform strategy based solely on reducing the numbers in custody are too simplistic, as even some critics acknowledge on reflection (Haines and Drakeford, 1998). There is no doubt, though, that some youth justice initiatives did come to be driven primarily by the negative aim of *reducing* custody, rather than the positive aim of *replacing* it with sustainable alternatives (see, for example, Stevens and Crook, 1986). The principal shortcoming of a pure reductionist strategy is that it provides no defence against those who simply argue that 'prison works' (Howard, 1995), because it offers no clear set of alternative principles for intervening to deal with the problems associated with offending behaviour.

Importantly, as we shall see, it is the emerging lessons about developing new models of intervention not dictated by narrow preoccupations with justice, due process, and the 'numbers game' that, in reality, offer a way forward for practitioners and agencies today.

Chapter 2

Where did it all go wrong?

Continuity or Change?

As already noted, the decision to structure an account in a particular way itself conveys implicit messages about the author's own preconceptions. In this instance, the insertion of a notional dividing line between the 1980s and the 1990s is conscious and deliberate. It does seem to me that there is evidence of a quite dramatic shift in the shape of youth justice in England and Wales, which can be located in the early 1990s. This view appears to be shared by a number of others (Goldson, 1997; Haines and Drakeford, 1998; Pitts, 1999), although some are more inclined to think in terms of continuities (Hudson, 1996; Smith, D., 1999; Muncie, 2000; Pickford, 2000).

In addition to accepting the idea that there was a significant change of direction at the beginning of the decade, the present account is also written from a perspective that identifies that change as the beginning of a period in which earlier gains were rolled back and some quite important achievements undone. From this viewpoint, the 1990s can be characterized as a period of 'unlearning'. While many of the drivers of this reversal can be located outside the justice system itself, the consequences can be identified quite clearly in changes in practice and outcomes. However, this is not intended to be a critical account of poor practice, and it will be possible to identify some important achievements on this level, in adverse circumstances. Overall, though, the picture will emerge of a youth justice system in retreat, where traditional susceptibilities to self-righteous populism have proved once again to be the Achilles' heel of competent and committed practitioners.

Gathering Clouds: Politicians, Policy and the Law

As already observed, the 1980s culminated in a series of policy developments which appeared to provide an effective underpinning for youth justice practices based on principles of minimum intervention. Home Office Circular 59/1990 (Home Office, 1990a) on cautioning once again endorsed the use of measures to deal with offences falling short of prosecution, even in the face of some resistance from police and magistrates. The White Paper *Crime, Justice and Protecting the Public* (Home Office, 1990b) offered further support for the provision of alternatives to custody, extending some of the principles established for young offenders to adults. The White Paper made explicit commitments to the 'punishment' of more offenders in the community, and it was dismissive of the reformative powers of custody. Instead, it tried to establish clear demarcations between serious offences (violence, domestic burglary or sexual offences), and other offences that could be dealt with effectively by way of community punishments. These principles were incorporated in the Criminal Justice Act 1991, setting out a new framework for the dispensation of youth (and adult) justice: 'Arguably the CJA 1991 represented the first time that a British government clearly enshrined in a piece of criminal justice legislation a single coherent sentencing philosophy and policy' (Haines and Drakeford, 1998, p. 77).

This philosophy is characterized as one of 'just deserts', whereby disposals would be proportionate to the offence(s) committed, and would take no account of either prior criminality or personal circumstances. This appeared to be no more than an extension of the offence-based approach that had informed much of the thinking in juvenile justice practice in the 1980s. This assimilation of policy-orientations for young and adult offenders also facilitated the restructuring of the courts, so that those below the age of 18 would be dealt with by the newly established Youth Court. In one respect, at least, this appeared to be a recognition of the principles set out in the UN Convention on the Rights of the Child (ratified by the UK in 1991), which requires all children (defined as those under 18) to be recognized and treated as such.

At the same time, however, some sentences previously reserved for adults would become available for 16-year olds for the first time (such as Community Service Orders and Combination Orders). Interestingly, the

29

Guidance associated with the 1991 Act also promoted a greater degree of inter-agency cooperation to enable these more flexible arrangements to work effectively (Haines and Drakeford, 1998, p. 84). For Haines and Drakeford, the 1991 Act represented the high-point of a developing consensus 'around the desert-based approach to sentencing'. Specific indicators of this could be found, for example, in the replacement of welfare-oriented Social Inquiry Reports with more offence-focused Pre-Sentence Reports to courts at the sentencing stage, and an emphasis on court disposals such as bind overs to emphasize 'parental discipline and control' at the expense of social factors (Macmillan and Brown, 1998). For some, at least, the erosion of the concern with social and environmental factors in the justice system laid the foundations for the increasingly punitive atmosphere of the 1990s and beyond (Haines and Drakeford, 1998). This appears to be a reversal of the argument advanced previously, which suggested that it was the inappropriate focus on welfare concerns that had contributed to the increasingly punitive treatment of young people in the 1970s (Thorpe *et al.*, 1980).

In any event, the 1991 Act had barely passed into law before it became the subject of intense criticism. The fragile penal consensus was broken. A number of factors appear to have contributed to this, including the higher profile that justice issues came to assume around this time. While it is too simplistic to attribute every twitch in the law-and-order apparatus to a 'political' reaction to public opinion and the media, there is no doubt that these are perennial influences on policy and practice in the youth justice arena. In particular, in the early 1990s a number of factors seem to have combined to create a climate of instability and retrenchment. Even as the achievements of the 1980s appeared to be cemented in place, trouble was brewing.

First, a change in key political personnel occurred, with the replacement of Margaret Thatcher as Prime Minister by John Major, and the appointment of a new Home Secretary, David Waddington, who was acknowledged as more right-wing than his predecessors. It seemed, indeed, that he was not wholly supportive of the 1991 Act even during its passage through Parliament, emphasizing its more punitive aspects, and contradicting the stated aim of reducing the prison population (Macmillan, 1998).

Second, the early 1990s saw renewed outbreaks of rioting, for instance in Cardiff, the Blackbird Leys estate in Oxford, and Meadow Well estate in North Shields. As already noted, such phenomena were not new, and rioting had been a matter of concern on a number of occasions during the 1980s. Interestingly, the areas in which these 1991 riots were reported were predominantly white. Perhaps it was easier to ascribe 'criminal' rather than political motivation to these, in contrast to disturbances occurring in predominantly black areas, such as those occurring in Brixton, Toxteth or Handsworth in the 1980s.

Third, it has been suggested that around the same time the police initiated a 'sophisticated campaign' focused on 'persistent offenders' – that small minority consistently held responsible for the great bulk of criminal activity. The riots were associated with joy-riding, and a number of young offenders were accorded national notoriety, including a 10-year old from Hartlepool (Brown, 1998), 'Rat Boy' on Tyneside, and a number of other similarly lurid characterizations. The police provided more reasoned support for their arguments in the evidence submitted to the Home Affairs Select Committee by the Association of Chief Police Officers, suggesting that the trends in youth crime represented an increased offending rate (54% up from 1980 to 1990) but a smaller number of offenders (Children's Society, 1993). In addition, police reported concerns that a large number of offences were being committed by young people while on bail (up to 40% in Northumbria, for example).

Fourth, it rapidly became clear that courts did not accept the constraints placed on their sentencing powers by the 1991 Act (Hudson, 1996). In particular, the requirement to focus almost exclusively on the current offence limited their ability to deal more severely with persistent offenders. The requirement to base sentences first and foremost on the 'seriousness' of the offence was seen as unacceptable political interference in the independence of the judiciary (Goldson, 1997), and, it ran counter to more intuitive feelings about responding more severely to repeated acts of defiance, whether for reasons of deterrence or of 'exacting the price' of crime.

The fifth reason often advanced for the dramatic shift of direction was the killing of the toddler James Bulger by two boys aged 10 and 11. While this traumatic event definitely added impetus to the new direction of youth justice, and influenced specific outcomes such as the abolition of *doli incapax*[1], it was not, as is sometimes assumed, the originating cause, coming as it did early in 1993.

Finally, and also more pertinent to the emerging trends, was the development of a political consensus, at least between the two leading parties, about being 'tough on crime'. This can perhaps be associated with the emergence of political heavyweights on both sides (Kenneth Clarke as

---

[1]Prior to its abolition by Section 31 of the Crime and Disorder Act 1998, the common-law presumption of *doli incapax* was that children aged between 10 and 14 in criminal proceedings did not know the difference between right and wrong, and were thus incapable of acting with criminal intent unless it could be proved otherwise.

Home Secretary, Tony Blair as Shadow Home Secretary), each anxious to make a reputation for himself, and establish a 'position' for their own party. In February 1993, shortly after the Bulger killing, the Prime Minister, John Major, said: 'society needs to condemn a little more and understand a little less'. This slogan has come to typify the behaviour of politicians in the youth justice arena, it could be argued. Writing in the *Daily Mail* at around the same time, Kenneth Clarke stated that: 'the courts should have the power to send really persistent, nasty little juveniles away to somewhere where they will be looked after better and where they will be educated' (*Daily Mail*, 22 February 1993). And, later in the year, contributing to the *Mail*'s competitor, the *Daily Express*, Tony Blair wrote that: 'no one but a fool would excuse the commission of a crime on the basis of the offender's upbringing; and no one but a bigot would ignore the impact of that upbringing on the individual's behaviour' (*Daily Express*, 31 August 1993).

Despite the acknowledgement by both politicians that other factors should be taken into account when dealing with the crimes of the young, these statements were clearly designed to attract public support for a 'tough' position rather than to add any real depth to the discussion of what to do about offending by young people. Indeed, in subsequent years, political posturing has come to characterize public debates about youth crime to the exclusion of rational or informed argument.

One immediate consequence of the rush to denounce the liberal trends of the 1980s and early 1990s was the Aggravated Vehicle-Taking Act 1992, which was the government's response to the problem of joy-riding and a reported increase in car crime (Home Affairs Committee, 1993; Children's Society, 1993). The highly specific nature of this piece of legislation is perhaps also symbolic of another tendency demonstrated in the political sphere as the decade unfolded, a kind of 'knee-jerk' reaction to perceived social problems, resulting in precipitate, poorly-targeted, and sometimes unworkable legal solutions.

The government also announced plans to tighten up on persistent young offenders more generally. Within months of abolishing custody for 14-year olds under the 1991 Act, the Home Secretary, Kenneth Clarke, was announcing plans to create 200 new custodial places in Secure Training Centres, which would be available for children as young as 12. Clarke informed the House of Commons:

> The Government are determined to continue to strengthen the powers of the courts to deal with persistent offenders. We must also take other measures to tackle the problem on a broader front ... The secure training orders will be different from anything that has ever

been provided before. (House of Commons Debates, col. 139–40, 2 March 1993)

Backtracking: Laying Down the Law

The government's U-turn took more concrete shape with the passage of the Criminal Justice Act 1993, which reinstated the powers of the courts to take account of an offender's previous record by the rather elegant device of inserting two words into Section 1(2) of the 1991 Act, so that rather than 'one' other offence 'one *or more*' offences 'associated' with the current one could be considered at the point of sentencing. Other aspects of the 1993 Act demonstrated an intention to create a more punitive climate, including the provision (Sec. 66(6)) that offences committed while on bail would be treated as an 'aggravating factor' in determining sentences.

Just in case there should be any doubt about where all this was heading, the new Home Secretary, Michael Howard, speaking to the Conservative Party conference, proclaimed that 'prison works' (Rutherford, 1996). He advanced two justifications: that prison protects the public from 'murderers, muggers and rapists', and that it acts as a deterrent. He did not make any claims for prison's reformative, rehabilitative or correctional powers. Not only did this signal a new legislative onslaught, but it also demonstrated that political decisions in this context were unlikely to be unduly influenced by the evidence, for example about the efficacy of custody (Rutherford, 1996). 1994 saw two further blows against the achievements of the 1980s, at either end of the youth justice 'system'.

At one end of the scale, in the face of professional advice the incoming Home Secretary sought to stamp his authority by pushing through Home Office Circular 18/94 (Home Office, 1994), which effectively blocked the practice of repeat cautioning, except in very tightly defined circumstances. The Circular also put more explicit restrictions in place to ensure that 'serious' offences would not be dealt with by way of a caution. It was emphasized that the decision to caution should remain exclusively with the police, and should not be shared with other agencies. Effective multi-agency approaches, such as those developed in Northamptonshire, felt themselves to be under threat: 'although previous Home Office circulars on cautioning ... had positively encouraged the police to consult with multi-agency partners ... this circular went a long way in retracting this policy commitment' (Bell *et al.*, 1999, p. 99).

The net (or net-widening!) effect of this kind of policy shift was always likely to be an increase in the numbers of young people being formally processed and made subject to prosecution. As always, it seems that where

33

liberalizing measures need copious evidence to demonstrate that they 'work', moves in a more punitive direction can often be decided on hearsay, or whim, as seems to have been the case here. Macmillan (1998) suggests that this particular measure was prompted by a BBC television programme, in which a young offender spoke of a caution being meaningless, and in which police and magistrates speculated about increased use of cautioning leading to an increased crime rate.

At the other end of the scale, the Criminal Justice and Public Order Act 1994 did, as promised, expand the range of custodial options available to the courts. Under the Act, courts were to be given the power to make Secure Training Orders on 12–14 year olds of up to 2 years, of which half would be served in newly constructed Secure Training Centres. Establishing these centres within the prison estate, rather than under child care regulations, appeared to put the government at odds with the Beijing Rules on the administration of juvenile justice (United Nations, 1985), to which the UK is a signatory. This was no deterrent to Mr Howard; neither was the projected cost of the new institutions, estimated then at £75 million of capital expenditure, and another £20 million for each year's running costs (Children's Society, 1993).

The 1994 Act also extended the scope of Section 53 of the Children and Young Persons Act 1933, and gave powers to the courts to pass long-term sentences on 10–13 year olds for a wider range of offences than previously. Maximum sentences for 15–17 year olds were doubled, from 12 to 24 months, and it was made easier for courts to override the presumption of bail incorporated in the Bail Act 1976.

Not satisfied with this substantial shift towards a youth justice policy dominated by the principle of punishment, pure and simple, the Home Secretary proceeded to announce further plans to confront criminal behaviour. Despite the lack of any evidence to support their efficacy, he became a convert to the American model of 'boot camps', the introduction of which into the UK he announced in February 1995. The same year, a further policy document was issued by the Home Office, advocating tougher forms of 'punishment in the community' (Home Office, 1995). This was entirely consistent with the government view that punishment should be the motif for all forms of formal action against young offenders, and it included plans for the expansion of forms of 'community restraint', such as electronic tagging and curfews. As we shall see, this created further difficulties for youth justice services. The problem originated in the 'trade-off', by which those providing community supervision for young people had accepted more intrusive conditions, in exchange for the recognition of such community sentences as genuine alternatives to custody (arguably dating back as far as 1982 and the introduction of

Supervised Activity Orders; Pitts, 1988). Having accepted this compromise, it became difficult to argue, in principle, against the introduction of more stringent conditions, in a more hostile climate. In addition, the underlying weakness of this position, namely that 'alternatives to custody' cannot be equated to custody itself, meant that these could still be portrayed as a 'soft option' by the Home Secretary (Muncie, 1999).

The strategy of the Major administration was defined by the legislative changes of 1994 as one of increasing both the flow and the intensity of the processing of young people by the justice system. More young people would be drawn into the system, on the assumption that pre-court diversion had been ineffective, and courts were to be encouraged to use custody not as a last resort, but more freely, as a positive option, because, in Michael Howard's words, it 'works'. This approach was taken one step further in the final days of the Conservative government with the Crime (Sentences) Act 1997, which included provisions to extend curfews, and to 'name and shame' convicted young offenders for the first time.

As we have observed, a number of factors contributed to this punitive turn, but the cumulative effect was to create a new 'feel' to the youth justice system as a whole, one typified by the phrase 'revenge justice', according to Macmillan (1998).

Diamonds in the Mud: Practice in a Hostile Climate

For those working in, and managing, the youth justice system, the speed and intensity of the policy reversals of the early 1990s felt like an onslaught, undermining many of the principles on which their practice was based. The consensus between different elements of the youth justice apparatus had broken down, and there appeared to be little room for manoeuvre in the face of policies that embraced the principle of punishment, apparently regardless of cost, efficacy, international obligations or moral considerations.

Not only was the climate increasingly hostile, but there was also a sense in which the delivery of youth justice interventions was changing at the same time. This can partly be attributed to an environment in which attention and money were diverted elsewhere. The achievements of the 1980s perhaps contributed towards an assumption that the battle was won, and for hard-pressed local agencies scarce resources could be diverted elsewhere, for instance into child protection, or towards the implementation of the community care legislation (in 1993). In addition, the substantial investment of money and energy represented by the 1983 IT initiative had gradually tapered off towards the end of the 1980s, and the 110 projects established under that programme were either in-corporated into mainstream practice, or were wound up (Smith, D., 1999). There is perhaps something in the argument that the task itself had changed, from one of developing and establishing new forms of inter-vention, to one of 'managing' those interventions as part of routine practice. Some (for example, Muncie, 1999) have argued that this is, in any case, consistent with an emerging strand of 'managerialism' in the delivery of public services, which can be traced to the incoming Conservative administration of 1979. Pratt (1989) argued that even in the 1980s debates between 'welfare' and 'justice' were little more than a smokescreen for the emergence of a 'corporatist' agenda, which was primarily concerned with efficient, effective (and cheap) forms of service delivery. These developments were associated not only with the emerg-ence of new forms of public management, but also with the emergence of multi-agency partnerships in youth justice, which had been a central feature of many of the successful initiatives of the 1980s:

> By the 1990s such corporate, multi-agency strategies were to become subsumed within a much broader process of public sector managerialization. This … has generally involved the redefinition of political, economic and social issues as problems to be managed rather than necessarily resolved. (Muncie, 1999, p. 288)

A further development, which resulted in more explicit expectations of those responsible for delivering youth justice, was the initial publication of National Standards for the Supervision of Offenders by the Home Office (Home Office, 1992). This set in motion a conveyor-belt which periodically delivers a new or revised set of standards for a particular aspect of the justice system; but its impact in terms of imposing centralized constraints on agencies and practitioners in the name of consistency and good practice should not be underestimated.

The central problem arising from these developments is the de-politicization of youth justice. The challenge becomes one of delivering an effective, well-managed, service function, rather than an informed and principled approach to producing 'just' outcomes: 'Social issues were depoliticised. Policy choices were transformed into a series of managerial decisions. Evaluations of public sector performance came to be dominated by notions of productivity, task remits and quantifiable outcomes.' (Muncie, 1999, p. 288). Accounts of practice during this period appear more likely to highlight improvements in efficiency and 'system manage-ment' than the development of new models of intervention, or the achievement of greater fairness in service provision. Thus, The Children's

Society (1993) reports an inter-agency initiative in South Wales that claims, as indicators of success, a 'speeding up' of the judicial process and a consequential reduction in offending while on bail. Although these achievements seem to have their own distinctive merits, they are, at best, interim targets, which *might* contribute towards more substantial aims, such as the general reduction of youth crime. Another initiative highlighted by the same report claims as its principal achievement the adoption of a comprehensive approach to managing the youth justice system, while nothing is mentioned about substantive outcomes (Children's Society, 1993, p. 55).

In this context of policy reversal and creeping managerialism, practice innovations took on rather different characteristics than in the preceding decade, it would seem. They were no longer concerned with bringing a vision of minimum intervention, informal justice, and improved social cohesion into being; rather, they took on a tactical and defensive character, typified by projects aimed at moderating some of the more damaging examples of injustice or inappropriate treatment. Foremost among the organizations developing this kind of initiative were the Howard League and The Children's Society (see, for example, Ashton and Grindrod, 1999; Moore and Smith, 2001). Both were voluntary organizations with an explicit commitment to end the use of custody for young people, and to promote children's rights. In this sense, they represented a spirit of continuity with the 'anti-custody' movement of the 1980s identified by Haines and Drakeford (1998). Unlike providers based in statutory agencies, they did not experience the constraints and realignments that impacted so significantly on practice in the early 1990s, and they began to develop a role as defenders of the key elements of a 'liberal' approach to youth justice. They sought to act strategically to promote the interests of children and young people at the most acute pressure points, specifically targeting arbitrary and discriminatory use of custody. This, it has been suggested, helped to compensate for one of the shortcomings of existing multi-agency strategies:

> The current orthodoxy ... is inclined towards holistic and multi-agency approaches ... but there has been a tendency for those agencies who are working with children who are at risk of entering the penal system to regard their involvement as being at an end if a child is remanded or sentenced into prison custody. (Ashton and Grindrod, 1999, p. 170)

The Troubleshooter Project *and Beyond: Drawing the Line*

The context for the Troubleshooter Project was, ironically, determined by the recognition that the number of 15-year olds remanded in custody in

England and Wales at any one time was at an all-time low, some 25 in the period when the project was being planned (Ashton and Grindrod, 1999). There was also increasing concern for the well-being of young people in custody because of a series of widely reported prison suicides around this time. The scheme, then, was conceived at the peak of the movement to replace custody for young offenders with alternative disposals. Numbers had fallen to such an extent that this objective now seemed feasible. Despite these aspirations, even as the Troubleshooter Project itself got under way in the autumn of 1993, the custodial tide had turned. By June 1991, as the furore about persistent young offenders began, the number of 15-year olds remanded to custody was 102; by June 1993 this figure had risen to 126, and even after the project had begun, the number continued to grow, to as many as 278 by June 1997. Thus it seems that far from being 'one last push' to secure the abolition of custodial remands for 15-year olds, the Troubleshooter initiative found itself struggling to stem this rapidly rising tide.

The Project was established with five key objectives: to 'rescue 15-year olds from prison custody'; to provide them with support and advocacy while in custody; to assist youth justice agencies; to monitor outcomes; and to promote good practice. The Project was put into practice with young offenders in Feltham Young Offender Institution and Remand Centre. Project staff were able to meet young people as soon as possible after reception, both on remand and post-sentence, and to establish grounds for seeking an alternative non-custodial option. Intervening directly in this way enabled the Project to identify shortcomings in existing processes, as well as providing positive support for the negotiation of alternative placements. From its inception, the Project was able to secure the release of significant numbers of 15-year olds remanded to Feltham, largely by remedying failings in the youth justice system. Some young people were found to have been remanded to custody illegally, some were let down by agencies who did not offer alternatives, and in some cases custodial remands were made simply because there were no suitable alternatives. In undertaking this role, the Project was also able to demonstrate the ability to tackle one of the further consequences of these problems, which was institutional discrimination on racial grounds. Black or Asian young people were found to be substantially overrepresented in both remanded and sentenced populations, and by intervening as it did, the Project was able to make a contribution to challenging this.

The initial achievements of the Troubleshooter Project led to the development and expansion of the scheme by The Children's Society under the title of the Remand Rescue Initiative. At this point, it was decided to extend the scheme to cover 16-year olds on custodial remand as well. The scheme was subsequently funded to provide much wider geographical coverage by the Youth Justice Board (which required the word 'Rescue' to be replaced by the rather less heroic sounding 'Review'). The scheme developed a mode of working which involved making initial contact with the young person on remand, assessing the young person's circumstances and 'state of mind', and evaluating documentation accompanying the young person. On the basis of this initial investigation, the response could be one of the following: to enable the young person to challenge the legal basis for the remand; to liaise with other agencies to provide information and advice to support alternatives to custodial remands; or sometimes to take on a direct advocacy role where agencies might need to be encouraged more actively to meet their responsibilities. Intervention thus took place on three levels – correcting system failures, addressing young people's needs, and promoting their rights. From January 1997 to November 1999, Remand Rescue dealt with 1,666 cases of 15- and 16-year-old boys on remand, and of these 32% were released as a result of this intervention (Moore and Smith, 2001).

Bail Support: Working Tactically

Another example of the kind of tactical intervention that emerged in the 1990s was 'bail support'. As we have already observed, the emergence of fears about 'persistent' young offenders, and changes in government policy, created a climate in which courts became increasingly reluctant to released suspects on bail. Prompted by the evidence of a rapid increase in custodial remands (Nacro/ACOP, 1995), programmes were developed which aimed to increase courts' confidence in the use of bail. One such scheme was the Manchester Youth Bail Support Project established in 1996, and extended to the entire Greater Manchester area in 1999. This scheme was the product of a wide-ranging inter-agency, and indeed inter-sector, partnership, including The Children's Society, the probation services and social services. The project aims to deliver 'individually tailored programmes to provide support and supervision to young people, addressing in particular the grounds for potential refusal of bail' (Moore and Smith, 2001, p. 67).

The programmes are targeted at young people who would otherwise be refused bail; it is not the intention to increase levels of surveillance and control over those who would, and should, be granted bail as a matter of course. The overarching aim of the project is to reduce the numbers of young people remanded to any form of secure setting, including both custody and local authority secure accommodation. In order to achieve this, however, the project recognizes the need to provide a comprehensive bail support service acceptable to the courts. It thus aims to provide the courts with an assessment of risk, need and suitability for the programme, on the basis of which, specific elements of support and supervision are offered as part of the package. These include measures to ensure that the young person returns to court at the end of the bail period, and to reduce reoffending, and to encourage family support, counselling, and educational opportunities. Courts are provided with progress reports and evidence of successful completion of programme components. In addition to this, the project also operates a breach procedure, which is enforced where necessary, again in the interests of maintaining credibility with the courts.

Following its establishment, the project was subject to an extensive evaluation, during 1998. During this period 136 referrals were made to the programme, and 102 young people were accepted. Of these, only 51 were granted bail on condition that they attend the programme, with 39 of the remainder being remanded to custody, and three to local authority accommodation. From these figures, it was possible to draw the conclusion that the bail support packages offered were appropriately targeted at those at risk of a custodial remand. At this stage, however, it was also noted that Black and Asian young people were relatively less likely to be recommended for, and thus accepted, onto the bail programme, which gives some cause for concern.

A total of 37 young people completed the programme during the evaluation period, of whom 8 (22%) failed, that is, breached the conditions of attendance, or re-offended, and were taken into custody. The others (78%) all completed the programme without being incarcerated, although five of these did not keep strictly to the terms of their bail requirements. For those where a final sentence was known, 63% of those completing the programme successfully were not sent to custody. The project could therefore claim a degree of success in both securing young people's compliance, and avoiding custodial outcomes. Similar schemes have been developed elsewhere (Audit Commission, 1996), and again the emphasis is on containment, compliance, personal development, and the prevention of further offences. The South East Kent Bail Support Scheme, for example '… is offered as a condition of bail to all those under 18 years who risk having bail refused. It aims to satisfy the courts that remand to custody or local authority accommodation is unnecessary, provided the young person complies with the rules and requirements of the scheme, and to offer appropriate control within the community' (Audit Commission, 1996, p. 31).

Supervision in the Community: Close Control?

The increasingly explicit 'punishment' agenda of the government also influenced the development of schemes designed to provide alternatives to custody, usually in the form of strengthened and more restrictive supervised activities imposed as additional requirements attached to Supervision Orders. The Audit Commission (1996) provides an account of one such programme for young people, required to attend for 30 or 60 days. Attendance requirements on the programme are described as being strictly monitored, with two failures to attend resulting in a return to court for breach proceedings. The programme itself is reported as having five 'compulsory modules', covering: offending behaviour; social skills; numeracy and literacy; job search/education; and substance abuse and HIV. Other 'options' are also reported as being available, including the ubiquitous 'constructive use of leisure time', and information technology.

In providing a strict correctional framework, the project could be said to reflect the concern of the government of the time to intensify the punitive elements of community programmes. By the middle of the 1990s, there were 'over 150 diversionary community programmes operating in England and Wales designed to address offending behaviour through victim awareness, anger management, drug awareness and positive leisure schemes' (Muncie, 1999, p. 283). Ironically, however, the example cited by the Audit Commission did not appear to be fulfilling the aim of providing an effective means of diverting young people from custody. Only 38 (25%) of 153 considered suitable for the scheme were accepted onto it. Of the others, only 34 (22%) received a custodial sentence, while the remainder received a variety of less intrusive options, including supervision and probation orders without conditions (29%), and in some cases attendance centre orders, fines and even conditional discharges. Not only was the project relatively unsuccessful at persuading courts to make use of it, but it also seemed to be some way from offering a pure alternative to custody. For those not initially at risk of custody but who subsequently breached the conditions of the programme, it might indeed have heightened the risk of being locked up. We cannot draw too much from one example, but this example does at least pose the question as to whether a strategy of intensifying 'punishment in the community' (Hudson, 1996) can be justified in any way if it is unable to show that it offers a convincing alternative to custody.

'Defensive' Practice: Messages from the 1990s

From these diverse examples of developing practice in the 1990s we can perhaps draw out some emerging themes. First, there are some positive messages: despite disparaging comments from some quarters (Haines and Drakeford, 1998), the 'anti-custody' philosophy of much youth justice practice does appear to have survived the political onslaught of the Conservative government. Second, a concern with promoting children's rights appears to have emerged, perhaps encouraged by the development of international frameworks such as the UN Convention on the Rights of the Child (United Nations, 1989), and the Beijing Rules (United Nations, 1985). Third, we have observed the increasing recognition of, and commitment to, tackling discrimination within the youth justice system, which was also reflected by projects such as Right Track in Bristol, specifically designed to address structural inequalities in the administration of justice, such as institutional racism. There is also a sense in which the programme-content of the kind of projects identified retained a concern with promoting opportunities for the personal and social development of young people in trouble. It should perhaps be remembered that young people's own aspirations for education, work and a sense of achievement are not too dissimilar to the objectives of many of the structured programmes offered in the context of Supervision Orders (see, for example, Graham and Bowling, 1995).

Despite these positive observations there are also clearly some rather more difficult lessons to be learnt from the experiences of this time. Notably, the acceptance of the 'punishment' agenda made it difficult to offer principled opposition to increasingly restrictive forms of community sentence. At the same time, alternative objectives for the justice system, such as 'growing out of crime' (Rutherford, 1992), became more difficult to sustain. In addition, it must be a matter of concern that the loss of flexibility meant that it became more difficult to adjust interventions to the changing needs and circumstances of young people. The 'welfare' agenda had been written out of youth justice almost entirely, it would seem.

There was a sense, too, of interventions being constrained by their having to operate in foreign territory, and according to rules imposed from outside. For example, despite its success, the Troubleshooter / Remand Rescue / Remand Review initiative could only function within a framework that treated the use of custody for *some* young people as legitimate. As always, advancing 'special-case' arguments for some individuals indicates a tacit acceptance that these do not apply to the entire population concerned. Similar implications, too, could be drawn from an increasing inflexibility and the greater reliance on breach procedures, where 'failures' falling short of re-offending expose young people to more stringent forms of punishment.

The Rising Tide: Trends and Outcomes

How, then, did the changes in policy and practice impact on the delivery of youth justice in the 1990s? What does the evidence from published sources show us about the changing climate, given that in the 1980s political rhetoric and experiences 'on the ground' were somewhat divergent?

As far as it is possible to rely on official sources, it appears that the diversionary trends of the previous decade were sustained until about 1993, when the pattern of disposals went rapidly into reverse. However, this does not appear to have been a reflection of changing patterns of offending, at least in terms of the very small proportion of offences that come to official attention (19%), or the even smaller proportion (3%) that leads to any form of formal action against reported offenders (Audit Commission, 1996).

The context for changing practices in the youth justice system is established by what we know about patterns of crime generally. It appears, for instance, that both officially recorded crime and crimes recorded by the British Crime Survey increased to a high point in the early 1990s, and then began to fall steadily. Recorded crimes rose from 4.5 million in 1990 to 5.6 million in 1992, before declining to 4.5 million again in 1998/9, when new counting rules came into effect. The revised figure remained more or less constant over the next two years (Home Office, 2001b). It is, of course, impossible to identify the exact proportion of offences that can be attributed to young people, but the Audit Commission (1996) has estimated that, based on the proportion of people under 18 among known offenders, this can be put at around a quarter.

Over the same period detection rates fell, and it is also believed that police continued to use informal warnings in some cases (Home Office, 1996). The net effect has been a reduction in the proportion of young offenders who are the subject of formal action (caution or prosecution) per 100,000 population over the course of the decade (Home Office, 2001b). This is not the same, of course, as indicating that the number of young offenders has decreased, or that this represents wider changes in patterns of behaviour. It does mean, however, that progressively fewer young people are being processed formally by the justice system.

For those who are cautioned (Reprimanded/Warned from June 2000) or prosecuted there have been significant changes in the pattern of outcomes. In common with other trends, cautioning as a proportion of all formal disposals increased to a peak in the early 1990s for all age groups, and for both sexes (Home Office, 2001b, p. 105), but then declined steadily to the year 2000. Cautioning rates fell for all categories of indictable offences between 1999 and 2000, except criminal damage and robbery.

Table 2.1 Cautioning rates (cautions as a percentage of all offenders found guilty or cautioned) 1990–2000

Year	Males			Females		
	10–11	*12–14*	*15–17*	*10–11*	*12–14*	*15–17*
1990	95	84	53	99	93	73
1992	96	86	59	99	96	81
1994	95	81	56	100	94	77
1996	94	77	51	99	91	72
1998	91	72	48	97	88	67
2000	86	68	43	95	86	63

Source: *Criminal Statistics England and Wales 2000* (Home Office, 2001)

With the rate at which children and young people were proceeded against falling, and the cautioning rates moving in the same direction, the net effect was that the number of cautions administered was also declining fairly steeply.

On the other hand, the *number* of young people (aged 10–17) being proceeded against in court for indictable offences was on the increase. After an initial decline from 66,000 in 1990 to 60,000 in 1993, the figure then rose steadily to 81,000 in 2000. While the overall number of those being dealt with formally did not change substantially, this clearly represented a much larger proportion of all young people processed by the justice system than in the early part of the 1990s.

Not only was there a clear increase in those being dealt with by the courts (both numerically and proportionally), there was also an increase in the rate of custodial sentencing, from 10% to 15% of all sentences over the period 1990–2000 for 15–17 year-old males, and from 2% to 7% for 15–17 year-old females.

In numerical terms the increases are more striking than in percentage terms, with an increase from 3,600 to 5,200 for young men (15–17), and from 100 to 400 for young women in this age group.

For 12–14 year olds, custody had been available only under Section 53 of the Children and Young Persons Act 1933 (now replaced by Sections

Table 2.2 Custody rates (percentage of children and young people sent to custody as a proportion of all those sentenced) 1990–2000

Year	Males			Females		
	10–11	12–14	15–17	10–11	12–14	15–17
1990	0	2	10	0	0	2
1992	0	3	11	0	0	2
1994	0	0	14	0	0	4
1996	0	1	16	0	1	4
1998	0	2	16	0	0	6
2000	1	6	15	0	2	7

Source: *Criminal Statistics England and Wales 2000* (Home Office, 2001)

90–92 of the Powers of Criminal Courts (Sentencing) Act 2000) at the start of the decade, and was reserved for the most serious offences. With the introduction of Secure Training Orders (now Detention and Training Orders) from 1997, this option has become much more widely available, and unsurprisingly has been used increasingly by courts. For example, by 1993, the proportion of sentenced 12–14 year-old boys going to custody had declined to 0% (but not zero in numerical terms); but by 2000 this had increased to 6%, of which 4% was represented by DTOs. Of sentenced girls of the same age 2% received this disposal as well.

In short the 1990s, and particularly the latter half of the decade, saw a reversal of the 'double gain' identified in the 1980s (Haines and Drakeford, 1998). Previously, diversionary strategies had reduced the numbers of young people coming to court, and at the same time greater use of alternatives to custody had reduced the proportionate use of custody achieving a multiplication of the initial benefit. By the late 1990s the reverse was occurring. The courts were processing more young people as a proportion of those dealt with by the justice system, and a greater proportion were receiving custodial sentences. At the same time there were big increases in the use of community sentences (Supervision Orders, and the new disposals available from June 2000 such as Action Plan Orders and Reparation Orders), and these were at the expense of other, lower-tariff disposals, such as fines and discharges (Home Office, 2001b). This trend is likely to be compounded by the effective removal of the Conditional Discharge as an option following a Final Warning.

The evidence from this brief summary of trends in the exercise of police discretion and sentencing patterns is that the youth justice system has taken an increasingly punitive turn since the early 1990s, and that this shift was not modified, at least initially, by a change of government in 1997.

Explaining the U-turn

In order to understand what is possible in youth justice today, it is important to try to make sense of the contrasting experiences of the 1980s and 1990s. As already noted, some authors have taken the view that it has been a period of continuity rather than change. Hudson (1996), for example, argues that the outcomes observed can best be seen as reflections of broader social and ideological trends, with the emergence of 'actuarial regimes' geared to manage and control the risk represented by those identified as potential offenders. Concerns with strengthened mechanisms of surveillance and control can be seen as a reworking of the perennial contest between 'penalizing and normalizing responses to crime' (see also Garland, 2001, on 'inclusionary' and 'exclusionary' criminologies). Hudson argues that the kind of 'technologies' advocated by both perspectives are similar, but that the 'actuarial' perspective is more widely acceptable: 'Who could argue against policies and practices designed to help people avoid suffering from criminal victimization?' (Hudson, 1996, p. 154). According to this perspective, the 'back to justice' movement of the 1980s opened the way for the segregating and repressive form of actuarial justice by removing any concern with the social origins of crime in inequalities of money and power. Offender characteristics are reinserted into the calculative process only as a means of determining future risk and of calibrating sentencing decisions. Haines and Drakeford (1998) agree that a continuing commitment to an 'anti-custody' philosophy at the level of practice is in evidence, but that this is out of step with changing political realities, thus incurring the risk of unintentional collusion with increasingly repressive tendencies. Muncie (1999), too, highlights continuities in the emergence of 'corporatist' and authoritarian strands in the treatment of young offenders: 'one notable feature of English youth justice in the 1980s and 1990s has been a consistent copying of punitive measures from America' (Muncie, 1999, p. 298).

Others have argued that the trends of the 1990s represent no more than the continuation of a penal strategy based on notions of 'bifurcation' (Pickford, 2000). The 1990s, by these accounts, saw a much sharper representation of that distinction between minor offences committed by inexperienced offenders and those offences suggesting that their perpetrators are serious and/or persistent social threats. Improved techniques for identifying the point at which this distinction can be made provide for a more sophisticated approach, which may in turn be reflected in the disposals administered.

For example, the Audit Commission (1996; see also Home Office, 2001a) has advanced the argument that cautioning becomes progressively less effective than prosecution (in the sense of preventing re-offending), which lends support to the government's discouragement of repeat cautioning. Despite the fact that the evidence in support of this conclusion is limited and untested (Audit Commission, 1996), it has become an accepted truth.[2] It appears that the message was also taken into account by the police, with cautioning rates increasing for first-time offenders, and declining for those who were found to re-offend, even before the introduction of Reprimands and Final Warnings sought to set absolute limits to the number of pre-court disposals available to individual young offenders (Home Office, 2001a).

Notwithstanding the evidence of continuities in youth justice, some authors (for example, Goldson, 1997, 1999) appear to share the view that the events of the early 1990s represent a dramatic shift in both ideology and practice in dealing with youth crime. Thus the abandonment of the central elements of the Criminal Justice Act 1991 and the commitment to redevelop custodial regimes for 12–14 year olds seemed to represent 'a death blow to the non-interventionist delinquency management strategies of the 1980s' (Pitts, 2001b, p. 17). Goldson attributes the backsliding of the government to a combination of elements, which created a 'moral panic', with the result that 'a reactionary U turn was launched which rapidly dismantled the successful practice orientation of the previous decade and set a harsh new tone in relation to state responses to children in trouble' (Goldson, 1997, p. 79). The evidence for this, in Goldson's view, is the renewed commitment to incarcerating children in defiance of the UN Convention on the Rights of the Child, which the government itself adopted only in 1991.

To some extent, the judgement as to whether this was a period of rapid reversal or steady continuity is a matter of interpretation, as Cohen (1985) reminds us. As he puts it, developments in the criminal justice sphere can readily be characterized according to one of three perspectives: 'uneven progress', 'we blew it', or 'it's all a con'. Indeed, it is likely that an effective analysis will draw on all three (see Chapter 7). There is no doubt that the 1990s did witness significant changes in the political climate, with the two

[2]More recent evidence (Kemp et al., 2002) questions this assumption, suggesting that action short of prosecution is likely to be more effective than prosecution itself in reducing re-offending by young people, even when administered for offences committed subsequent to their third or fourth criminal 'proceedings'.

leading political parties seeking to outbid each other to appear the 'toughest' on youth crime; and, at the same time, there was a clear and substantial change in the way that young offenders were treated. While Smith, D. (1999) cautions us against overstating arguments based on out-come indicators alone, the coincidence of political 'noise' and more punitive practice is not accidental, and it does form an important backdrop for thinking about the future of youth justice. At the same time, one is forced to acknowledge that other trends, such as creeping 'corporatism' (Pratt, 1989), the continuing commitment to providing offence-focused alternatives to custody, and the persistence of the sentencing tariff (notwithstanding the 1991 Act), suggest that the organization and delivery of youth justice may feel little different in the sphere of practice, even as dramatic contextual shifts occur.

This last observation is an important one, as it seems to indicate that even as political and strategic forces may have quite a significant impact on the nature of the target population for youth justice interventions, the management and delivery of these interventions might show a substantial degree of consistency over time. This sense of continuity, in turn, may serve to mask some of the more problematic shifts demonstrated, towards more intrusive, and earlier, interventions with young people identified as offenders.

Chapter 3

Old wine, new bottles –
New Labour and youth justice

'Tough on crime, tough on the causes of crime ...'

Although this quotation has become something of a cliché, it is still a valid
starting point for a consideration of the New Labour project in the area of
youth justice, and for a number of quite distinct reasons. It is indicative of
a wider trend towards 'soundbite' politics, whereby persistent and
substantial social problems are identified, diagnosed and solved in a
matter of seconds. But aside from this, the quotation's author, Tony Blair,
writing at the time (1993) as Shadow Home Secretary, went on to become
Prime Minister, with both a high degree of interest in and, of course,
substantial influence over policy in relation to young people. In addition,
it seems that the emergence of a distinctive 'New Labour' position in
relation to youth crime can be traced to this time, when a perceived
political imperative of challenging Tory dominance in this area of policy
began to be translated into a coherent strategy. Events since that point, and
particularly since Labour's acquisition of power in 1997, must be seen in
this light of attempting to establish hegemony in an area where
traditionally the Conservatives had been identified as having the best
policies.

Central to this political strategy was the linking of criminal behaviour
with its antecedents and underlying causes, although, as time goes on,
there is less and less evidence of an explicit attempt to sustain this

connection by leading members of the government. In 1993, though, Tony Blair, writing in the *Daily Express* (31 August), made the connection between individual responsibility for the commission of crime and the social factors which might account for this behaviour.

Importantly for an analysis of the youth justice system, this attempt to address the context of offending as well as criminal act itself should lead us to consider specific policies related to youth offending as but one element of a wider strategy to address factors associated with it, such as poverty, family problems, wider criminal influences, and school performance, or, more broadly, 'social exclusion'. It might be argued that attempts to criticize the operation of the youth justice system under New Labour irrespective of the impact of broader policy initiatives are misleading, in that they do not take account of the 'joined up' nature of Labour's approach (Clark, 2002). On the other hand, as we shall see, an understanding of these wider strategies to tackle social exclusion might view them as conflicting with the aims and impact of youth justice policy, thus amplifying more narrowly focused criticisms. The extent to which different aspects of Labour policy are complementary or contradictory is an important question. The aim of this chapter is to provide a brief account of the broader policy canvas, particularly in relation to the political aims of reducing crime by tackling social exclusion, before concentrating more directly on the emerging picture in relation to youth justice, so that these issues of consistency and conflict between the two can be taken into account.

Social Inclusion and Crime Reduction

In many ways the approach adopted by Labour reflected a well-established consensus, which associated the incidence of youth crime with a number of predisposing factors, including various forms of disadvantage such as 'inadequate parenting', 'lack of training and employment', 'unstable living conditions' and 'drug and alcohol abuse' (Audit Commission, 1996). The incoming government established the Social Exclusion Unit (SEU) in 1997 to develop an integrated strategy to address these issues, both individually and collectively. The SEU's initial analysis confirmed the assumption that specific problems tended to be associated with others, and that they had a compound effect, generating a pattern of 'social exclusion', that was concentrated in particular communities and neighbourhoods:

... the poorest neighbourhoods have tended to become rundown, more prone to crime, and more cut off from the labour market. The national picture conceals pockets of intense deprivation where the problems of unemployment are acute and hopelessly tangled up with poor health, housing and education. (Social Exclusion Unit, 1998, paragraph 1)

Given the interrelated nature of many such problems, and their significance in their own right, the advantage of tackling them in a coherent fashion appeared self-evident:

Above all, a joined-up problem has never been addressed in a joined-up way. Problems have fallen through the cracks between Whitehall Departments or central and local government. And at neighbourhood level, there has been no one in charge of pulling together all the things that need to go right at the same time. (Social Exclusion Unit, 1998, paragraph 7)

Further support for this kind of strategy was offered by historical evidence, which suggested that tackling one type of problem might create a kind of 'virtuous circle' with other benefits following. The evidence from the Headstart programme in the USA has long been taken as suggesting that early-years interventions to support families and children can have long-term benefits across a number of areas, including improved educational attainment, more employment and reduced levels of offending. Thus, the investment in family support and improved parenting skills through the Sure Start programme (£1.4 billion by 2003/4; Social Exclusion Unit, 2001) is at least partly justified by its anticipated contribution to the reduction in youth crime in years to come (Sure Start, 2000).

Equally, high rates of teenage pregnancy, school non-attendance, unemployment and neighbourhood decay are all seen as interwoven and likely to be associated with increased crime rates:

This 'joined-up' nature of social problems is one of the key factors underlying the concept of social exclusion – a relatively new idea in British policy debate. It includes low income, but is broader and focuses on the link between problems such as, for example, unemployment, poor skills, *high crime*, poor housing and family breakdown.' (Social Exclusion Unit, 2001, paragraph 4)

So, we can observe a range of initiatives developed under the umbrella of promoting social inclusion, which address social problems with established links to offending rates. For example, it has been noted that offending is associated strongly with 'non-attachment to school' and lack of 'parental supervision' (Graham and Bowling, 1995). High crime areas are observed to demonstrate characteristics of *'compound social dislocations* – that is, an accumulation of social problems alongside crime, including drug-misuse, family violence, teenage pregnancy, children taken into care, and school failure ...' (Hope, 1998, p. 53). At the same time it is observed these are *'areas of concentrated poverty* .... Here, low skilled and otherwise disadvantaged youth often fail to gain access to the primary labour market. Such conditions bring together vulnerable victims and potential offenders ...' (Hope, 1998, p. 52).

It is interesting to note that many of the initiatives undertaken by government in its social inclusion programme address factors that have been linked with an increased likelihood of offending, whether at the level of individual predisposition or community susceptibility. It could thus be argued that these broader initiatives were intended to contribute to the aim of 'preventing offending', to which the government had committed itself in its policy statements on youth justice (Home Office, 1997a; 1997b). Indeed, as the strategy developed, it appeared that 'prevention' was being pursued on three levels – general social programmes, targeted schemes for 'at risk' groups, and individual interventions with known offenders (or 'troublemakers').

Generalized Crime Prevention

By 2001 the government was able to boast a range of initiatives directed at aspects of social exclusion linked to the risk of crime, including: truancy and school exclusion; neighbourhood renewal; teenage pregnancy; and new employment opportunities for young people (Social Exclusion Unit, 2001). For example, a series of initiatives was introduced to address school exclusion and truancy, at a cost of £300 million over the first four years (1997–2001). This programme included the establishment of Learning Support Units, additional places in Pupil Referral Units, and the addition of incentives to schools to retain students at risk of exclusion. In addition to these wide-ranging measures, however, targeted schemes to reduce truancy, including 'truancy sweeps', negotiated between police and Local Education Authorities, were put in place following the extension of police powers in December 1998. It was reported that 'in York, when truancy sweeps were launched in 1999, youth crime fell by 67 per cent, and in parts of Newham, car crime fell by 70 per cent' (Social Exclusion Unit, 2001 Annex B, paragraph 16). Here, the link between dealing with educational

Table 3.1 Government youth crime prevention strategies

Category	Generalized	Targeted	Individualized
Object of intervention	Disadvantaged neighbourhoods, problem populations, 'crime' in general	'At risk' groups, marginalized young people	Known offenders, anti-social individuals
Methods of intervention	Family support, Community development, education and training	Leisure schemes, project work, work, learning opportunities	Offending behaviour programmes, surveillance, restrictions of freedom
Intervention programmes / mechanisms	Sure Start Teenage Pregnancy Initiative, Connexions, Social Inclusion: Pupil Support (SIPS)	'On Track', Youth Inclusion Programme, 'Summer Splash'	Criminal justice system, sentences, other sanctions (e.g., bail conditions)
Outcome targets	Long-term, general reduction in crime figures	Medium-term, area based, reduced offending rates	Short-term stop / reduce individual offending

problems and youth offending is made quite explicit, and the reduction in crime is advanced as a justification for the strategy of getting young people back into school.

In a different sense, the teenage pregnancy initiative developed in response to an earlier SEU report (Social Exclusion Unit, 1999b) is linked to youth crime, in that:

A module on sex and relationships education for *young offenders* [my emphasis] has been developed as part of the Life skills package with the Prison Service. The Sex Education Forum has produced supporting materials. The sexual health education course for young offenders will be rolled out from April 2001 .... (Social Exclusion Unit, 2001, Annex D, paragraph 8)

Here, too, it seems that intervention to address concerns about teenage pregnancy and early parenthood are linked to a belief that this can help to promote 'responsible' behaviour and conformity.

The concern about the implications of unemployment for young people was addressed early on in the SEU's existence (Social Exclusion Unit, 1999a), and this work led to the establishment of the Connexions Service[1], which would ensure that every young person had access to a Personal Adviser to support her/him in the transition to the world of work and adult responsibilities. The government launched the Connexions Service in 2000, with a spending commitment of £420 million, aiming to provide better access to careers advice, and opportunities for personal development for young people leaving school:

> Connexions will provide information, advice, support and guidance to all teenagers through a network of Personal Advisers based in schools, further education colleges and elsewhere. The service has a range of ambitious targets to improve participation and achievement in education and training, and to reduce drug abuse, *offending* [my emphasis] and teenage pregnancy rates. (Social Exclusion Unit, 2001, paragraph 5.22)

It was reported that this approach showed early signs of positive outcomes:

> Thirteen Connexions pilots have already demonstrated how a Personal Adviser can make a real difference. There are examples within the pilots of young people at risk being pulled back from the brink of chaos and set up to achieve greater success in later life. (Social Exclusion Unit, 2001, Annex E, paragraph 3)

Specific funding was also earmarked to improve educational opportunities for young offenders (Social Exclusion Unit, 2001).

The government also promised a 'revolutionary approach' to the problems of disadvantage and deprivation in specific neighbourhoods. This would be fuelled by the creation of a £900 million Neighbourhood Renewal Fund, and targets included improved educational attainment and reductions in crime, specifically domestic burglary (to be cut by 25% during 2001–05).

---

[1]There is increasingly a divergence of terminology between England and Wales. The Welsh equivalent to Connexions is Extending Entitlement, (National Assembly for Wales, 2000).

Targeted Youth Crime Prevention

As well as establishing an approach to social exclusion that was intended to provide a range of social benefits, including a reduction in youth crime, the incoming 1997 Labour government focused on a number of more specific crime reduction initiatives, targeted at young people on the margins. Some of these, admittedly, represent extensions or additions to existing programmes, including drug education and crime prevention in schools, Safer Cities programmes, and youth crime prevention initiatives, focusing on specific issues such as bullying, graffiti and vandalism (Home Office, 1997b). New initiatives, to promote a more 'joined up' approach at local level, included the establishment of a new requirement for local authorities and police to work together to reduce crime and improve community safety (through the establishment of Crime and Disorder Reduction Partnerships), 'so that the Government expects that measures to tackle youth crime will figure wherever that is a problem locally' (Home Office, 1997, p. 10).

The implication of this was that while government would expect local agencies to act to reduce crime, the precise means adopted should be based on local factors, such as the nature of the community and the specific problem identified.

Additional funding was provided for such initiatives by further government programmes aimed at specific groups of young people. These included On Track, launched in December 1999, aiming to provide preventive interventions for children aged 4–12. The menu of methods to be used is cited as including 'home–school partnerships, home visiting, parent training, structured pre-school education and family therapy' (Children and Young People's Unit, 2002).

In an approach that carries echoes of the 'Catch 'em Young' ideas espoused by the Conservative government of the early 1980s, and of the early pioneers of Intermediate Treatment in the late 1960s, On Track aims to ensure that 'children at risk of offending are identified early and they and their families provided with consistent services through the child's development' (Children and Young People's Unit, 2002). Similar sentiments are also expressed for the Youth Inclusion Programme (YIP), whose target group is 'the most disaffected young people in the 13 to 16 age range' (Morgan Harris Burrows, 2001, p. 1). The aim of this series of projects, launched in 2000, was to identify 50 young people at greatest risk of offending in the highest crime areas in England and Wales, and to incorporate them in a variety of interventions involving young people in general, including holiday schemes, sport, after-school activities, informal education, and social-skills training. Early results from the YIP were said

55

to be encouraging (Morgan, Harris Burrows, 2001), with a 32% fall in crime reported in Doncaster and a 14% fall in Gateshead and Wrexham.

Further development of this kind of approach is evidenced by schemes such as 'Splash', initiated by the Youth Justice Board in 2000 to provide Summer activities for young people at risk – borrowing, it seems, from the much-praised French model of the *étés jeunes* (Pitts, 2001b).

In their broad-based approach and aspirations towards promoting social inclusion, these programmes could be said to demonstrate a degree of consistency with the wider aims of the government of avoiding setting individuals and groups apart, and of providing opportunities for growth, development and personal achievement, leading to social acceptance. While there have been criticisms of 'targeting' (Percy-Smith, 2000) and the viability of an 'administrative' approach to tackling structural problems (J. Clarke *et al.*, 2000), these programmes do appear to offer both a substantial investment in, and a clear commitment to, the principles of an inclusive approach to crime prevention.

Individualized Crime Prevention

However, alongside the inclusive measures detailed above, both gen-eralized and targeted, the new government also put forward a range of 'crime prevention' measures that focused on identified offenders and troublemakers, and appeared to reflect more a concern with social control than with social inclusion. For example, Labour's White Paper *No More Excuses* (Home Office, 1997b) proposed a range of measures under the heading 'Effective Intervention in the Community' that aimed to intervene directly with children and young people 'at risk' of becoming offenders, and their parents: 'the child safety order is designed to protect children under ten who are at risk of becoming involved in crime or who have already started to behave in an anti-social or criminal manner' (Home Office, 1997b, p. 15). Presumably here the word 'protect' is intended also to imply the words 'from themselves'! The order (for children under 10, it should be emphasized) would allow the court to require a child to comply with a range of specific instructions, such as 'to be home at certain times' or to attend 'a local youth programme', with the option of instituting care proceedings for failure to comply. In addition to the order targeted at specific children, the government also proposed the introduction of a 'local child curfew', with the dual aim of protecting children from the risk of harm and preventing 'crime and disorder' (Home Office, 1997b, p. 16).

These measures would be complemented by the proposed 'parenting order', which would require parents to attend training and ensure compliance by their children, the justification for this being that 'inadequate parental supervision is strongly associated with offending – in a Home Office study, 42% of juveniles who had low or medium levels of parental supervision offended, but only 20% of juveniles with a high level of supervision' (Home Office, 1997b, p. 12).

Thus, the New Labour government's youth crime prevention strategy could be argued to have three distinct elements: one with a focus on the social factors associated with crime, and developed as an integral element of an overarching social inclusion programme; one that aimed to target and intervene with individuals 'at risk' within their communities and neighbourhoods; and one to address antisocial and pre-criminal behaviour directly by imposing a range of control measures on 'problem' children and their parents. This latter measure, of course, would also be supplemented by the extensive range of criminal sanctions proposed under the government's reform programme for the youth justice system, to which we will now turn.

The End of Tolerance – the Roots of Reform

The specific project of tackling youth crime, which formed such a central element in the incoming Labour government's reform programme in 1997, can be traced back to a number of emerging strands of thought, linking research evidence, direct experience and political ideas. These coalesced to provide a coherent and politically attractive rationale for the change strategy, which subsequently emerged in the White Paper *No More Excuses* (Home Office, 1997b).

It had become increasingly apparent over the previous decade or so that the impact of crimes committed by young people was a major social issue (Lea and Young, 1984; Kinsey *et al.*, 1986). 'Left realists' argued that 'criminality' should not be seen simply as the political and ideological consequence of the imposition of state control on young people, but also as a feature of the everyday experience of most communities, and especially those experiencing a range of disadvantages. Not only do the official figures conceal a huge number of unrecorded offences, but these are also likely to affect certain individuals and groups in society disproportionately, with poorer people more likely to be burgled, and young Black men being more likely to suffer violent attacks, for example (Lea and Young, 1984, p. 22). The victimization of specific groups, such as women and ethnic minorities, and the concentration of specific crimes in poorer areas, was seen as requiring an active range of responses to tackle these forms of behaviour in their own right, in order to pursue social justice:

57

> Law and order ... is a radical issue. It is an issue for the poor and the old, least able to resist the impact of crimes that ... may appear trivial. It is an issue for ethnic minorities suffering racial harassment and racial attacks. It is an issue for women suffering ... male harassment and violence. ... All these social groups, despite their many differing interests, have a common interest in combating crime.' (Kinsey *et al.*, 1986, p. 73)

This realization in academic circles found its echo in the direct experience of Labour politicians (notably those 'from working class backgrounds' according to Taylor (1981), who tended to represent those very areas that were experiencing the multiple impacts of a range of disadvantages, including the kind of 'intra-group' (Lea and Young, 1984) crimes that compounded communities' sense of injustice and abandonment. This recognition, combined with Labour's traditional vulnerability to the accusation of being 'soft on crime', led to a significant reappraisal during the party's long period in Opposition.

The first clear indication of a shift in position emerged with Tony Blair's contributions to the debate in the climate of moral panic prevailing in 1993 (see Chapter 2). Moves to develop a new and credible centre-left strategy on youth crime were further intensified with Jack Straw's promotion to the position of Shadow Home Secretary in 1994. His willingness to consider new anti-crime initiatives seemed at least partly to derive from his own history and personal inclinations. His experience of being brought up in relative poverty, and his awareness of his constituents' concerns about crime, led to a reluctance to make excuses for those who offended, whatever their own circumstances. A visit to New York in 1995 enthused him with the notion of 'zero tolerance' policing (Newburn and Jones, 2001). According to the principles of this approach, any and all signs of anti-social behaviour and community disintegration must be tackled swiftly and resolutely (Kelling, 1998). This message was put across quite bluntly, and with a distinct shift of emphasis, away from the causes of crime and towards its manifestations:

> In conjunction with tackling the underlying causes of crime, the community has a right to expect more responsible and less anti-social behaviour from its citizens. That means less intimidation, bullying and loutish behaviour on the streets and in our towns and city centres. (Straw, 1995, quoted in Charman and Savage, 1999)

These aspirations were quickly transformed into statements of policy in preparation for the forthcoming General Election, at least partly in order to neutralize the Conservatives' perceived advantage in this area of public policy (Pitts, 2001b). So, by 1996, the language of 'blame', 'responsibility' and 'punishment' had entered Labour Party rhetoric. In launching its pre-election drive to take the initiative, Labour's policy document on youth offending stated that:

> Recognising that there are underlying causes of crime is in no way to excuse or condone offending. Individuals must be held responsible for their own behaviour, and must be brought to justice and punished when they commit an offence. (Straw and Michael, 1996, p. 6)

Equally importantly, a shift away from traditional Labour concerns with children's welfare needs was also signalled: 'the welfare needs of the young offender cannot outweigh the needs of the community to be protected from the adverse consequences of his or her offending behaviour' (Straw and Michael, 1996, quoted in Goldson, 1999, p. 9). The contrast with Labour's attempt to address offending behaviour *through* addressing welfare needs under the Children and Young Persons Act 1969 could not be more explicit. The consequences for government policy when New Labour took power were clear. Youth offending would be dealt with directly in its own right, and at face value. As Goldson (1999) puts it: 'the (re)politicization of youth crime has ushered in a new agenda moulded and fixed around the imperatives of punishment, retribution and re-moralisation' (Goldson, 1999, p. 9).

No More Excuses – the Road to Discipline

The rhetorical separation of youth crime from other areas of policy had a number of other consequences. In particular, it meant that there was emerging a clear distinction between youth justice strategy and the incoming government's broader programme to promote social inclusion, and to tackle those factors identified as the 'causes of crime'.

Arguing, however, that its youth justice policy would complement its social inclusion initiatives, the new Labour government sought to 'shake up' the administration of measures for dealing with young offenders. The 1997 White Paper *No More Excuses*, published swiftly by the government on taking office, set out its vision for the youth justice system clearly and in detail, claiming again that it represented a clean break with the past. This does not do justice to the inevitable historical continuities both political and practical, (for example, the inheritance and adaptation of tagging from

59

the previous Conservative administration), but it does offer us a clear picture of a determined attempt to stake out a distinctive philosophy of youth justice. Indeed, the White Paper made a strong bid to achieve radical change, claiming to herald a 'root and branch reform of the youth justice system', in the words of the Home Secretary's Introduction.

Of particular significance here was the statement that the principal aim of the youth justice system should be purely and simply to prevent offending, thus extending the theme of prevention into the ambit of the justice system itself, and attempting to re-establish a link with pro-grammes aimed at reducing crime by promoting social inclusion (Social Exclusion Unit, 2001).

The aim of preventing offending would be delivered by the realization of a number of key objectives, including requiring offenders and their parents/carers to take responsibility for their behaviour, earlier intervention with first offenders and pre-delinquents, more efficient administrative procedures, and improved partnerships among youth justice agencies. These aims set the parameters for the planned reforms, and it should be noted that they bear some resemblance to the strategies of control set out by authors such as Foucault (1979) and Donzelot (1979), specifically in the attempt to put into operation the notion of parents as agents of intervention, and in the creation of an extended network of agencies with the common objective of preventing crime. The focus, too, on early intervention could be equated with a desire to extend the mechanisms of control, both to earlier stages of individual young offenders' careers, but also into families and communities[2].

Importantly, in tying all aspects of the planned reforms together with the aim of preventing offending, the government's proposals performed the same reductionist sleight of hand as attributed to Foucault (Garland, 1990):

> ... the Government does not accept that there is any conflict between protecting the welfare of a young offender and preventing that individual from offending again. Preventing offending promotes the welfare of the individual young offender and protects the public. (Home Office, 1997b, p. 7)

Apart from conjuring up rather worrying rationalizations along the lines of 'we're only doing this for your own good', this also rather too neatly subsumes two quite distinct and potentially contradictory objectives

[2]Foucault's (1979) graphic term for the extension of the logic and practices of the penal system into the community itself is the 'carceral archipelago'.

under the banner of preventing crime. Conflating rights and responsibilities in this way has significant implications. Once this conceptual
adjustment has been achieved, the scope for justifiable intervention across
all aspects of young people's lives is significantly increased.

The subsidiary aims linked to the prevention of offending also show
signs of representing a more proactive, intensive and intrusive approach.
The responsibilities of parents and young offenders would be reinforced
according to the White Paper; punishment would be made proportionate
to the seriousness and/or persistence of offending; interventions would
be administered swiftly and surely; and young people would be
confronted with the consequences of their behaviour (Home Office, 1997b,
p. 8).

The White Paper proceeded to develop these principles of intervention
in more detail, identifying ways in which the prevention of youth
offending could be achieved under each heading. Thus, for example,
parents' responsibilities could be reinforced through programmes of education and guidance, much in the way envisaged by Donzelot (1979). For a
13-year-old offender who does not attend school, for example, 'a parenting
order might be imposed which required his [sic] parents to attend training
and included additional requirements that they ensure his attendance at
school ...' (Home Office, 1997b, p. 14). As well as the delivery of control by
proxy through the development of parents' role in supervising and
containing young people's behaviour, the White Paper also argues for
effective intervention in the community, as we have already observed,
signalling that 'disposals should focus on changing behaviour as well as
punishment' (Home Office, 1997b, p. 15). Thus, as we have seen, for pre-
delinquent children under the age of 10 the 'Child Safety Order' was proposed, which would incorporate requirements to comply with explicit
instructions, and to attend school.

More widely, child curfews could be applied to an entire
neighbourhood, in order to 'provide an effective immediate method of
dealing with clearly identified patterns of anti-social and disorderly
children who are too young to be left out unsupervised late at night'
(Home Office, 1997, p. 16). These purportedly preventive measures were
targeted at pre-delinquents, extending the scope of the youth justice
system into areas of behaviour management previously beyond the reach
of the criminal law. The distinction between 'prevention' and 'crime
control' appears increasingly blurred here.

Moving up the scale, for those at the early stages of delinquent careers,
the White Paper proposed more stringent, but finely graded, forms of
intervention, including 'Reprimands' for a first and minor offence, and
then the 'Final Warning' for a second offence. Unlike their predecessors,

Informal Action and Cautions, these would represent explicitly progressive steps up the offending tariff, and in the case of the Final Warning would be accompanied by planned programmes of corrective intervention with the young person concerned. Here the concepts of assessment and targeted intervention can easily be equated with Foucault's (1979) vision of systematically organized and closely managed mechanisms of discipline, where the intervention is aligned to the behaviour of the specific offender.

Further proposals contained in the White Paper also reflect these principles in certain key respects. Thus, there is an identifiable degree of continuity of purpose as young people move through the system. For example, the proposed 'Action Plan Order' for convicted young offenders was designed to ensure that precisely tailored programmes, involving a range of options, could be applied to individual young offenders, depending on a detailed assessment of their particular characteristics and behaviour.

Taken further again, into the custodial setting, the Government's approach was reflected in proposals for a new framework for penal facilities, with changes both in the scope and purposes of the secure institutions. As a result, new regimes were to be developed. The government expressed the intention of seeing that greater emphasis would be placed on preventing offending and responding to progress:

> The Government believes that a custodial sentence should not be an end in itself – it protects the public by removing the young offender from the opportunity to offend, but the fundamental aim of both custodial and community sentences, in line with the aim of the youth justice system, should be to prevent offending. (Home Office, 1997b, p. 19)

According to the White Paper, sentences should be closely related to the nature of the offence, and should reflect concerns about both seriousness and persistence of offending. They should also be designed to provide a disciplinary framework to encourage and promote compliance and good behaviour. Thus, the proposed 'Detention and Training Order' would build in flexibility, both of sentence length and release date, combined with post-release supervision, to ensure continued compliance under scrutiny. Sustained evidence of responsible behaviour could be rewarded with rights to reduced levels of restriction and surveillance.

In order to support its substantive proposals, the White Paper also promoted two further measures to improve the administration and effectiveness of the youth justice system: the speeding up of the judicial process and the establishment of effective inter-agency partnerships to achieve better coordinated action to prevent offending. In particular, the latter proposal bears a degree of similarity to Foucault's portrayal of an army of professional experts, all geared to identifying, classifying and regulating offenders' behaviour.

Thus, throughout (and beyond) the youth justice system, the government's proposals could be seen to represent 'a kind of carceral continuum', which:

> covers the whole social body, linked by the pervasive concern to identify deviance, anomalies and departures from the relevant norms. This framework of surveillance and correction stretches from the least irregularity to the greatest crime and brings the same principles to bear on each. (Garland, 1990, p. 151)

The Crime and Disorder Act 1998 – the Micro-politics of Social Control

Most of the proposals set out in *No More Excuses* were incorporated in the 1998 Act itself, and this, in turn, was implemented almost in its entirety by June 2000.

The Act develops the proposals in the White Paper, particularly in areas such as the creation of inter-agency frameworks to implement youth offending strategies. The establishment of Youth Offending Teams, local inter-agency partnerships and statutory plans to tackle youth crime are all put on a statutory footing. The Act has thereby created the structures within which a corporate approach to crime control can be pursued.

In addition, the Act has put in place a series of mechanisms and procedures for ensuring detailed implementation of its objectives. This is where the machinery of scrutiny and regulation is realized. For example, the requirements relating to assessment of young offenders (and alleged young offenders in the pre-trial phase) has led to the development of the ASSET form (in several versions), which serve to measure and classify individuals for the purposes of determining the specific intervention to be applied.

Further than that, the Act is quite precise in attempting to link specific programmes of intervention with the particular circumstances and criminal careers of individual young offenders. It seems to be highly prescriptive in this respect, leaving little room for discretion among either criminal justice practitioners or judicial decision-makers. Thus, the progression through Reprimands and Final Warnings for first- and second-time offenders is closely prescribed, and leaves little room for manoeuvre, as some Youth Offending Teams are already finding (Pragnell, 2001). The Act also seeks to preclude the courts from considering a Conditional Discharge in circumstances where a Final Warning has been administered previously, thereby impinging on their discretion as well.

In these ways, there appears a:

> ... continuous gradation of the established specialized and competent authorities ... which, without resort to arbitrariness, but strictly according to the regulations, by means of observation and assessment, hierarchized, differentiated, judged, punished and moved gradually from the correction of irregularities to the punishment of crime. (Foucault, 1979, p. 299)

Interestingly, this distinction between misdemeanours (*délits*) and crimes (*crimes*) remains embedded in the French justice system (Ministère de la Justice, 2001). However, we can also see just such a process of gradation and progression set out in the detailed prescriptions of the Crime and Disorder Act:

1. Protective orders are put in place to deal with the anti-social tendencies of those individuals (or communities of young people) identified as pre-delinquent: the Child Safety Order, the Curfew Order, the Parenting Order, and the Anti-Social Behaviour Order.

2. Progressive pre-court disposals, accompanied in some cases by corrective programmes are made available *only* for those at the early stages of their offending careers: Reprimands, Final Warnings, then fettered court discretion (no discharges available).

3. A range of disposals available to the courts once the options above have been exhausted. These incorporate both traditional and new disposals, but the sense of progression is clear and unavoidable: the Referral Order (an additional option provided by the Youth Justice and Criminal Evidence Act 1999), for first-time court appearances, Discharges (where permitted), Fines, the Reparation Order, the Supervision Order, the Action Plan Order, the Community Service Order (for those over 16). In some of these cases, it is possible to apply additional conditions, or build up combined disposals, but this does not detract from the central principle of a graded and targeted response.

4. An array of custodial sentences that form the apex of the penal structure. It is the use and form of custody that sets the tone for all

other aspects of the justice system. Thus, we can observe, once again, recurring themes: progression, assessment and the application of tailored disciplinary regimes – the Detention and Training Order, the Youth Custody Order, the Section 53 Order – although in practice, the Prison Inspectorate has shown that the performance of the various regimes is rather more uniform (uniformly oppressive, that is – see Goldson, 2002; Joint Chief Inspectors, 2002).

Further Reform: Extending Control or Muddying the Water?

Following the passage of the Crime and Disorder Act, the government attempted to develop and improve on its youth justice reforms even further. Despite the ostensible ideological and operational coherence of the major reforms of 1998, subsequent developments have appeared rather more inconsistent. While there have been some interesting and promising new initiatives, at the core of the Labour government's strategy to date there appears to lie a continuing preoccupation with improving the machinery of control.

The Referral Order – the advance of restorative justice?

Immediately following the 1998 Act, the government introduced a further piece of legislation, which duly became the Youth Justice and Criminal Evidence Act 1999, notable for the introduction of the Referral Order. The Referral Order was signposted by the White Paper *No More Excuses*, which proposed that for young people pleading guilty on their first court appearance, the court should, apart from exceptional cases, refer them to a 'youth panel', for their offences to be dealt with outside the framework of the justice system. It was argued that this would enable the application of principles of 'restorative justice' within the context of youth offending. According to the White Paper, these principles are:

restoration: young offenders apologising to their victims and making amends for the harm they have done;

reintegration: young offenders paying their debt to society, putting their crime behind them and rejoining the law abiding community; and

responsibility: young offenders – and their parents – facing the consequences of their offending behaviour and taking responsibility for preventing further offending.
(Home Office, 1997, p. 32)

Despite this attempt to provide a rationale for the new approach, it should be noted that neither the definition nor the principles of restorative justice are the subject of wide agreement (Haines, 2000), a discussion to which we shall return subsequently. For the moment, however, the important point is that the policy and legislative context is framed by the aims set out in the White Paper.

On referral to the youth panel, the young person and parents would be expected to attend a 'panel session', with attendance by victims and other relevant people where appropriate. Legal representation would not be allowed, in order to ensure that the panel was able to engage 'directly' with the young offender.

The expectation would be that a 'contract' would be drawn up between the panel and the young person, setting out the requirements placed on her/him and her/his parents. These would 'always include an obligation to make **reparation**. This might be achieved through a letter of apology or a direct meeting with the victim; by putting right the damage caused by the offence; or through financial compensation' (Home Office, 1997, p. 32). Reparation could also be made to the 'community' where direct means were inappropriate. In addition, the contract might be expected to include requirements to participate in specific activities, such as counselling or drug rehabilitation, unpaid community work, and educational programmes. It might also specify that the young person should *not* participate in certain activities, or attend particular places. According to the White Paper, although the youth court would have no control over the content, it could determine the length of time for which the programme should operate, with three-monthly progress reviews by the panel.

These proposals were enacted, largely as they stood, by Part I of the Youth Justice and Criminal Evidence Act 1999 (consolidated in the Powers of Criminal Courts (Sentencing) Act 2000), so that referral to a 'youth offender panel' (the term adopted in the legislation itself) is made mandatory on a young person's first court appearance, except where the court intends to impose a custodial sentence (or hospital order), or deal with the case by way of an absolute discharge. Thus, the youth offender panel and the Referral Order are established as central features of the youth justice system, but only at this particular point in the young person's offending career.

It should also be noted that the nature of the process itself places the Referral Order in a very specific relationship to the youth justice system as a whole, with associated implications for the restorative principles to which it aspires. Failure to attend the panel, failure to agree a contract, failure to comply, and failure to complete the agreed programme satisfactorily are all grounds for the return of the young person to court for an alternative sentence. This, in turn, may well be influenced by the connotations of failure to cooperate with the Referral Order itself.

Tightening the grip – further measures of control

Despite the innovative approach to resolving the problems of youth offending heralded by the Referral Order, many other measures following the Crime and Disorder Act convey much more strongly a sense of 'business as usual', with a raft of changes in law and government policy which have intensified the punitive aspects of the youth justice system. This process has been accompanied by rather florid rhetoric from senior Labour government ministers, including the Home Secretary, David Blunkett:

> One of the biggest challenges we face is how to deal with young offenders who believe that their age makes them untouchable, who flout the law, laugh at the police and leave court on bail free to offend again. The public are sick and tired of their behaviour and expect the criminal justice system to be able to keep them off the streets. (David Blunkett, Labour Party Election Broadcast, 24 April 2002)

These sentiments complement Labour's published plans to continue to address the need to dictate young people's behaviour at all stages of the judicial process (Home Office, 2001c). The government's vision statement for the justice system as a whole, *Criminal Justice: The Way Ahead*, was published in February 2001, and offered some pointers as to imminent changes for young offenders, including the introduction of more restrictive community programmes, tighter surveillance of alleged offenders on bail, and increased availability of places in custody. Announcing the new Intensive Supervision and Surveillance Programme (ISSP), with funding of £45 million from April 2001, the document states:

> The Youth Justice Board is making grants to around fifty YOTs (or groups of YOTs) for each to work with 50–60 hardcore repeat young offenders a year.

> An ISSP will last at least six months for each offender. It will combine close surveillance by the police and other agencies with a highly structured intensive daily programme tackling the causes of the offending. During the first three months the supervision programme will be for at least five hours a day on weekdays with access to support during the evenings and weekends.

> The whereabouts of each young offender on the programme will be checked at least twice daily with 24 hours a day, seven days a week surveillance where this is necessary. Techniques may include electronic tagging, voice verification ..., tracking ..., and intelligence led policing. (Home Office, 2001, p. 32)

There is a strong sense in this proposal that surveillance and containment dominates at the expense of any underlying factors linked to the young person's offending, and there is no recognition of the importance of addressing need.

The ISSP was launched initially in 41 areas of England and Wales, and subsequently its availability was extended to young people at risk of being remanded to custody. Thus, a highly intensive and intrusive programme comes to be applied to young people prior to conviction and sentence.

In addition to the ISSP, proposals were included in *Criminal Justice: The Way Ahead* for a further extension of courts' powers 'to refuse bail to youngsters with a history of committing or being charged with imprisonable offences' (Home Office, 2001a, p. 32). As it stands, this represents a significant shift of emphasis, creating further doubt as to the government's commitment to the underlying presumption in favour of bail, established under the Bail Act 1976.

This reform was put in place by Section 130 of the Criminal Justice and Police Act 2001, which significantly relaxed the constraints placed on courts in making decisions to refuse bail. This provision effectively enabled courts to impose a 'security requirement' where young people (aged 12–16) had a 'recent history' of repeated offending, and where, in the court's opinion, they required to be kept in secure conditions (a remand centre, a prison, or local authority secure accommodation) to prevent the commission of further imprisonable offences. Earlier constraints relating to the seriousness of the alleged offences, or the level of risk to the public, were effectively removed by the way in which these new powers were framed. As the supporting guidance observes 'the courts have not previously had the power to remand into secure detention those young people who have committed, or who are alleged to have committed, repeated offences of a less serious nature' (Home Office, 2002, p. 2).

In addition, the same piece of legislation provided courts with the power to require the 'electronic monitoring' (tagging) of young people on bail or remanded to local authority accommodation (Sections 131 and 132).

Finally, in this bundle of enhancements to the Labour government's earlier reforms, there was the commitment 'over the next five years to build 400 additional secure training centre places, providing intensive supervision and high quality programmes for young people in custody'

(Home Office, 2001a, p. 32). These places are presumably intended, in part, to meet the additional demand arising from the increased use of secure remands provided for by the Criminal Justice and Police Act (National Association for Youth Justice, 2001).

There seems no doubt, then, that this aspect of the government's reform programme in youth justice is characterized by a desire to intensify levels of control and restriction of liberty, both in community interventions and by extending the use of secure placements, especially for young people on remand. This represents a clear reversal of earlier commitments to minimize the use of secure provisions, particularly for those under the age of 15, thus continuing the erosion of safeguards for younger children initiated by the Crime and Disorder Act (Goldson and Peters, 2000).

The annual event of new crime legislation also saw the introduction of the Criminal Justice Bill 2002, which gave ample confirmation that the intended direction of government policy remained consistent. In particular, the Bill provided for earlier use of Parenting Orders (Clause 261) and the attachment of Individual Support Orders to Anti-Social Behaviour Orders, to require young people 'to undertake education-related activities' (Clause 259)[3]. In addition, for those aged 16 and over, a variety of orders would be consolidated under the catch-all term Community Order (Clause 160). According to the National Association for Youth Justice (2003), the Bill stands as a missed opportunity to ensure that criminal justice for children reflects international standards of fairness and decent treatment. At the same time, the introduction of additional sanctions for parents and children appears to represent a further tightening of control.

The State of Policy: Coherence, Camouflage or Confusion?

At this point it might be helpful to attempt to reflect on the meaning and impact of youth justice policy as constructed by the Labour government in its first five years of office (1997–2002). This in turn will help us to consider in subsequent chapters questions of implementation, impact and possibilities for the future.

The first question to consider in this context is perhaps the *intent* of the government's reform programme. As already noted, it is important to distinguish between 'youth crime' and 'youth justice' when considering policy aims and intervention strategies. The government maintains that its initiatives in these areas are complementary, and that they should be seen

[3]See also the White Paper, *Respect and Responsibility*, (Home Office, 2003).

as part of a coherent whole. According to the Prime Minister, a political consensus has emerged, based on a common understanding that while offending cannot be excused and must be dealt with, 'tackling the root causes is essential' (Blair, 2002). This understanding, he argues, underpins a comprehensive programme of reform, in which the parts are coherent and complementary. Summer activity programmes, for example, are mirrored by action to tackle anti-social behaviour head on, and tougher sentences for 'street crime'. This is part of a package of reforms intended to 'deliver a fair balance between the rights of victims, witnesses, the rest of law-abiding society and the defendant' (Blair, 2002). And he added that:

> Re-balancing the system means tackling the causes of crime – striving to give everyone in our society the rights and the opportunities they need to avoid a life of crime.
>
> It means tough legislation – backed up with police on the streets – to reduce crime and anti-social behaviour and reinforce people's responsibility to society.
>
> It means bringing our courts into the twenty first century, and making sure that they serve victims and witnesses as well as they serve defendants.
>
> And it means sentencing that keeps the public safe from the most dangerous prisoners, and which rehabilitates those who can be diverted from re-offending. (Blair, 2002)

Vision statements such as this have been supported by detailed policy documents, such as *Criminal Justice: The Way Ahead* and the White Paper *Justice for All*. The Criminal Justice Bill 2002 has further signalled the government's intentions. A range of 'tough' and authoritarian reforms within the justice system are explicitly presented as one half of the overall

Table 3.2 'Tough on crime, tough on the causes of crime' – the government's programme

Tough on crime	Tough on the causes of crime
Catching and convicting criminals	Sure Start
Prosecuting and rules of evidence	Neighbourhood Renewal
Review of the criminal courts	Raising standards (education)
What works (prison service reform)	New Deal
A better deal for victims and witnesses	Anti-Drugs Coordination Unit

Adapted from: *Criminal Justice: The Way Ahead* (Home Office, 2001a, p. 22)

crime reduction project, complementing a series of community safety initiatives, as the following table summarizes.

While these measures are presented as part of a coherent whole, it is clearly not sufficient simply to list them alongside each other in order to substantiate Labour's claims. A number of concerns must, indeed, be addressed here.

First, it has been argued that the 'managerial' approach to tackling social exclusion adopted by New Labour is itself inadequate to deal with the structural causes of crime. Pitts argues that dealing with partial and superficial 'manifestations' of poverty is unlikely to provide real or lasting solutions to the 'structural economic and political problems at the heart of social exclusion' (Pitts, 2001b, p. 147). He further suggests that this kind of approach has led to a concern with identifiable, and measurable 'risk factors' which provide, at best, only a limited understanding of the causes of offending (Pitts, 2001a). Thus, concerns with 'social exclusion' are translated into programmes designed to manage and control its surface manifestations in the form of '[poor] "parenting", "truancy", "drug abuse", "homelessness", "low income" and the like' (Pitts, 2001a, p. 9). As a consequence, initiatives based on tackling these issues, such as 'truancy sweeps', for example, are based on causal assumptions which are un-supported by the available evidence. Managerial indicators of per-formance, therefore, gloss over key questions about both their purposes and their efficacy. The attempt to deal with symptoms in the form of 'risk factors', means that:

> ... we are little nearer understanding the causes of youth crime and our choice of methods of intervention must remain haphazard. In the event, this, by no means insignificant, problem has been resolved by a process of political and scientific attrition. (Pitts, 2001a, p. 9)

Linked with these concerns is the fear that dealing with social problems by way of a 'targeted' approach has a number of unintended consequences. As Percy-Smith (2000) puts it, there are problems with both the techniques of 'targeting' and their impact on those individuals and communities they single out. It is, as she acknowledges, very difficult to find sufficiently accurate and sensitive tools to 'identify individuals, groups or areas who should be the focus of targeted actions' (Percy-Smith, 2000, p. 18). In addition, because these mechanisms are crude, people are inevitably going to be wrongly classified, with some of those being 'targeted' attributed with problems they do not have, and others being 'missed'. As the Audit Commission (1996, p. 58) acknowledges, there is 'no way of predicting accurately which individuals are going to offend'. And, as Pitts (2001b) reminds us, 'risk factors' linked to youth crime operate in quite different ways in different contexts. Apart from the practical difficulties associated with it, targeting of groups for specific types of interventions has other unhelpful consequences. It 'can exacerbate negative perceptions of particular areas or groups' (Percy Smith, 2000, p. 18). This, in turn, can be linked to additional problems, such as racial stereotyping and discrimination. This is an issue of particular importance in the present context, where young Black men are routinely overrepresented at all stages within the justice system (Goldson and Peters, 2000).

Not only are there potential limitations in policy approaches that are based on targeting and on managerial solutions to youth crime at the level of groups and communities, but also these shortcomings are intensified when applied to the youth justice system itself. The account of the criminal justice reforms already given in this chapter shows how the rhetoric of social inclusion is consistently undermined by the intensified focus on individuals who are either identified as offenders, or seen as potential troublemakers. Indeed, this process of singling out those who present the greatest threat, and concentrating interventions on them, might be based at least partly on assumptions about the failure of these individuals to respond constructively to the opportunities provided through broader inclusive programmes, as well as early interventions within the justice system. Thus, the Labour government makes it clear that its interventions will be intensified as young people progress through the stages of an offending career and become 'persistent young offenders' (Home Office, 2001a, p. 31). The government is concerned that 'offenders are returning to court again and again without seeing an appreciable increase in the severity of punishment they receive' (Home Office, 2001a, p. 21). The youth justice system, it seems, is increasingly seen as progressive, drawing on well-established notions of a tariff of disposals (Hudson, 1996), intensifying the mechanisms of scrutiny and control of the young person's behaviour for each offending episode (Foucault, 1979), and demonstrating less and less interest in the 'causes of crime', as far as that individual is concerned.

The final issue to be considered here in relation to developing youth justice policy is that of 'coherence, camouflage or confusion'. By which of these terms might the underlying nature of the New Labour strategy be characterized?

In the light of the overarching emphasis on progressive and targeted interventions that emphasize 'surveillance' and 'incapacitation' (Pitts, 2001a, p. 13), it is difficult to see how other principles espoused by policy-makers within the youth justice system, such as restorative justice and even, ironically, the prevention of offending, can be accorded much priority. The glimpse offered by the Referral Order of an alternative perspective appears less substantial when its limited role within the justice system is acknowledged. In reflecting on the relationship between the Youth Offender Panel in England and Wales and the ostensibly similar Children's Hearings in Scotland, Whyte has noted 'that attempting to define young people in criminal terms alone is an ineffective form of classification with limited predictive validity in terms of getting positive results' (Whyte, 2000, p. 187). This, however, is a major constraint of the Referral Order, which is implemented under the shadow of the court, where a considerable array of sanctions await 'failure', and where the tariff insists that it can only be invoked once, at a particular point in the young person's offending career. Whereas Children's Hearings have a primary concern for the child's welfare, such a concern is absent from the Youth Offender Panel agenda. Even where restorative principles are espoused, 'there is a potential for tension between the YOP and the youth court if the former is following a restorative justice philosophy and the latter is more inclined to punishment' (Bentley, 2000, p. 216).

While it may seem that distinctive but potentially complementary policy goals are espoused within strategies of youth crime and youth justice, the overriding impression is that scrutiny, behaviour management, and the restriction of freedom lie at the heart of New Labour thinking in this area; high profile pronouncements on 'tackling crime' (Blunkett, 2002), 'cracking down on anti-social behaviour' (Blair, 2002) and 'tough new' penalties (Youth Justice Board, 2001) are best characterized as 'an attempt to peddle simplistic, but politically acceptable, solutions to remarkably complex social, economic and cultural problems' (Pitts, 2001a, p. 14).

Overall, then, there is a sense of a confused and incoherent set of policy objectives juxtaposed in the hope that a fortuitous coincidence of positive outcomes will emerge. At the same time, the managerial preoccupation with certainty and control appears likely to ensure that coercive youth justice practices will take precedence over a more flexible and collaborative approach to resolving the problems, both individual and social, that are associated with the crimes of the young.

Chapter 4

Inside the machine

Between Policy and Practice

The previous chapter explored the policy aims and rationale(s) emerging from the New Labour project; but it is also important to consider the ways in which these aspirations have been put into operation. It will be helpful to develop an understanding of the procedures and structures that create the terrain for practice, and which mediate, interpret and amend policy goals. We cannot simply assume that policy as set out by government or other statutory bodies simply acts as a blueprint for the services that are provided on the ground, even in a context where it frequently feels as if practitioners are addressed directly by government, over the heads of intervening agencies and managers. Harris and Webb (1987), for example, develop the idea that the 'macro' level, meaning the legislative and policy framework, and the 'micro' level of direct practice are linked in a dynamic fashion by the 'mezzo' level, which acts not just as a conduit for information and instruction, but allows for interpretation, elaboration and in some cases, revision of policy, as it is transformed into operational guidance.

For a number of reasons, there is an inevitable tension between the general aims of policy and the practical requirements of creating arrangements for delivering these effectively. Most obviously, it is inevitable that general statements of policy will not be sufficiently detailed to inform practice in all circumstances. Practitioners might expect, and indeed require, broad aims to be developed with greater precision to provide a basis for their specific application. In addition, as we know from experience, policy goals might be unrealistic, or in conflict with each other, when it comes to implementation. Mediation is needed to set priorities and unravel contradictory expectations, such as the tension between demands for detailed assessments and limited timescales. We should also expect room to be allowed for variations in policy and procedures to take account of local circumstances, or the particular characteristics of certain groups of the population. Policy, for example, which is 'colour blind' runs the risk of compounding the impacts of racial discrimination experienced elsewhere. It might also be the case that the process of implementation itself runs counter to the overarching aims of policy, and that local adjustments become necessary. For example, the increasing formality of early disposals in youth justice might contribute to delays elsewhere, creating pressure for the extended use of short cuts, such as informal warnings.

There are, therefore, a number of essentially pragmatic and practical reasons for expecting policy at the level of law and national guidance to be developed and modified by agencies and managers to deal with the specific context of implementation. This, in a sense, is a relatively benign reading of the way in which 'bureaucracy', as originally conceptualized by Weber, adapts the intentions of the state in order to ensure that they are practical, realistic and deliverable. This may well be one way in which the machinery of youth justice, which we are shortly to consider, can be appraised: it may be evaluated to the extent that it is more or less efficient and effective in delivering explicit policy goals originating with government, such as the 'prevention of youth crime'.

However, there are other, rather less benign, perspectives on the mechanisms and structures put in place for the delivery of youth justice which must also be considered. Muncie (1999) and Pratt (1989; 2000), for example, have suggested that the increasing emphasis on the apparatus of management in this context should be seen as part of an emerging pattern of closer and more inclusive forms of control, which bind agencies together in a common strategy of containment and coercion. Pratt refers to this as the:

> ... 'dark side' of modernity. That is to say, the seeming humanity and rationalist of punishment in the modern world camouflaged a more intrusive and extensive modality of social control, based around tactics of discipline and surveillance: and at the forefront of such deceptions were the penal experts and the penal bureaucracies. (Pratt, 2000, p. 143)

While Pratt himself argues that this articulation of the machinery of youth justice might itself be superseded in time, there is no doubt that concerns about the impact of 'managerialism' (Muncie and Hughes, 2002) should be addressed in reflecting on the way in which services are organized and delivered.

Alternative perspectives on the management and administration of youth justice could be rather less monolithic than this, suggesting that New Labour, in particular, has established a framework intended to accommodate a range of interests, and to create room for creativity and innovation, as well as promoting the delivery of core programmes and the achievement of specified targets. In this sense, it might be argued, the establishment of a body such as the Youth Justice Board achieves a number of political and practical objectives. Cynically, it might be argued that the creation of such bodies skilfully locates the blame for failures elsewhere than at the doors of government ministers. However, by the same token this opens up space for a potentially greater degree of risk-taking and innovation, than might otherwise be the case. This, in turn, creates the basis for the incorporation into the government project of professional and policy interests that might otherwise be quite critical of some aspects of the reform programme. There is a sense here in which the structures of youth justice themselves constitute contested terrain, which could contribute to a belief that there is 'all to play for', as opposed to the assumption that they merely operate as an arm of government, extending control right down into the microscopic workings of the system.

These, then, are some of the issues that should be considered in reflecting on the procedures, structures and mechanisms put in place to secure the delivery of youth justice at the start of the 21st century.

National Standards: Prescribing Good Practice?

One important element in the changing landscape of the justice system is the development of prescriptive standards for agency management and practice. Like many other recent initiatives, this is not specific to the post-1997 Labour government, and dates back to the early 1990s, at least. This was the time when the criminal justice system in general saw the systematic publication of standards for work with offenders (Smith, D., 1999). In Smith's view, the development of National Standards represented an attempt to formalize interventions with young offenders, and in particular, to impose clear expectations as to the levels of control to be imposed. This, he argues, could also be seen as a progressive process, with the 1995 version of the Standards reflecting a clear shift of emphasis from the 1992 version, towards a concentration on behaviour management, and away from earlier concerns with welfare needs. These aims, he observes, are intended to be met by promoting compliance and responsible behaviour. These developments, he argues, emphasize young offenders' criminality, and accords them no real recognition as children or young people. In arguing for a creative response to the requirements of uniform standards of practice, he is: 'concerned with the recovery of forgotten possibilities, memories of social work's past which have been all but eradicated from practice today by managerial diktat and the rule-bound proceduralism of National Standards' (Smith, D., 1999, p. 163). Smith's concerns appear to be validated by the subsequent action of the Home Office, which showed a preoccupation with the enforcement of compliance with orders and sanctions for breach (Home Office, 1997). It is clear that he identifies the introduction and revision of National Standards as a vehicle for a more regimented approach to offenders and their behaviour, at the expense of issues to do with their welfare and social environment. In this sense, he seems to share the view of those who see corporatism as a vehicle for repression (Muncie and Hughes, 2002).

Are these fears borne out, then, by the revised National Standards for Youth Justice (Youth Justice Board, 2000), issued to coincide with the implementation of the Crime and Disorder Act 1998? Following the legislation, this document sets out, as the principal aim of the youth justice system, the prevention of offending by children and young people. Six objectives are identified in support of this aim, to which all youth justice agencies are expected to work:

the swift administration of justice so that every young person accused of breaking the law has the matter resolved without delay;

confronting young offenders with the consequences of their offending, for themselves and their families, their victims and the community and helping them to develop a sense of responsibility;

intervention that tackles the particular factors that put the young person at risk of offending;

punishment proportionate to the seriousness and persistence of the offending and which strengthens protective factors;

encouraging reparation to victims by young offenders; and,

reinforcing the responsibilities of parents.
(Youth Justice Board, 2000, p. 1)

Not only do the National Standards seek for the first time to provide an overarching framework for the delivery of youth justice services, but they are issued as a corporate document, on behalf of the Youth Justice Board, Home Office, Department for Education and Employment (now DfES), Department of Health, Lord Chancellor's Department and the National Assembly for Wales; and 'they are ... required standards of practice which youth offending teams and others are expected to achieve' (Youth Justice Board, 2000, p. 2). Without acknowledging these as explicit objectives, the preamble to the Standards document also makes a commitment to protecting children's rights and avoiding discriminatory practices in the delivery of interventions.

The Standards themselves cover all stages of the youth justice process, from preventive work through to the supervision of young people sentenced under Section 53 of the Children and Young Persons Act 1933 (now Sections 90 and 91 of the Powers of Criminal Courts (Sentencing) Act 2000). They are directed primarily, but not exclusively, to operational managers (mainly Youth Offending Team Managers), which is perhaps indicative of two emerging themes in government policy documents (and those of allied organizations, such as the Youth Justice Board) – their managerial tone and the fact that they are addressed directly to those responsible for service delivery, bypassing intermediary agencies or strategic bodies.

Preventive work

In keeping with the earlier observations about the government's broader crime prevention strategy, the Standards for preventive work refer directly to the need to establish links between youth offending teams (YOTs) and other services such as Connexions, as well as setting a spending require- ment for preventive work of 2.5% of the YOT budget. Unlike many of the other Standards, these are broad and general, and they are addressed to the local authority chief executive.

Work with young people following arrest

These Standards refer to the requirement to provide a service to young people following arrest, and while subject to police investigation. Most of this area of practice is governed by the Police and Criminal Evidence Act 1984 and associated Codes of Practice. The police have responsibilities to inform parents and involve the Youth Offending Team following the arrest of a young person; and The YOT manager is responsible for ensuring that 'appropriate adults' are available to accompany children during police interviews, where parents are unavailable, and that appropriate information is provided to young people who are charged with offences. The appropriate adult 'is not just an observer but has a responsibility to ensure that the young person's rights are upheld at all stages, understands what is going on, and is not the subject of any discriminatory action' (Moore and Smith, 2001, p. 33). This service, therefore, incorporates elements that reflect a commitment to children's welfare and the protection of their rights, within the justice system. As we shall observe, these detailed prescriptions do, indeed, retain some of the concerns with young people's needs which might appear to have been diminished in other respects.

Assessment

The National Standards document also sets out detailed requirements relating to the assessment of young people prior to any intervention with young people, whether at the point where decisions are made about bail, where disposals are imposed by the court, or on receipt of a custodial sentence. The shape of such assessments is determined by the ASSET form, adopted by the Youth Justice Board as the 'industry standard'. While initial experience and research is at best equivocal (see, for example, Roberts *et al.*, 2001), there is no doubt that this innovation is intended to bring uniformity to the assessment process. The assessment is intended to be comprehensive, and must be based on previous information available from official sources (for example, statements of special educational needs), and interviews with the young person and parents or carers. The responsibility for complying with these standards rests squarely with the YOT manager.

Work with victims of crime

Increasingly, formal standards are being set for work with victims arising from the operation of the youth justice system, and the National Standards document attempts to regularize these, locating them, logically, alongside assessment. Youth Offending Teams are expected to provide appropriate services to victims in parallel with their work with young offenders, including the range of reparation services: 'this must include, where appropriate, apology, explanation, and direct work by young offenders for the benefit of victims' (Youth Justice Board, 2000, p. 10). It is made clear that victims should be involved only on their own terms and to the extent that they wish, in an attempt to establish clearly the principle that the youth justice system should serve them rather than the reverse. However, it should also be noted that the focus of the document, as a whole, remains the processing of reported young offenders rather than the meeting of victims' needs. Williams (2000), for example, remains highly sceptical about the true implications of the apparent emphasis on placing victims more centrally in the justice process.

Pre-court interventions

The Standards covered by this heading relate to the administration and delivery of the pre-court disposals falling short of prosecution provided for by the Crime and Disorder Act 1998, reprimands and 'final' warnings. The YOT is responsible, in these circumstances, where the police have decided to administer a final warning, for carrying out assessments (using the ASSET form) and delivering 'rehabilitation' programmes, where appropriate. These programmes are to be directed only at dealing with the 'factors' contributing to the offending, and to securing reparation. Where continuing needs for other services are identified, then the child or young person must be referred elsewhere. In keeping with the broader trends already noted, this seems to draw a very restrictive line around the YOT in terms of its responsibilities to consider welfare needs.

Court work and remands

In this context, the Standards are concerned with setting out requirements in terms of efficient delivery of services to the courts, both in general through the establishment of effective inter-agency liaison, but also specifically through the provision of bail information and assessment, arrangements for making secure remands, court duty, and the provision of standard information. The production of Pre-Sentence Reports is specified in some detail, suggesting a concern with form and process rather than content:

> The YOT manager must ensure that Pre-Sentence Reports (PSRs) are produced using the following *standard headings* (their emphasis) :
> - sources of information;
> - offence analysis, including what is known about the impact of the offence on any victim, and assessment of the offender's awareness of the consequences to self, family and any victims;
> - offender assessment;
> - assessment of risk to the community, including risk of re-offending and risk of harm; and,
> - conclusion. (Youth Justice Board, 2000)

Again, the concerns with standardization and the limited scope for discussion of the offender's background, and any contextual factors related to offending or other needs, are significant. The other major concern of the document in this area of practice is to ensure that PSRs are produced on time, with a maximum limit of 10 working days allowed for reports on 'persistent young offenders' (young people previously dealt with by the courts on at least three occasions), and 15 days in other cases. Some reference is made in the context of PSRs to ethnic monitoring, as an aspect of 'quality assurance', although no guidance is offered on how to avoid discriminatory practice in the first place. Despite the very restrictive framework established for the writing of PSRs, at least one study has found that 'report writing remains idiosyncratic in nature' (Drakeford and McCarthy, 2000, p. 110).

Court-ordered interventions

National Standards are intended to provide for interventions undertaken with young offenders by Youth Offending Teams subsequent to a court disposal, or a Referral Order (including reparation orders, action plan orders, supervision orders, parenting orders, and child safety and anti-social behaviour orders).

Where offenders are placed under formal supervision under any of these orders, the Standards are much concerned with the speed of initial contact, the production of supervision plans, regularity of contact (at least twice-weekly in the first 12 weeks, for example), and breach action, which again is the only aspect of this part of the document strongly underlined. Missed appointments must be followed up, and formal warnings issued where there is no satisfactory explanation, leading quickly to breach action:

> *Breach action must be initiated within 10 working days of the most recent failure to comply, if the offender receives more than two formal warnings during the first 12 weeks of the order.* Breach action can only be stayed in exceptional circumstances with the authorisation of the YOT manager. (Youth Justice Board, 2000, p. 20)

Notwithstanding this apparent preoccupation, the Standards also specify that for orders involving supervision of one kind or another there must be a plan to address matters such as parental or carer involvement, work on offending behaviour, substance misuse, healthcare needs, educational needs, experience of discrimination, harm reduction, and reparation. Here there appears to be some recognition in the National Standards that there is a welfare role for those providing a youth justice service, albeit focusing on a limited range of possible needs. No connection appears to be made,

however, between the competing demands of these differing requirements, such as the impact of drug misuse on reliability and regularity in
keeping appointments.

Work with young offenders sentenced to a detention and training order

Standards are also set for work with young offenders subject to custodial
sentences, both for YOTs and for the institutions concerned. Here, much
greater emphasis is given to comprehensive planning, both during the
custodial element of the sentence, and on release. Regular contact is
required, and close supervision is to be offered at crucial transition points,
such as admission and release. Specific areas of concern should be
addressed, such as vulnerability and possible educational and health
needs.

The supervisor appears to be given the role of 'advocate' on behalf of
the young person, with an active role in securing delivery of planned
provision, such as education and personal support.

Section 53: supervision

For young people subject to longer custodial sentences, a similar
supervisory role is attributed to the YOT, giving it the responsibilities for
maintaining contact between the young person and her/his parents,
ensuring regular visits, planning for post-release accommodation, education and health needs, and providing personal support.

In a sense, then, the welfare responsibilities of the Youth Offending
Team appear to become much more explicit for young people subject to
custodial sentences, rather than those at other points in the youth justice
system.

Considered in this kind of detail, National Standards appear rather
more disparate than has been suggested previously (Smith, D., 1999),
including both broad aspirational aims, such as 'the provision of
preventive services' (Youth Justice Board, 2000, p. 7), and residual concerns with the rights and welfare of young people in the justice system,
such as the 'vulnerability assessment' (Youth Justice Board, 2000, p. 13).
On the one hand, this creates space for the imaginative and creative use of
the Standards framework in the interests of young people in the justice
system; but, on the other, this capability needs to be set against the political
and operational context, which might impose narrower and more restrictive interpretations of what is required. National Standards themselves
provide little help, in this respect, because, in paying lip service to
children's rights they do virtually nothing to put into operation require-

ments set out in human-rights legislation (e.g., Race Relations Act 1976, Human Rights Act 1998), or international conventions on children's rights (see, for example, United Nations, 1985; 1989). In the light of this shortfall, it is important to consider in more detail the two major vehicles for the delivery of the 'new youth justice': the Youth Justice Board and Youth Offending Teams.

The Youth Justice Board: a Quango in Search of a Rationale

Under the heading 'Partnership' in the White Paper *No More Excuses*, the incoming Labour government set out its proposals to establish the Youth Justice Board, which would provide 'clear national leadership ... to improve the performance of the youth justice system' (Home Office, 1997b, p. 2). Despite the Labour Party's aversion to quangos while in opposition, the advantages of such a body seemed attractive to the new government. It would allow for a concentration of expertise to oversee the entire youth justice system, including the operation of courts and the provision of secure accommodation. It would be the source of advice on standards for the delivery of youth justice services (as we have already seen). It could 'identify and disseminate good practice' (Home Office, 1997b, p. 26), and it could advise the Home Secretary on possible reforms to the system. This essentially advisory role was 'fudged' somewhat by the additional proposal that the Board be given responsibility for 'commissioning and purchasing ... secure facilities for young offenders' (Home Office, 1997b, p. 26).

The Youth Justice Board (YJB) was duly established by Section 41 of the Crime and Disorder Act 1998, with these provisions, but it was also provided with grant-making powers for the purposes of developing good practice. The Board was additionally given responsibility for receiving and evaluating annual youth justice plans submitted by local authorities (Section 40). This role, according to Pitts (2001a), put the Board in an extremely powerful position in relation to local providers of youth justice services, with the ability, in effect, to determine whether or not these were adequate. In sum, the YJB was established in a position of considerable influence.

It will be informative now to consider how these powerful levers (along with the National Standards) have been used by the YJB to shape the activity of agencies and practitioners within the youth justice system.

Performance management and youth justice plans

The Youth Justice Board retains tight control over the process of preparing local annual youth justice plans, each of which must be submitted for approval, in a process where sanctions can be applied if the plans are unsatisfactory. Thus, for example, where the YJB specifies a series of national objectives and performance targets, these are likely to be followed fairly closely by individual plans. For 2001/2 the key targets were:

1. The swift administration of justice …

2. To confront young offenders with the consequences of their offending

3. Interventions which tackle the particular factors which put a young person at risk of offending

4. Punishment proportionate to the seriousness of offending

5. Encouraging reparation to victims by young offenders

6. Reinforcing the responsibility of parents
(Leicester YOT, 2001; Northamptonshire YOT, 2001)

As a result, the aims and objectives of YOTs themselves are likely to be shaped to fit these requirements. Perhaps we should note, in passing, a number of potentially revealing omissions from this list. There is nothing, for example, about promoting anti-discriminatory practice or protecting the rights of young people in any other way; there is nothing about addressing welfare needs, even those which may underlie young people's offending behaviour; there is nothing about promoting opportunities for young people through education or any other form of positive activity.

Given these constraints, we might expect to find YOTs themselves reflecting YJB priorities in the way in which they prepare and implement their plans. For example, both bodies appear to share a commitment to speedy production of Pre-Sentence and Specific Sentence Reports for the courts, and to reducing delays in identifying and processing 'persistent young offenders'. Indeed, the 'provision of information to Police to execute warrants on Persistent Young Offenders' becomes a priority area of work for one YOT (Leicester YOT, 2001, p. 13).

In order to ensure that young people are 'confronted' with the effects of their crimes, plans focus on issues such as the implementation of reparation schemes and the development of effective monitoring pro-cesses. However, in some cases there appears to be a recognition of issues of diversity at local level, in spite of the Board's silence on this point: 'all minority ethnic young people in custody are referred to the Black Prisoners Support Group' (Leicester YOT, 2001, p. 17). In relation to inter-ventions to tackle risk factors, plans appear to focus on identifying and targeting areas of need, despite the YJB's apparent lack of concern about welfare issues, and improving assessment processes. In line with broader concerns about social exclusion, links are identified at the local level with drug misuse, educational/training needs, accommodation needs, and mental health. Plans can be seen to concentrate on identifying these needs and establishing links with specialist services. In this context, at least, there appears to be a 'reinsertion' of what might be seen as traditional youth justice concerns into the service-planning process.

In relation to the expectation of delivering punishment 'proportionate' to young people's offending, YOTs are placed in some difficulty by the Board, since they are responsible for *administering* some, but not all, punishments, rather than for their *imposition*, which rests with the courts. Interpreting this requirement in the form of performance targets presents real challenges, especially as the notion of 'proportionality' itself is slippery :

> Ranking offences according to seriousness and then establishing a scale of penalties of commensurate severity achieves *ordinal proportionality*, but gives little guidance on *cardinal proportionality* [her emphasis], the overall severity of penalty scales. Put simply, the problem is that deserts theory can help with the graduation of punishments within the most severe and least severe points, but can do nothing to tell us what these anchoring points should be. (Hudson, 1996, p. 45)

This is a fundamental problem for the youth justice system as a whole, and to require YOTs to produce meaningful targets in the absence of both an ability to control sentencing practice and an explicit understanding of what is 'fair' in any objective sense is simply unrealistic. Nevertheless, consistent with the spirit of keeping the YJB happy, most plans make the attempt to do so. One, for example, retains faith in the objective of reducing custody rates (see Leicester YOT, 2001, p. 25). Another invokes the spirit of diversion by seeking to 'obviate' the need for Anti-Social Behaviour Orders (Northamptonshire YOT, 2001, p. 40). Others appear to have concentrated on developing more intensive community programmes to work with persistent offenders, based on the model piloted by the Youth Justice Board as the 'Intensive Supervision and Surveillance Programme' (ISSP). There is evident among YOTs, a considerable degree of uncertainty about how to apply the concept of proportionality in practice, as we might expect.

In relation to the Board's objective of improving the service provided to victims by way of reparation, YOTs appear keen to improve links with colleagues in Victim Support, to improve offenders' understanding of the needs of victims, and to develop models of 'restorative justice', again, probably in response to specific prompting by the Youth Justice Board.

Finally, the commitment to developing work aimed at 'reinforcing' parents' responsibilities, required by the Board, finds its expression in YOT plans to develop 'parenting programmes', and to ensure more regular attendance by parents at police interviews and in court: 'the Youth Offending Team will extend its work with parents, supporting them to take greater control in the exercise of parental responsibilities' (Salford YOT, 2001).

In demonstrating a considerable degree of consistency, local youth justice plans indicate a high degree of compliance with the expectations of the Youth Justice Board. However, it is also true to say that, for some, there appears to be an active commitment to interpreting the requirements fairly broadly, and thereby incorporating services designed to address welfare issues, to minimize the use of custody, or to protect young people's rights.

Buying influence: the YJB funding strategy

Since its establishment in 1999, the YJB has held responsibility for administering a wide variety of funding programmes, on behalf of a number of government departments, although predominantly the Home Office. It has also acquired responsibility for commissioning all places in the 'under-18 secure estate' since April 2000. The way in which these funds are administered is clearly an important indicator, in practice, of the way in which the Board seeks to influence the delivery of youth justice and the realization of its primary objective of 'preventing youth crime'.

Firstly, it is clear that money was initially directed to all aspects of the youth justice system, from preventive programmes to investments in improving the quality of custodial regimes. By 2002, the YJB had been responsible for funding 70 Youth Inclusion Programmes (as already mentioned) and over 150 Summer Splash holiday programmes, intended to reduce offending by young people in high-risk areas. In arguing for more funding, the YJB claimed significant initial success for these programmes (Youth Justice Board, 2001a).

For young people entering the justice system, the Board invested in bail support programmes (129 by February 2002), which 'offer individually tailored programmes according to the risks and needs of young people on bail. In general, they provide help with education, employment and training, accommodation, social and life skills and work with families.' (Youth Justice Board, Press Release, 26 Febrary 2002). Early in its existence, too, the Board made £5 million available to develop the Remand Review

Project (see above), again with the express intention of reducing the use of custody for young people awaiting trial or sentence.

In the sphere of direct interventions with young offenders and their families, the YJB has also been fairly active in using its funding resources to shape practice. It has, for example, funded mentoring schemes, drug workers and accommodation schemes. It has also developed and evaluated new initiatives, such as the Referral Order, parenting pro-grammes, and the Intensive Supervision and Surveillance Programme, which is available both pre- and post-sentence. While the YJB appears committed to developing non-custodial options for dealing with young offenders (and *alleged* young offenders, it should be remembered), these are often characterized by a greater degree of intrusion and surveillance than may have been thought acceptable previously. For example, the use of electronic tagging as part of the ISSP menu is clearly not discouraged, according to the Board's Chief Executive:

> Electronic tagging is already available for young people as part of a curfew order and is being used on ISSPs as part of rigorous com-munity sentences and the community part of a Detention and Training Order. The new powers will extend to bail programmes, including the ISSP. (Youth Justice Board, Press Release, 26 February 2002)

The ISSP has not, therefore, been introduced as a new sentencing option, but rather as a delivery mechanism, applicable at any point of the justice system (pre-trial, as part of a community sentence, or post-custody):

> The ISSP is testimony to the fact that unprecedented levels of supervision, in the form of tagging and otherwise, does protect the public whilst the supervision element looks at the reasons for offending and challenging young people's behaviour. (Youth Justice Board, Press Release, 26 February 2002)

Although seeking to strengthen alternatives to custody, the YJB has also invested fairly heavily in custodial options. It has established a £40-million programme to improve educational, vocational and personal develop-ment provision in custody, but it has also announced plans to significantly increase the number of places available in a range of secure settings, including 400 additional places in secure training centres (Youth Justice Board, 2001a). Subsequently, this figure was increased again to 600 places in the 2002 Budget announcement. Despite claims from the YJB that these new places would ensure the transfer of young people from prison settings to alternative secure environments, there is little evidence of concern at the concurrent increase in the use of custody (see Chapter 3).

The Youth Justice Board has, it seems, used its distribution of funds to develop a strategy for youth justice that appears to rely heavily on targeting specific groups, at all stages of the process, and increasing the levels of intrusion and surveillance to which they are subject. At the same time, there appears to be only limited evidence of this as a kind of 'trade off' between community sentences and the use of custody, since there is a trend towards increased spending and increased capacity in both areas of delivery.

Apart from these very direct mechanisms employed by the YJB to try to shape and influence practice in the youth justice arena, there are also clear indications of a belief in the use of publicity as an attempt to signal desired changes, although evidence to demonstrate the effectiveness of exhortation of this kind is less than compelling. The YJB has, for example, expressed concern over the inappropriate use of custody: 'Short custodial sentences disrupt the lives of young people and make it more difficult to implement effective educational and behaviour changing programmes. They also waste resources' (Lord Warner, Youth Justice Board Press Release, 22 August 2001). Lord Warner also took this opportunity to criticize a 'wide disparity' in sentencing practice, which 'is inherently unfair'. On the other hand, the Board has seemed relatively undisturbed by the government's policy of increasing the number of custodial places available and by the courts' increasing eagerness to make use of them (Youth Justice Board, 2002, p. 15). It seems that direct spending on the custodial estate is more likely to have an impact than countervailing press releases issued during the summer holidays. The Youth Justice Board's position on the locking up of children should perhaps best be described as ambiguous.

The YJB has moved quickly since its creation to become a significant force in the field of youth justice. In taking on this role, it has begun to communicate a strategic vision for dealing with, and preventing, youth crime, based on central direction, targeting, and increasingly intrusive forms of intervention. As a consequence, it has tended to encourage a routinization of planning and service delivery at the local level, which has narrowed the scope for imaginative and creative professional responses to the problems associated with the crimes of the young.

Despite these concerns, more recent developments suggest something of a reappraisal of the Board's role. Some evidence has emerged of a readiness to assert an independent, and in some respects, young-person centred perspective. This has been marked most clearly by the statement that 'there are too many kids in custody' (Lord Warner, the *Guardian*, 28

July 2002). Associated with these sentiments are reports that the YJB has been lobbying government for greater investment in alternatives to custody such as the Intensive Surveillance and Support Programme, and crime-prevention projects, such as Youth Inclusion Projects and Summer Splash (White, 2002).

This trend was further emphasized by the Board's increasingly firm opposition to the use of short Detention and Training Orders (Youth Justice Board Press Releases, 27 January 2003; 4 February 2003), and the withdrawal of sentenced young people from Ashfield Young Offenders Institution, following a highly critical inspection report (Youth Justice Board Press Release, 5 February 2003). Perhaps these ventures into the public arena might be seen as straws in the wind, indicating early signs of the YJB developing an independent identity, and beginning to show a real commitment to the principles of community-based, community-led and inclusive youth justice.

YOTs: All at Sea?

Finally, in considering the new terrain of youth justice management and delivery we must consider the emergence and early experiences of the bodies charged with the task of making it all happen, the Youth Offending Teams. The establishment of the multi-agency YOTs can probably be attributed to the convergence of a number of strands of thought and practice. Firstly, the much-reported and well-regarded diversion initiatives of the 1980s, such as that established in Northamptonshire (see, for example, Smith, R., 1989; Audit Commission, 1996; Bell *et al.*, 1999), seemed to provide a 'working model' on which further developments could be based. The Northampton initiative perhaps provided grounds for optimistic assumptions that the good working relationships established in one area between agencies at all levels could straightforwardly be replicated elsewhere. It was made clear by participants, however, that effective partnerships are something that have to be worked for, and actively sustained: 'inter-agency strategy and working in partnership involve complex and dynamic processes which require intellectual, emotional and practical commitments' (Bell *et al.*, 1999, p. 101).

Others (Davis *et al.*, 1989; Pratt, 2002) have taken a more cynical view, arguing that what was in evidence in this sort of collaborative exercise was the emergence of a form of 'corporatism'. The suggestion has been made that this in fact represented:

[a] third model of juvenile justice: *corporatism*. This sociological concept refers to the tendencies to be found in advanced welfare societies whereby the capacity for conflict and disruption is reduced by means of the centralization of policy, increased government intervention, and the co-operation of various professional and interest groups into a collective whole with homogeneous aims and objectives. (Pratt, 2002, p. 404)

This analysis is supported by broader reviews of welfare state formations (Esping-Andersen, 1990), which suggest that corporatism plays an increasingly central role in the structure and delivery of statutory services in general, and youth justice in particular (Smith, D., 2000).

This developing trend found its echo in New Labour's diagnosis of the problems of social exclusion, as we have already seen, with the view rapidly emerging that these were 'joined up problems' requiring 'joined up solutions': 'in the past, governments have had policies that tried to deal with each of these problems individually, but there has been little success at tackling the complicated links between them, or preventing them arising in the first place' (Social Exclusion Unit, 2000, p. 1). In this context, then, the establishment of Youth Offending Teams, or something like them, was almost inevitable, and they have taken their place alongside an array of inter-agency, inter-professional and inter-sectoral initiatives put in place by the Labour government from 1997 onwards, such as Education Action Zones, Health Action Zones, New Deal, Neighbourhood Renewal Programmes, Connexions and Drug Action Teams.

YOTs were created by the Crime and Disorder Act 1998 (Section 39), with the local authority as lead body, but requiring the 'co-operation' of the police and health authorities. They were required, under Section 39 (5) to include as members:

at least one of each of the following, namely –

(a) a probation officer;

(b) a social worker of a local authority social services department;

(c) a police officer;

(d) a person nominated by a health authority any part of whose area lies within the local authority's area;

(e) a person nominated by the chief education officer appointed by the local authority under section 552 of the Education Act 1996.

Other people could be recruited to the team, depending on local circumstances. The task of the YOT would be to 'co-ordinate the provision of youth justice services' and to deliver the youth justice plan. In a display of commitment to the principles of inter-agency working, the guidance on establishing Youth Offending Teams was issued jointly by the Home Office, the Department of Health, the Welsh Office and the Department for Education and Employment (subsequently Department for Education and Skills, or DfES). It was made clear that the YOTs were 'not intended to belong exclusively to any one department or agency' (Home Office *et al.*, 1998), and that local authority chief executives should ensure that they were established *'corporately'*. The YOT manager was intended to be a pivotal figure in bringing together a disparate team, and establishing a common approach. Where necessary, the partnership approach could be extended to include voluntary organizations, victim organizations, or the youth service. Some aspects of the overall task could, indeed, be delivered by other organizations, 'such as bail support, reparation or mediation work or specified activities under a supervision order' (Home Office *et al.*, 1998). The brief was also extended beyond that specified in the legislation to include preventive work with young people, reflected, as we have seen, in the requirement to dedicate at least 2.5% of the YOT budget to this area of activity. The guidance also issued a reminder of the 'joined up' nature of government thinking, with the explicit linking of the YOTs' work to other aspects of government policy, including: crime reduction, Youth Action Groups, tackling school exclusion and truancy, parenting and family support, tackling drug misuse, neighbourhood renewal, and 'welfare to work'.

The guidance goes on to describe the scope of the YOTs' duties (broadly consistent with the tasks identified by National Standards), and the preferred structure for managing and delivering their programmes of work. In spite of the commitment to linking with other initiatives, the distinctive nature of the youth justice service is emphasized, with the advice that the YOT managers may be drawn from any, or none, of the participating agencies, and ought not to be '"buried" within the management structure of any of the partner agencies; it is essential that they are able to engage, as appropriate, with all the relevant local agencies ...' (Home Office *et al.*, 1998, p. 14).

Thus, a degree of independence from local parent agencies (if not the Youth Justice Board) appears to be vested in the YOT manager, who is also accorded a significant role in recruitment of team members and allocation of tasks. The intention is not simply to have team members who replicate their previous roles or activities: 'while the skills that different professionals bring to the team are likely to reflect their occupational background, rigid boundaries within the team would be inefficient and limit the benefits of joint working' (Home Office *et al.*, 1998, p. 21). However, the tension between maintaining a distinct professional identity and contributing, in a collaborative manner, to a joint service is inevitably a recurrent theme in inter-agency initiatives, and it is unlikely that it can easily be resolved through guidance alone. The guidance itself goes on, rather confusingly, to list a series of distinct tasks which, it suggests, would best be carried out by specific professionals – thus cementing in place, for example, the view that police officers are best equipped to carry out victim-oriented tasks.

In conclusion, the guidance reminds YOTs of their obligations to the Youth Justice Board, including the submission of youth justice plans for review and the ensuring compliance with the legislation, production of monitoring information, and delivery of expected levels of training.

In parallel with the development of the guidance, pilot YOTs were established in 9 areas (Nacro, 2001), to run from September 1998 to the full implementation date of 1 April 2000. Out of these, 4 were given the full range of powers of YOTs, while 5 pilots were given selected responsibilities, with the aim of testing specific aspects of the new legislation more fully. These pilots were subject to extensive evaluation, with one large study commissioned by the Home Office (Holdaway *et al.*, 2001), and parallel investigations carried out by other researchers (Bailey and Williams, 2000). The Home Office study reported broadly positive outcomes, after some initial difficulties. YOTs are applauded, for example, for responding to fundamental changes in the organization and delivery of services in a very short timescale. They are commended for overcoming initial tensions, and for moving towards a common approach to the task: 'there was a 14% increase in the numbers of staff who, when surveyed, saw the team as having a shared view of work' (Nacro, 2001, p. 2). This, it is suggested demonstrates that: 'YOTs have been successful at melding the skills and expertise of members from different agencies to create the possibility of a distinctive culture for the delivery of youth justice' (Holdaway *et al.*, 2001, p. 113).

The pilot YOTs are also commended for undertaking a 'systematic' approach to case management, record keeping and the use of IT, for using pooled budgets creatively, and for drawing on 'specialist services' in tackling offending behaviour and 'criminogenic factors'. However, the report appears more critical in its detailed observations than in its conclusions, arguing that assessment forms were found to be diverse and subjective, and that some of the content of intervention programmes was 'questionable' (Holdaway *et al.*, 2001, p. 33). In addition, the study observes that some participants appeared uncommitted to the idea of joint working, budget disputes persisted, and service delivery was both 'formulaic' and 'inconsistent'! Nacro's overview of the evaluation also notes that the pilot YOTs appeared to have little impact on more tangible outcomes, such as the use of custody for young offenders, with one area, at least, demonstrating a sharp increase. The evaluation concludes:

> It would be wrong to blame the apparent increase in the use of custody on the new orders since a slight upward trend in the number of custodial disposals was apparent from early 1997. It would be equally mistaken, however, to dismiss the possibility that the changes associated with the Crime and Disorder Act might have helped to intensify the drift in Wessex [the pilot area of Hampshire and the Isle of Wight] towards a more punitive approach towards young offenders. (Holdaway *et al.*, 2001, p. 69)

Other research into the development of YOTs also attributes some of their difficulties to an over-simplistic view of the new legislation: 'The [Crime and Disorder Act] is a complex one, capable of being interpreted in a variety of ways. In practice, this presents some difficulties for agency managers in establishing youth offending teams' (Bailey and Williams, 2000, p. 18). The researchers observe, for example, that the belief among agency managers in the diversionary potential of the new legislative framework is not shared by academic commentators. Not only do they comment on differences of perception of this kind, they also draw attention to continuing disputes of a more traditional nature, such as budgetary wrangles, access to confidential information, and the 'ownership' of YOT members, who remain members of their parent agencies. They note that conflicts appear to arise on a number of levels: between organizations; between professional interests; and between practice ideologies (for example, over the issue of the management of risk). These issues are also linked to questions of professional status, organizational power, and public standing, on which there are clearly differences, and which affect the extent to which team members can expect to enjoy a genuine spirit of partnership. Despite all this, the researchers' conclusions are not wholly pessimistic, although they argue that there is much to be done to generate an effective and productive arrangement for inter-agency working in the field of youth justice:

> The pressure of getting youth offending teams off the ground has meant that practitioners have largely stuck to doing what they know. Only when they have the time and resources to share their expertise

and develop new skills will the real benefits of inter-agency work be seen. (Bailey and Williams, 2000, p. 83)

Whilst both studies quoted above identify some of the practical difficulties in delivering a truly 'corporate' approach to youth justice services, interestingly neither appears to question the underlying rationale for such a strategy. D. Smith (2000) concurs, despite what he terms the 'negative connotations of corporatism'. Reflecting on the experiences of the 1980s, he reminds us that inter-agency initiatives, like the Northamptonshire Juvenile Liaison Bureaux, were 'in large measure a creation of practitioners', and that the lack of effective cross-agency commitment can undermine creative and progressive projects with young offenders. He concludes:

> The Labour government's version of corporatism is based, in part, on the kinds of criticism of established practice which youth justice practitioners have themselves made over the years, and it deserves, at least, a serious collective attempt to make it work in practice. (Smith, D., 2000, p. 142)

Against this optimistic analysis of the development of corporatism, however, we must also set the arguments of those who see it merely as an extension of centralized state control, which stifles professional creativity, and enforces a uniformly punitive straitjacket on those who deliver or receive youth justice services. For some, uniformity and control lie at the centre of the New Labour project, where the government finds: 'conflict uncomfortable and threatening and it therefore strives to characterise the new youth justice system it has brought into being as one in which such conflict has been "designed out"' (Pitts, 2001b, p. 142).

Thus, the relationship between National Standards, the Youth Justice Board and multi-agency Youth Offending Teams is supposedly seamless and internally consistent, with procedures and structures complementing one another towards the achievement of the agreed and uncontentious end of reducing youth crime. Muncie (1999) argues that corporatism is not unique to the New Labour reform programme, and is rather a continuation of trends extending back over at least a decade:

> By the 1990s it was already clear that traditional welfare or justice-based interventions had become peripheral to much youth justice practice. The ... setting of performance targets and the establishing of local audits does indeed suggest a depoliticization and de-humanisation of the youth crime issue such that the sole purpose of

youth justice becomes one of delivering a cost-effective and economic 'product'. (Muncie, 1999, p. 290)

Corporatism: Constraint or Catalyst?

In summary, then, we can perhaps draw the conclusion that the mechanisms put in place by the Labour government to deliver the youth justice reforms in 2000 and beyond can be seen as part of a coherent and centralized structure, which bears some of the characteristics of a 'corporatist' or 'managerial' approach. This is perhaps illustrated by the observation from one study that senior managers from different agencies could be heard to parrot the stated aims of the Youth Justice Board in setting out their own local aims and objectives (Bailey and Williams, 2000, p. 21). The evidence cited above of youth justice plans following precisely the template provided by the Board suggests a similar conclusion.

Despite this view, some care must be taken not to draw simplistic conclusions. It is also clear from the available research that tensions remain, and that agencies and managers still experience conflict and still espouse competing objectives. Tensions can, of course, be creative, and at the same time, it would seem that there remains a degree of latitude for those in practice when it comes to implementing overarching policy goals.

Also, however much policy-makers might aspire to delivering consistent and coherent prescriptions for the organization and delivery of services, there will always remain a degree of uncertainty, and in some cases, clear contradictions in statements of policy. While the Youth Justice Board might claim that its six objectives for the youth justice system are consistent with the 'principal aim' of preventing crime, this is by no means self-evident. 'Proportionate' punishment, for example, may even be criminogenic, given what we know about the effects of custody. These contradictions, in turn, present both challenges and opportunities to those responsible for implementing youth justice policies.

Finally, as we have already noted, it is clear that commentators (and even some academics) disagree as to whether 'corporatism' is beneficial or damaging in its effect on outcomes in youth justice. Perhaps it makes more sense to conclude that a corporatist approach to service delivery is likely to be powerful and effective in achieving its goals, but that the crucial questions are the nature of these goals, and the likelihood of unintended consequences, such as the net-widening potential of formalizing collectively agreed local strategies to achieve pre-court diversion (Bailey and Williams, 2000; Goldson, 2000).

Chapter 5

Making it happen: practice in the new era

Effective Innovation or Routinization of Control?

At the level of practice, two competing portrayals of youth justice are now on offer. One suggests that the extensive reform programme of the late 1990s and early 2000s has established, perhaps for the first time, a sound and sustainable basis for the delivery of interventions which 'work', building on a very substantial body of national and international research evidence. This evidence includes policy analysis (Audit Commission, 1996), systematic reviews (Goldblatt and Lewis (eds), 1998), and the copious evaluative research carried out into the pilot schemes put in place following the Crime and Disorder Act and other initiatives (e.g., Holdaway *et al.*, 2001; Newburn *et al.*, 2001a; Newburn *et al.*, 2001b; Roberts *et al.*, 2001; Farrington *et al.*, 2002). This body of knowledge, it is suggested, provides the soundest possible grounding for the implementation and development of new models of practice consistent with the new policy regime, which are the most likely to deliver effective outcomes (see, for example, Goldblatt and Lewis (eds), 1998).

The alternative perspective takes the view that much of this evidence is little more than a smokescreen for the implementation of routinized forms of control, which require very little professional imagination, but rely rather on standardized processes to deliver fixed and measurable levels of compliance. This view claims that too much reliance is based on studies that have a clear vested interest in producing positive findings:

Unsurprisingly, perhaps, the evaluations of mentoring cited by the Youth Justice Board, which is funding over 100 such programmes, are remarkably upbeat, deriving as they do mainly from studies undertaken by members of the US-based National Mentoring Association. (Pitts, 2001a, p. 12)

In Pitts's view, it is not that 'nothing works' – indeed a wide variety of interventions can be shown to work with some young people, some of the time. He cautions against excessive claims of efficacy, however, arguing that not only does this create unrealistic expectations, but that it also feeds a government agenda of reducing the available range of interventions to 'a narrow range of correctional techniques'.

We are thus confronted with two widely divergent perspectives on the aims, delivery, impact and efficacy of current practice, and it will therefore be important here to begin to build up a realistic picture of just what is going on in the field. Then it might be possible to generate a clearer understanding of what is being (and what could be) achieved.

First Impressions

As already noted, a substantial body of evidence is already being generated on the impact of changed working arrangements, innovations in practice, and the administration of new orders. In addition, there are a number of other sources of evidence available, including local evaluations and accounts from the perspective of practitioners and managers themselves, and these should be accorded due weight, even in the presence of the rather more comprehensive findings delivered by professional researchers. What sort of practice, then, can be observed in the light of the recent changes in the policy and structures that shape the youth justice arena?

Firstly, we will focus on the routine and the ordinary, to avoid the trap of concentrating only on those rather more peripheral aspects of the new system that appear exciting and glamorous. It is the impact of the system, as a whole, that gives us the best picture of what is going on, and we should avoid reading too much into experimental programmes, however successful, which do not represent the norm.

Reducing delays

It might be instructive, for example, to consider the impact on practice of the procedural changes resulting from Labour's 1997 commitment to reduce delays in the youth justice system, highlighted as one of the Party's five election 'pledges' in that year. This commitment was based on the legitimate arguments advanced in particular by the Audit Commission (1996), that delays in dealing with young people's offending were both wasteful of resources and damaging to young people, in that they might contribute to re-offending, and reduce the impact of any punishment administered. These concerns had crystallized into a clear commitment by the time of the White Paper *No More Excuses*:

> The Government is determined to end these delays. They impede justice, frustrate victims and bring the law into disrepute. And delays do no favours to young offenders themselves; they increase the risk of offending on bail and they postpone intervention to address offending behaviour. The top priority will be to halve the time taken between arrest and sentence for persistent young offenders. (Home Office, 1997, p. 23)

Pilot schemes to cut delays were established in a number of areas following the passage of the 1998 Act, and the Youth Justice Board published a guide on *Speeding Up Youth Justice* (Youth Justice Board, 1999). In addition, the National Standards set explicit limits for the completion of Pre-Sentence Reports, as we have already noted. Ironically, the time period (10 days) allowed for 'persistent young offenders', and therefore those more likely to have more complex needs, was less than that for other offenders (15 days). Implicitly, more pressure was placed on YOT staff in just those cases where a more considered approach might have been required.

Such pressures have been amplified by the advice offered by PA Consulting Group on behalf of the Youth Justice Board, citing 'unnecessary adjournments between verdict and sentence' as one of the 'five major causes of delay' (PA Consulting, 2002). In order to reduce these, requests for Pre-Sentence Reports should be made 'selectively', and should 'only be considered where a custodial or community sentence is a serious option' (PA Consulting, 2002). Even then, it is suggested that 'existing' reports may be acceptable to courts, rather than always requesting a new one in subsequent cases. The concern here must be that professional issues to do with the quality and thoroughness of the assessment process for young offenders are being subsumed under the need to hurry things up to meet politically inspired deadlines. Reviewing a number of pilot schemes to reduce delay, Ernst and Young (1999) found no real impact on the 'quality of justice', although, strangely, they do not appear to have considered the implications for assessment and sentencing decisions. On the other hand, the team reviewing the pilot YOTs observed that:

... there is evidence from all of the pilots that the perceived need to speed up the system of youth justice is being treated as an end in itself. This is having the unintended consequence of jeopardising the attainment of other important objectives. (Holdaway *et al.*, 2001, p. 25)

Among those objectives at risk were found to be 'the need to ensure just outcomes' based on a full and informed understanding of the circumstances, but also proper attention to the interests of victims and the promotion of the 'accountability of the offender'. Although the team seem happy with the idea of a 'corporate approach to the task of sentencing', they remain concerned about the impact of 'fast-tracking', commenting that 'courts have demanded increasingly tight schedules for cases and YOT members have had to accommodate them within workload constraints' (Holdaway *et al.*, 2001, p. 111).

The ASSET form(s)

Routinization seems to have influenced practice in other important areas as well, notably assessment, with the introduction of the ASSET form, to be completed at most stages of the process. As the relevant National Standard states 'before *any intervention* is made with a young person, including via a Youth Offender Panel, an assessment must be undertaken using the Youth Justice Board ASSET assessment (my emphasis)' (Youth Justice Board, 2000, p. 9). The aims of the ASSET form are set out by the YJB as being both to assist practice decisions and to improve management information. Most importantly, the principal 'function of the ASSET is to help YOTs assess the needs of young people and the degree of risk they pose and then to match intervention programmes to their assessed need' (YJB quoted in Roberts *et al.*, 2001, p. 28). In this sense, then, the ASSET form and the associated assessment process appear to share the orientation and commitment of comparable material, such as the *Framework for the Assessment of Children in Need and Their Families*, issued by the Department of Health under the Children Act 1989 and endorsed by the Home Office (Department of Health, 2000). This, too, focuses on assessing children in an integrated manner, balancing risk and need, in order to ensure that all aspects of the case can be addressed. In addition, the guidance issued by the YJB makes it clear that it sees a use for the ASSET form as a management tool, as a source of data from which to judge the needs of offenders locally and nationally, and thereby to support better service planning.

The ASSET form itself runs to 12 pages (although there are shorter versions for specific circumstances, such as bail assessments), covering basic information about the offender, including ethnic origin, and including on its first page a space for the 'gravity score' of the primary offence and basic victim information. The young person's 'care' and 'criminal' histories are also treated as key background information. The form then concentrates on the young person's offending behaviour, before addressing social and personal factors in more detail, which provide the basis for an aggregate ASSET score, intended to indicate the level of risk the young person presents. 'Positive factors' and 'indicators of vulnerability' are also provided for, but are not scored in the same way. A self-assessment section is also included, called 'What do you think?', for completion by the young person: this has been received positively by practitioners (Roberts *et al.*, 2001). Despite this, the ASSET form uses a 'tickbox' approach throughout, and concentrates to a very substantial extent on negative indicators, which may, of course, influence overall perceptions of the young person and her/his behaviour.

The ASSET form and procedure have been piloted and evaluated (Roberts *et al.*, 2001), while at the same time YOT practitioners and managers have been able to form their own views about its value. The evaluators identify a clear dichotomy between the form as a management tool and the form as aid to understanding young people and their offending behaviour. The expectations of the YJB that the form will be completed 'fully' and 'on all young people entering the justice system' (Allan, 2001) seem to conflict with the views of the evaluators that:

> ASSET was not intended to be used as an inflexible interview schedule or just a checklist to run through with a young person. Whilst there appeared to be some staff using the form in this way, most recognised that this was not a helpful approach' (Roberts *et al.*, 2001, p. 33).

The evaluation report notes 8 different approaches to completion of the form demonstrated by practitioners, who often preferred to use it as a 'framework' for interviews, rather than a rigid format.

When considering the relationship between ASSET forms and the more traditional professional practice of completing reports to inform courts' sentencing decisions, practitioners were found by the evaluators to express a range of views. Most thought there was some value in the ASSET form in that it provided a comprehensive framework for the preparation of a Pre-Sentence Report, but others felt that it added little to the process, and oversimplified the task of providing an 'individual' picture of the young person (Roberts *et al.*, 2001, p. 38).

While practitioners had some concerns about the appropriateness and relevance of some of the detailed questions included in the ASSET form, their main worries related to the validity and value of being required to use these as a basis for 'rating the risk of re-offending' (Roberts *et al.*, 2001, p. 45). This procedure appeared to many to be arbitrary and unreliable. It also appears to sit oddly with the earlier suggestion that the form should not be used too rigidly, but should inform a more refined approach to interviewing and assessment. As an illustration of the difficulties likely to arise from over-reliance of the rating system, the evaluators quote the following example:

> One police officer described how he would always give a rating of 4 [greatest likelihood of reoffending] if a young person admitted using cannabis because this, by definition, meant that they were likely to re-offend. Other colleagues who regarded cannabis use as low risk and low priority did not accept this approach. (Roberts *et al.*, 2001, p. 45)

The concerns of YOT members about the spurious use of an apparently objective scoring system such as this focused on a number of specific issues: uncertainty about what a specific score actually means; lack of ability to 'weight' some sections which might be more or less relevant; the negative impact of finding out more about a young person (especially significant because of the overall negative bias of the ASSET form); and possible misuse of the aggregate data by the Youth Justice Board. These concerns crystallize the conflicts inherent in a standardized instrument such as ASSET, which confronts professional judgement with a routinized scoring system in such a way as to challenge many of the core beliefs of those who see a role for individual discretion and creative decision-making in the youth justice system. Unsurprisingly perhaps, staff were found by the evaluators to be making limited use of completed ASSET forms to inform subsequent interventions. While most questionnaire respondents said they were using ASSET 'in some way' to inform their practice', in group discussions this did not appear to be the case (Roberts *et al.*, 2001, p. 48), and one despairing respondent was observed to comment: 'nothing is done with completed ASSETs, so what are we doing it for?' (quoted in Roberts *et al.*, 2001, p. 51). This kind of perception may have informed the cynical view of some staff that the main purpose of the exercise is to provide statistical information for the YJB and government. The evaluators also note that their findings may have been influenced by the self-selecting nature of their sample, so that the views of others with a more critical perspective may not have been reflected (Roberts *et al.*, 2001, p. 61). Such concerns did not, however, appear to impact on the thinking of the YJB which announced that 'it would now make completion of the assessment tool a key condition of funding provided by the board' (Allan, 2001, p. 3). Concerns about the routinization of practice, the unreliability and inadequacy of the rating system, and the contradiction between standardization and professional discretion were swept aside, it seems.

New Orders – Redefining Practice?

In the light of this attempt to routinize the initial stages of the youth justice process, in the interests of reducing delay and establishing a standardized assessment system, it will now be helpful to consider some of the issues arising in the context of practice interventions under the changing legislative and organizational structures of the early 2000s.

It is to our advantage that the new forms of intervention have been heavily evaluated, usually in their status as pilot projects. Although the government and the YJB appear to have made little use of the findings which have emerged, they do convey some important lessons for those concerned with the delivery of good and effective practice in the context of youth offending. Overall evaluations have been undertaken of YOTs and their practice (Bailey and Williams, 2000; Holdaway et al., 2001), and specific investigations have been carried out into key aspects of the new portfolio of interventions (Newburn et al., 2001b; 2002).

The study by Holdaway et al. (2001) offers the most comprehensive overview of the new practice environment, and elaborates in some detail the general and specific aspects of the 'new disposals' (specifically, the Final Warning, the Reparation Order, the Action Plan Order, the Parenting Order and the Child Safety Order). They locate their observations within an analytical framework, which emphasizes the value of knowing and delivering interventions that 'work':

> At many points of [our] report we comment on the importance of evidence-based practice to the routine work of YOT staff. By 'evidence-based practice' we mean work with offenders to reduce offending, the success of which has been demonstrated through rigorous evaluation. (Holdaway et al., 2001, p. 1)

In so doing, they link this orientation towards achieving practical and effective outcomes to a belief in the need to ensure that risk assessments are systematic and sound, in order to provide a strong basis for evaluation of the services delivered. Unlike most research and evaluation, which makes claims of objectivity, the researchers here start from an openly committed position, arguing that:

> YOT managers need to be very knowledgeable about practice-based research and ensure that their staff understand it
>
> YOT staff should base their work with offenders on systematic evidence of 'what works'
>
> ... YOT managers need to be involved in 'evidence generating' practice. This means that they need to evaluate systematically the work of their team.
>
> Whatever the outcome of an evaluation, results should be disseminated ... The dissemination of systematic evidence about what does not work is as relevant as that which does work
>
> Evaluation should be a standard feature of professional work ... (Holdaway et al., 2001, p. 1)

Clearly then, this orientation will influence the researchers' attempts to understand practice in the reformed youth justice system, and one would expect a pragmatic orientation towards a focus on outcomes rather than processes. We have already considered these researchers' observations and concerns about the YOTs as delivery mechanisms (Chapter 4), and we will now address their findings in relation to practice interventions, while noting that they are also fairly prescriptive in this respect, too. For example:

> YOTs need to ensure that they are able to offer a sufficient range of meaningful and effective reparative interventions, whether these are intended to meet the needs of individual victims or to ensure that reparation is made to the community at large. Such interventions should be sufficiently flexible to cater for different types of offenders and offences ... YOTs need to take particular care to avoid the use of 'tokenistic' or 'formulaic' interventions ... (Holdaway et al., 2001, p. 28)

On the basis of seeking evidence of effectiveness in reducing the likelihood of further offending, the research team undertook to examine the impact of a number of interventions by YOTs.

The Final Warning

The Final Warning is seen as an important innovation, reflecting a desire to keep young people who offend out of court by giving them a 'last chance', while at the same time providing the basis for formal intervention where necessary. Thus, where identified as appropriate, it could be expected that a specific programme of intervention would be offered to young people to supplement the administration of a Final Warning by the police. These 'change programmes' would have the central aim of addressing offending behaviour in order to prevent further offences by the young person. On this basis, the research team questions the wide variation between YOTs in determining whether such a programme should be put in place, with up to 80% of offenders not being considered for further intervention, a figure contrary, in their view, to the intention of the Crime and Disorder Act (Holdaway *et al.*, 2001, p. 33).

Change programmes put in place in support of a Final Warning might include counselling in respect of alcohol or drug misuse, letters of apology, reparation, mentoring, youth club attendance, education support, 'general offence' work, and to a lesser extent, counselling or family support. Programmes were usually undertaken within 2.5 months of the Warning being administered, and 74% were recorded as being completed satisfactorily. Despite this, the researchers express concern about YOTs' failure to offer programmes in some instances, or their offering of standardized responses that might be inappropriate to the circumstances of the offender. They question:

> The considerable use of a letter of apology as an element of a change programme ... In some pilot areas, staff dealing with change programmes were requiring all young people to write letters of apology, irrespective of the circumstances ... This is surely inappropriate in many cases and a less than satisfactory way of meeting the needs of offenders and victims. (Holdaway *et al.*, 2001, p. 78)

Concern is expressed about the 'questionable' relationship between change programmes and the nature of the offence or the young person's circumstances. Additionally, it is suggested that sometimes the focus of programmes is too narrow, and that some offenders would benefit more from interventions beyond the scope of the YOT to provide. In some cases, parents' needs for support were not being recognized or addressed in Final Warning change programmes. While the researchers conclude with positive support for the Final Warning scheme, they raise concerns about whether YOTs' practice is sufficiently flexible to address the diverse range of circumstances of young offenders receiving this disposal. Interestingly, these concerns are supported by the findings of related research, which, while claiming that Final Warnings do appear to reduce the level of young people's subsequent involvement with the legal system, also offer no support for the efficacy of specific programmes of intervention:

> There was no statistically significant difference in further criminal proceeding rates between those who the youth offending team assessed as appropriate for a 'behavioural change programme', those who were assessed as not appropriate, and those who were not seen by the youth offending team. This result calls into question the nature and role of assessment procedures and the programme delivered as part of a final warning during the pilot period. (Hine and Celnick, 2001, p. 1)

It seems, then, that we are left with a somewhat inconsistent set of findings: a range of interventions is used to support Final Warnings; these interventions appear to be used somewhat arbitrarily; Final Warnings are nevertheless effective in reducing the level of further proceedings against young people; but, we are told, they should still be supported by change programmes in more cases (Holdaway et al., 2001, p. 33). This rather speculative conclusion sits oddly with the researchers' exhortations that we should be concerned to promote 'evidence-based practice'.

Reparation Orders

The Reparation Order was included in the Crime and Disorder Act 1998 as a new disposal, but it built on a fairly long tradition of intervention in juvenile/youth justice, stretching back at least as far as the early 1980s (Smith, R., 2002a). In some ways, then, it might be expected to be based on a stronger foundation than some of the other innovative inventions of New Labour. According to Holdaway et al. (2001, p. 35), the Reparation Order needs to be seen as part of a series of interventions introduced by the 1998 Act, incorporating principles of 'Restorative Justice' for the first time into the English and Welsh criminal justice process. Although originally the government had planned to require courts to consider Reparation Orders in all cases (Home Office, 1997, p. 14), the Crime and Disorder Act restricted their use to being 'entry level' disposals for relatively minor offences. Despite this, the new order would require YOTs to develop or extend their repertoire of interventions to include work with victims. YOTs would be expected to arrange reparation directly or indirectly where courts required it, and this, according to the researchers, represented:

> one of the most important and far-reaching cultural changes required by the Crime and Disorder Act ... [An] essential pre-requisite ... is the need to ensure that all who are involved in the imposition and delivery of reparative interventions ... are fully conversant with the restorative justice ethos that underlies the Act. (Holdaway *et al.*, 2001, p. 36)

The evaluation of YOT pilots showed that practitioners and managers had responded positively and creatively to the requirements of the new order, establishing new methods of working to accommodate the interests of victims. These included the development of 'victim consultation procedures', offering support to victims, the establishment of mechanisms for securing direct reparation, and direct and indirect mediation, all of which required the development of means of approaching and involving victims. In addition, offenders could be involved in 'restorative' measures such as writing letters of apology, undertaking victim awareness programmes, and indirect reparation projects. Clearly, those interventions that necessitate the involvement of victims introduce a new dynamic into the practice arena, and it has become a matter of concern over time that victims' interests should not be subsumed under the priorities of the youth justice system, which are to process young offenders (Davis *et al.*, 1989; Williams, 2000). Most victims in the pilot evaluation felt that offenders' interests were prioritized (Holdaway *et al.*, 2001, p. 81).

Despite this, the research team states a clear preference for taking a proactive approach to involving victims, primarily because of concerns about a low response rate: 'it seems probable that some form of personal contact with victims (either by telephone or by a follow-up visit) is more likely to elicit a positive response than a simple letter, requiring the victim to 'opt-in' to the process' (Holdaway *et al.*, 2001, p. 37). There also appears to be an emerging separation in YOT responsibilities in this respect, with police officers on the team taking primary responsibility for making initial contact with victims, on the basis that they are more likely to have prior experience of such work. With the introduction of the Referral Order, this separation of roles has become more strongly entrenched, at least in some areas (Smith, R., 2002a). The need for this separation of responsibilities remains questionable, at least in the present author's experience (Smith, R., 1989), and has clear implications for the interprofessional model of working espoused for the YOTs.

The reparation undertaken by young offenders, under the supervision of YOTs, can include 'community reparation', that is, indirect reparation that makes amends for the offence where the victim cannot be, or does not wish to be, involved. However, questions are raised about the 'meaning' of some of these activities, especially where they bear little relationship to the offence:

It appears easier to set up general reparative tasks, such as the per-formance of basic conservation work, than ones that are particularly suited to particular types of offences or offenders ... there is a risk that it could degenerate into a somewhat tokenistic response ... (Holdaway *et al.*, 2001, p. 38)

Generally, the pilot YOTs were found to have established some form of direct reparation service as well. However, in the initial stages at least, this was found to be limited largely to writing letters of apology. In addition, the pressures on YOTs to reduce delays, as we have already observed, created countervailing pressures to the need to develop sensitive and negotiated methods of engaging victims. Such difficulties also affected YOTs' ability and willingness to establish 'mediation' as a means of bringing victims and offenders together to resolve the issues arising from an offence, and to facilitate direct apologies.

In the light of these difficulties and concerns, it is perhaps not surprising that YOTs were observed to be turning to other options, such as victim awareness exercises, designed to 'challenge' the young person's offending behaviour. These allow for the incorporation of more established forms of intervention, with which practitioners may be more comfortable. In one area:

The standard programme is based on a cognitive behavioural approach, but this can be adapted if necessary to encompass anger management or drugs therapy. In other areas the victim awareness programmes are mainly linked with victim empathy and apology exercises. (Holdaway *et al.*, 2001, p. 39)

Clearly, it would be unfair to criticize too strongly work undertaken at the development stage of a new order, and in the early days of a new delivery mechanism (the YOT), but there are a number of key issues raised by this evidence, many of which are not new. These include: the status and treatment of victims; the pressures of time as against the demands of consultation and negotiation; the extent to which reparative activities are meaningful; the implications of compulsion; and, once again, the routinization of a specific and specialized form of intervention.

The Action Plan Order

As Holdaway *et al.* (2001) remind us, the Action Plan Order is a core element in the youth justice reforms of the New Labour government. The intention was to create a short-term intervention that would allow for 'individually tailored' programmes to be delivered to young offenders 'at an early stage', in order to tackle the causes of their offending (Home Office, 1997a). The order could impose a series of requirements, of greater or lesser specificity, such as compliance with 'educational arrangements', reparation to victims, participation in specified activities, or avoidance of particular places (Home Office, 1997a). The evaluators of the YOT pilots argue that the Action Plan Order is intended not to replace, but to supplement other sentences, although they also note a tendency for the order to displace the Attendance Centre Order, which is perhaps unsurprising, since attendance centres are included as one of the options within the Action Plan Order (Home Office, 2000). They argue, contrary to the aspirations of the Home Office, that the Action Plan Order is not intended to occupy a particular place on the tariff. This is difficult to reconcile with the guidance issued in support of the Crime and Disorder Act:

> The action plan order is ... intended to be imposed for relatively serious offending, but it is also intended to offer an early opportunity for targeted intervention to help prevent further offending. Courts may wish to consider the action plan order when a young person has *first* been convicted of an offence serious enough for a community sentence. (Home Office, 2000, p. 4)

Despite the apparent constraints on its use, the Action Plan Order is reported as being well received by courts and youth justice workers. Courts apparently appreciate the opportunity to specify the content as well as the nature of the order. In addition, it is noted, offenders and their parents also appear to appreciate the structure offered by the order (Holdaway *et al.*, 2001, p. 41).

The approach typically taken by YOTs to delivering the order is to offer a 'core programme', with other elements constructed around the specific circumstances of individual offenders. The core programme includes elements that appear at other stages, and under other orders, such as addressing the consequences of offending behaviour, victim issues, and work on family and relationships. Additional requirements to be added where appropriate include a range of options, such as mentoring, reparation and motor projects. The overlap with other parts of the repertoire of interventions is particularly noticeable in the context of reparation, with the same activity likely to be available to young offenders subject to Final Warnings, Reparation Orders, Action Plan Orders and Supervision Orders.

The elements of the individualized package are combined to provide an overall programme, which is found to extend to around 25 hours in total, representing a fairly substantial time commitment in a short order. The evaluation of YOT pilots found considerable variation in the content and delivery of orders, although, as noted, the response was generally positive, except where victims felt that they were not being well served.

Interestingly, the evaluation team is critical of the approach they observed in some areas, which is attributed to staff from previous youth justice teams bringing 'old ways of working' with them, and turning Action Plan Orders into 'mini-supervision orders' (Holdaway *et al.*, 2001, p. 42). This, they state, is not what the legislation intended. On the other hand, both the 'menu' of activities documented, and the individualized nature of the programme to be delivered, are reminiscent of the content of Supervision Orders stretching back over a considerable number of years (see, for example, Children's Society, 1988; 1993; Audit Commission, 1996). In this sense, the models of intervention observed could still be characterized as 'correctional', although the more central role attributed to reparative activity under the Action Plan Order might suggest the emergence of a more restorative orientation. Despite this, evaluation of YOT activities undertaken elsewhere seems to suggest that much of the work carried out in the course of an Action Plan Order could be construed as a compressed attempt to deliver some of the standard interventions associated with Supervision Orders, including some attempt to address 'welfare' needs, such as family problems, accommodation difficulties, or the consequences of exclusion from school (Smith, R., 2002a). Where this approach is adopted by YOTs, clearly it will be important to seek to avoid the imposition of orders by the courts which are over-prescriptive in their content.

The Referral Order: Moving Restorative Justice Centre Stage?

Introduced and implemented after the Crime and Disorder Act, the Referral Order represents a further attempt to make fundamental changes to the terrain of youth justice. Like its immediate predecessors, the Referral Order was also extensively piloted and evaluated before its full implementation in April 2002 (Newburn *et al.*, 2001a; 2001b; 2002; Earle and Newburn, 2002). Early impressions, at least, are available as to the impact of the order on practice, and the implications of it for youth justice in general.

The centrality of the Referral Order is guaranteed by the place assigned it in the sentencing tariff by the Youth Justice and Criminal Evidence Act 1999 (and consolidated in the Powers of Criminal Courts (Sentencing) Act 2000). On a first conviction, with minor exceptions, the court is required to make a Referral Order on a young offender (under 18) except where it is considering a custodial sentence. On the face of it, this seems to represent something of a duplication of the Action Plan Order in the repertoire of disposals available to the court.

The effect of the Referral Order is to transfer responsibility for the disposal to a Youth Offender Panel, consisting of a YOT member and two independent persons. The task of this panel is to agree and oversee a 'contract' with the young person, specifying a programme of requirements to be undertaken during the period of the order (3–12 months). Under Section 23 of the 2000 Act, the order 'may include' one or more of a by now familiar list of requirements: reparation; mediation; community service; school/job attendance; 'specified activities'; attendance at specified times and places; avoidance of specified places and people; and compliance monitoring. Again, the overlap with the Action Plan Order appears substantial.

The supporting guidance for the Referral Order (Home Office, 2001c), clearly emphasizes the centrality of the victim to the process, and makes it clear that her/his involvement in the process will be expected: 'it is essential that all victims be given the *opportunity* to become involved in the referral order process, and to facilitate their involvement where they do wish it' (Home Office, 2001c, p. 22). Victims should be encouraged and enabled to attend Youth Offender Panel meetings, so that they can express their views about the offence and their expectations of the offender. It is expected that the contract will be agreed with the young person at this meeting, and that it will 'always include an element of reparation' (Home Office, 2001c, p. 35). Other elements of the programme to be agreed will depend on the factors 'leading to the offending behaviour'. The 'principal' aim of the youth justice system, preventing youth crime, appears in this instance to have been subsumed by the principle of restoration.

Evaluation of the Referral Order pilots has produced a broadly favourable conclusion: 'possibly the most encouraging result to date is the fact that within a year YOPs appear to have established themselves as deliberative and participatory forums in which to address a young person's offending behaviour' (Newburn *et al.*, 2001b, p. x).

Over 1,100 orders were made in the 11 pilot sites in the first 9 months of their operation. Most were made for six months or less, although this has not subsequently proved to be the case everywhere (Smith, R., 2002a). Because of the inclusive nature of the legislation, many orders appear to have been made for traffic offences, which might technically constitute a first finding of guilt, but do not appear to warrant referral to a Youth Offender Panel. Other relatively minor offences, such as shoplifting, are also reported to result in referrals (Newburn *et al.*, 2001b, p. 10).

In terms of the operation of the panels, the researchers note almost complete compliance with the requirement to attend by young offenders, but very low involvement (around 6%) of victims. Thus, a key aspiration of the new disposal appears not to have been met to any great extent in the initial stages. Despite this, the panel meetings held are reported as agreeing contracts with the young offender in nearly all cases (97%), with some form of reparative activity being the most common element of the programmes agreed (41%). Most contracts have a relatively small number of elements, so there were rather fewer instances of programme components such as 'addressing educational issues' (8%), 'exploring career options' (7%), and addressing offending behaviour (7%) being included. Again, these are fairly familiar elements in the correctional portfolio. Of the reparative elements identified, community reparation and letters of apology were the most frequent, which is perhaps unsurprising in the light of the low rates of direct victim involvement. In addition, panel meetings seem to be relatively successful in securing expressions of regret from young people, with around two-fifths offering apologies at panel meetings themselves (Newburn *et al.*, 2001b, p. 29).

The implementation of agreed programmes is supervised by the YOT, subject to reports to 'progress panels', which are reconvened to assess compliance with the contract and to determine whether to vary the terms, refer young people back to court for unsatisfactory progress, or agree that the contract has been fulfilled satisfactorily. The evaluation found that the initial non-completion rate was 26%, with non-compliance or re-offending being the main reasons for this (Newburn *et al.*, 2001b, p. 12).

The overall picture generated from these findings, and supported by other evidence (Smith, R., 2002a), is of the framework created by the Referral Order generating a range of familiar forms of intervention, tempered to a limited extent by a greater degree of 'reparative' activity. However, on closer examination, much of this activity is 'community reparation' (44%), which is not necessarily clearly or closely linked to the offence committed (Holdaway *et al.*, 2001). Beyond this, a concern is reported by the evaluators that YOT members believe that the new order might lead to a range of responses that is 'disproportionate' to the offence. It is noticeable, for example, that contracts can, and do, impose a variety of fairly stringent requirements over periods of time of up to 12 months. One YOT member is reported as saying:

This is processing young people when a conditional discharge would have been sufficient … Intensive supervision with over-loaded contracts to address lots of issues which are resource intensive should be reserved for higher risk offenders, in line with 'what works' principles, not low-risk one-time offenders. (Quoted in Newburn *et al.*, 2001b, p. 61)

Meanwhile, Back at the 'Heavy End'

So far we have concentrated on a range of new requirements and orders introduced for relatively minor and early offenders. But it will also be important to give some consideration to the changing expectations of practice for those deemed to be more serious or 'persistent' young offenders. The Intensive Supervision and Surveillance Programme (ISSP), launched in June 2001, is perhaps the most far-reaching example of this. The programme is deliberately and explicitly targeted at those persistent young offenders who are 'estimated' to be responsible for 25% of all youth crime, and directed towards those police-force areas 'worst affected by street crime' (Youth Justice Board Press Release, 30 April 2002).

ISSPs are available to be attached as additional requirements to Supervision Orders, Community Rehabilitation Orders, the community part of Detention and Training Orders and as bail conditions. Young people are eligible for an ISSP if they are:

> … charged with or convicted of an offence and have previously:
>
> Been charged, warned or convicted of offences committed on four or more separate dates within the last 12 months and received at least one community or custodial penalty;
>
> In addition, young offenders can also qualify for ISSP if they are at risk of custody because:
>
> The current charge or sentence relates to an offence which is sufficiently serious that an adult could be sentenced to 14 years or more;
>
> Or they have a history of repeat offending on bail and are at risk of a secure remand under section 130 of the Criminal Justice and Police Act 2001.
> (Youth Justice Board, Letter to ISSP Managers, 19 June 2002)

The YOT is to be responsible for delivering the 'intensive supervision' element of the programme, involving at least 25 hours contact time for the first three months of the programme (ironically, equivalent to the norm for an Action Plan Order, as we have already observed). Supervision then continues at 'reduced intensity' and includes (predictably) 'packages of education and training, offending behaviour programmes, reparation to victims, inter-personal skills and family support' (Youth Justice Board Press Release, 30 April 2002).

In addition, however, those on ISSPs are to be subject to 'surveillance', consisting of 'either tracking, electronic tagging, voice verification or intelligence-led policing', as we have already noted (Chapter 3). These elements of the ISSP are to be contracted out to private providers of security services, although overall responsibility for compliance and breach decisions would remain with the YOT (Home Office, 2002, p. 11). The framework and delivery requirements set out for ISSPs are highly prescriptive, leaving little scope for the exercise of professional discretion by YOT practitioners. The overall aim is to provide a demanding programme, which can reassure courts and the public that it will be a more 'effective' response than custody. It is thus of crucial importance to the rationale for the programme that 'early anecdotal evidence suggests it is having an impact on re-offending rates' (Youth Justice Board Press Release, 30 April 2002) – presumably in a downward direction!

Practice and the New Youth Justice: a Recipe for Success or 'Korrectional Karaoke'?

In order to generate a systematic understanding of the shape and meaning of practice as it emerges and develops under the New Labour reform programme, it might be helpful to start by characterizing what we have observed in the form of Weberian 'ideal types' (Weber, 1957). That is, by developing idealized models of alternative constructions of what has been happening, we may be able to use these as the basis for a realistic interpretation.

On the one hand, then, we are offered the 'official' version, which suggests that new models of practice can best be seen as part of a coherent and comprehensive package of innovations, which, even in the first few years, can be demonstrated to have achieved remarkable levels of success (Youth Justice Board, 2002). The framework for this is established by the administrative and procedural improvements intended to reduce delay and provide a standardized model for assessment and planning (typified by the ASSET form). It is reported that the ASSET form has demonstrated its diagnostic value, by achieving almost a 70% success rate in predicting the likelihood of re-offending:

This means that offenders who are most likely to continue to offend can be identified at the earliest stage and steps can be taken to prevent it with confidence. More than any other aspect of the reformed system, this tool, properly used is capable of preventing further offending. (Youth Justice Board, 2002, p. 9)

The comprehensive nature of the ASSET form means that a wide range of factors contributing to the likelihood of further offences can be identified, and used as a basis for further intervention by the YOT. The multi-professional nature of the YOT means that a 'case management' approach can be adopted, with the specific skills of the appropriate team member being applied to the individual circumstances of any case (Holdaway *et al.*, 2001, p. 112). Thus, practical interventions can be explicitly and directly linked to the evidence that suggests that certain factors in young people's background, attitudes and personal characteristics are linked with a likelihood of offending (Graham and Bowling, 1995: Youth Justice Board, 2002). For example, where young people's offending is linked strongly to drug use, according to Section 7 of the ASSET form (Youth Justice Board, 2000, p. 7), the appropriate skills of the Youth Offending Team health worker (Holdaway *et al.*, 2001, p. 112) can be utilized to respond to this specific issue. In addition, the team member concerned will also be able to call on the resources of the parent agency to supplement this provision. The flexibility and eclecticism of the framework for disposals available means that this service (or any other appropriate element of an intervention programme, such as the social work task of working to improve family relationships) can be incorporated at any point in the young person's offending career, from Final Warning through to ISSP. In other words, it is the contribution to preventing offending that the intervention offers which determines whether or not it is made available, rather than its position on the sentencing tariff. In this sense, the questions of surveillance, control and the restriction of freedom are viewed as distinct from the preventative work undertaken with the young person.

To complete the virtuous circle, evidence from research suggests that targeted interventions of this kind are working. In a context where overall reconviction rates are reported to be falling dramatically (Jennings, 2002), specific interventions are also credited with similar achievements. The rate of further proceedings for those receiving Final Warnings is reported to be 6% better than expected (Hine and Celnick, 2001). For the Reparation Order, a re-offending rate of 49% is highlighted (Youth Justice Board, 2002). Referral Orders are reported as the most effective disposal, with no further offences reported in 60% of cases within a year of the court hearing; 69% of contracts are complied with, and only a quarter of young people subject to Referral Orders are reported as re-offending during the lifetime of the order (Holdaway *et al.*, 2001, p. vi). Similar achievements are claimed for Bail Support Schemes and ISSPs (Youth Justice Board, 2002).

A rather gloomier perspective on practice with young offenders has been taken by a number of commentators (for example, Goldson, 2000; Jones, 2001; Muncie, 2001; Eadie and Canton, 2002) to a greater or lesser extent. Claims of effectiveness for particular programmes or methods of intervention are frequently found to be overstated, thereby contributing to a standardization of practice that is not justifiable: 'we are witnessing the emergence of a 'one-size-fits-all' national (correctional) curriculum for offenders in prison and the community ...' (Pitts, 2001a, p. 11). Pitts argues that the effectiveness of the programmes that underpin the models adopted by the Home Office and the Youth Justice Board is at least open to question; he also reminds us that practice must be seen in context. The idea that similar programmes can be delivered at different levels of the youth justice system assumes that they will be received and acted upon consistently by the young people on which they are imposed. It is equally likely, however, that as 'surveillance' and 'incapacitation' become more central to youth justice practice, these will become the most significant aspects of intervention from the perspective of the young person to whom it is applied. Using the ISSP as a gauge of this kind of development, Pitts argues that: 'it is inconceivable that this move will not undermine still further the capacity of YOTs to deliver the 'holistic' regimes which were their original raison d'être' (Pitts, 2001a, p. 13).

The problems with practice as it has developed under the post-1998 reforms are two-fold, according to this analysis. First, it develops a range of specific programme elements to be dropped into any proposed disposal according to the identified characteristics of particular young people, but for which its claims of effectiveness are unrealistic. Second, and partly as a consequence of this, it incorporates a range of coercive measures to ensure that these components of individual programmes are delivered. Young people's noses are metaphorically held as the medicine (which is good for them) is forced down. The consequence, however, is that coercion and surveillance inevitably subvert the correctional and reformative aims of the specified intervention. This is evident in even quite mundane ways, for example in the manner of delivery, whereby home visits are supplanted by requirements to attend the office at specified times. At the same time, the threat of further penalties for non-compliance will almost inevitably compromise young people's motivation, commitment and sense of personal responsibility.

The fact that characterizations of youth justice, as it is delivered in the early 2000s, are so widely divergent presents some very real challenges for those engaged in the business of direct interventions with young people in trouble. In the real world of practice, of course, as we are reminded, the task remains to work creatively and constructively with young people, negotiating the tensions and contradictions that arise:

> Wherever practice is tightly prescribed, practitioners will repeatedly discover that an uncritical application of the rules would be oppressive and unfair. Reflective youth justice workers draw on their knowledge and skills, but also give expression to their values. They are guided by awareness of the constraints upon young people, and of the differential impact of 'the same' penalty on those whom they supervise. They continue to offer opportunities to change even when these appear to be rejected. Throughout, they respect both substantive and procedural justice, working openly and honestly with young offenders and with their managers. If workers behave officiously or take enforcement action prematurely, this not only constitutes poor social work, but is also reductively ineffective and unjust. (Eadie and Canton, 2002, p. 23)

Chapter 6

Failing to deliver

How Can We Measure Success and Failure in Youth Justice?

As we have seen, the context of this discussion is one in which a substantial programme of reform has been implemented over a relatively short timespan, from 1998 onwards. These reforms have operated at all levels, including law and policy, strategic and operational delivery systems, and front-line management and practice. They have been driven strongly from the centre, by the Home Office and Youth Justice Board, and they have been governed by one overarching principle, namely, 'to prevent offending' (Youth Justice Board, 2002, p. 8). At the time of writing, most of the specific reforms put in place have been operational for some time, and claims of success in meeting the objective of reducing youth crime have already being widely publicized (e.g. Home Office *et al.*, 2002, p. 29). For these reasons, then, it would not be unreasonable to subject the 'new' youth justice system to a more detailed, more wide-ranging and more comprehensive examination.

For a number of reasons, relying on one, single measure of achievement is both risky and methodologically unsound. It is important, for example, to consider the impact of the reforms on a number of constituencies, who may have quite legitimate objectives which cannot be equated simplistically with a reduction of offending as reflected in official statistics. As has been recognized, for example, fear of crime and public confidence are not related straightforwardly to rates of crime, whether measured by official records or crime surveys (Home Office, 2001b). It might be thought quite legitimately, too, that the youth justice system itself, dealing with a very small proportion of all crimes as it does (Audit Commission, 1996; Home Office, 2001a), is not ideally placed to take a leading role in the prevention of offending. In other words, we must be careful, once again, to distinguish between policies and initiatives to address 'youth crime' and the policies and practices of the youth justice system which has a much narrower and more specific role.

Given these observations, it is arguably important to consider a range of impacts of youth justice practices, of which its role in reducing crime is just one. Indeed, as we have already observed, this need is tacitly acknowledged by the Youth Justice Board (Youth Justice Board, 2000) – for example by including a series of objectives that modify the principal aim of reducing offending in its National Standards document. These include victim reparation, proportional punishment, avoidance of delay, and addressing the 'factors that put the young person at risk of offending'. In addition, the document notes the importance of protecting the rights of children, and ensuring 'that all intervention is delivered fairly, consistently, and without improper discrimination, in a way which values and respects the cultural and racial diversity of the whole community' (Youth Justice Board, 2000, p. 3).

In reality, then, the pure aim of reducing crime by young people is an impractical objective for the youth justice system alone, since it does not deal with most youth crime, whilst there are additional expectations incorporated into the operational standards set for service delivery. In moving on to consider the impact of the reforms on specific interest groups, then, we should bear in mind that it is reasonable to consider a wider range of outcomes than purely the recorded levels of youth offending, particularly given the contested nature of these figures themselves (Muncie, 1999). In this context, we shall consider first the outcomes and impact of the youth justice system on specific groups, and then, drawing on these observations, the wider question of just what the New Labour reforms have delivered in this arena.

Young Black People: Institutionalized Discrimination?

In some respects, the prospects for young people from ethnic minorities in the youth justice system appear quite promising. The inquiry into the death of Stephen Lawrence, for example, prompted action to instigate wide-ranging reforms in the police and other agencies. The Labour government, having initiated the inquiry, accepted without question 56 of the 70 recommendations made (Bowling and Phillips, 2002). In particular, the inquiry had, for the first time, identified 'institutional racism' as endemic in the practices of the police and other organizations responsible for the delivery of the justice system. Partly as a result of this, the Race Relations (Amendment) Act 2000 was introduced, applying anti-discrimination principles much more actively to public services than had previously been the case, and removing some of the immunities from liability that had previously applied to chief police officers. This specific legislation is supported by the Human Rights Act 1998, and the requirement for ethnic monitoring in the justice system introduced by Section 95 of the Criminal Justice Act 1991. This provision has been criticized for being relatively weak (Bowling and Phillips, 2002), but it does, in principle, provide for a much greater openness about discriminatory practices within criminal justice.

Although it may be too early to tell whether these legislative and policy initiatives, taken together, will have a significant impact, the current picture is relatively bleak:

> Racial oppression may be real, morally repugnant, and pervasive, but when the new managerialism takes it on, it becomes little more than a dysfunctional organisational residue amenable to the kinds of administrative techniques developed to solve many other kinds of 'human resource' problems. (Pitts, 2001b, p. 137)

This process of turning a major social evil into a legal-rational problem has produced limited gains in the past, and, as Pitts observes, does little to address underlying factors.

As a result, the experiences of young Black people in the justice system, and the research evidence available, continue to demonstrate real and persistent discriminatory outcomes. The starting point, we should perhaps recall, is that offending rates among young people of all ethnic groups are largely similar. According to their own accounts of participation in crime, the differences between 'white and Afro-Caribbean respondents' are not great overall (44% and 43% respectively), although there is some variation in the pattern of offences (related to socio-economic status, in part, it would seem). For young people of Asian origin, self-reported crime rates overall are much lower (Graham and Bowling, 1985). As a consequence of these observations, it is argued that 'the answer to the question as to why black (young) people are over-represented in the … system as 'subjects' is likely to lie somewhere other than with their rates of 'participation in offending' (Goldson and Chigwada-Bailey, 1999, p. 54).

The evidence of overrepresentation of young Black people at each stage of the youth justice system, however, produces an overall picture of progressively intensified discriminatory practices. This is described by Goldson and Chigwada-Bailey (1999) as a 'multiplier effect'. As they observe, this comes into operation at the first point of contact between young Black people and the justice system. This has been a persistent feature of the experience of the Black population, as Muncie observes: 'In England and Wales in 1993–4, 25 per cent of all stop and searches were of ethnic minority populations ... Nationally black and ethnic minorities are five times more likely to be stopped and searched than white people.' (Muncie, 1999, p. 233). This pattern does not appear to change substantially over time. In 1999, for example, Black people were more likely than those from other ethnic groups to be 'approached by the police' – 28% as compared with 24% of the white population – and there were just slightly smaller proportions for young people of Asian origin. For young Black males, in particular, there was a greater chance of being stopped by police while on foot than their white counterparts (a third as compared to a quarter), and at the same time a much smaller proportion of those from ethnic minorities were likely to report that they had been treated 'well' by the police (Clancy *et al.*, 2001). These findings were significantly reinforced by the additional evidence that Black and minority-ethnic individuals have been found to be up to 7 times more likely to be 'stopped and searched' than their white peers (Home Office, 2002c).

At the next stage in the process, the proportion of Black people arrested for 'notifiable offences' in 1999/2000 was 4 times higher than that of the white population (Home Office, 2001, p. 19). A relatively smaller proportion of Black people arrested was subsequently cautioned (Reprimands and Final Warnings had not been implemented at this point) – 11% as compared to 16% of white people charged with notifiable offences. Decisions made by the Crown Prosecution Service and the courts are reported to 'reflect decisions made at earlier stages of the criminal justice process including charging, cautioning and also the circumstances of the offences' (Barclay and Mhlanga, 2000, p. 1). This, indeed, highlights one of the most contentious aspects of the debate about racism and criminal justice. Some commentators argue that the system itself merely 'reflects' inequalities elsewhere in society, producing unequal outcomes because of the greater likelihood of Black people coming into the ambit of the judicial process; while, it is also argued that the system itself amplifies or compounds those discriminatory forces that operate outside of, and prior to, the instigation of criminal proceedings (Goldson and Chigwada-Bailey, 1999). Barclay and Mhlanga argue that 'the ethnic group of the suspect was not found to be a significant predictor of post-arrest decisions'

(Barclay and Mhlanga, 2002, p. 2). Their evidence suggests that arrests of young (under-22) Black (69%) and Asian (68%) people are less likely to lead to a conviction than those involving young white people (78%). The implication is that the overrepresentation of young Black people in the criminal justice system is most significantly influenced by antecedent factors. If anything, the criminal justice system itself appears to modify these influences by applying principles of due process. Barclay and Mhlanga conclude that it is 'not possible' on the basis of their findings to say whether the differences in outcome they identify 'reflect the result of discrimination in the criminal justice system' (Barclay and Mhlanga, 2000, p. 1). By contrast, the Commission for Racial Equality is reported to have found that decisions to prosecute are weighted against young Black people (Goldson and Chigwada-Bailey, 1999, p. 65), which might, in itself, partly account for the greater number of 'not guilty' pleas entered by them. Similar anomalies are also revealed when decisions about the use of bail and custodial remands are made prior to court hearings. The evidence from local initiatives, for example, provides an indication of an attritional effect, even within programmes. The Manchester Youth Bail Support Project, developed by The Children's Society, was able to demonstrate over its first year of operation that from the point of referral onward, Black and Asian young people were progressively screened out of the programme (Moore and Smith, 2001). Of the initial 136 referrals, 29 (21%) were from ethnic minorities; of the 102 accepted for the programme, 17 (about 17%) were Black or Asian; of the 52 bailed on condition they attend the project, 6 (about 12%) were Black or Asian. While these 6 then went on to complete the programme successfully, this example illustrates quite well an institutionalized selection process that appears to be based on objective criteria, but which still has a racially discriminatory impact.

The consequences of this apparently impersonal and scientific decision-making process can be demonstrated more graphically still. The Howard League's *Troubleshooter Project* (described previously) was based in Feltham Young Offender Institution and Remand Centre with the aim of securing the release of 15-year olds wrongly or inappropriately remanded or sentenced to custody. Of the 650 referrals received from December 1993 to June 1996, '45% were ... Black or Asian' (Ashton and Grindrod, 1999, p. 176). This is not an isolated finding, as it is reported that in 1999: '16.2% of children and young people remanded in HMP and YOI Doncaster; and 31.6% of those similarly remanded in HM YOI and RC Feltham were Black' (Goldson and Peters, 2000, p. 15).

These trends are, in turn, found to be compounded by sentencing decisions, with studies repeatedly demonstrating an independent race effect on court outcomes (Goldson and Chigwada-Bailey, 1999, p. 65).

These findings are supported by the statistics on the use of custody for different ethnic groups, with 15% of all 15–17 year olds in custody on 30th June 1999 being recorded as 'Black' (Home Office, 2001, p. 45). In addition, young Black offenders are likely to receive disproportionately long sentences. On the same date, they accounted for 6% of young offenders serving sentences of 12 months or less, but 16% of those serving longer sentences. While these figures might partly be accounted for by antecedent factors (such as the nature and context of the offence), they are also partly attributable to the 'amplification' effect of the justice system itself, as Bowling and Phillips argue: 'The empirical evidence demonstrates the existence of both direct and indirect discrimination in the criminal justice process' (Bowling and Phillips, 2002, p. 241). They argue that some aspects of the reform programme instigated by the Labour government are likely to intensify the discriminatory impact of the justice system itself. These include the creation of new and finer 'nets', through the introduction of Reprimands, Final Warnings and the Referral Order. The tendency to 'over-charge' young Black people may be intensified, for example. In addition, the increasing use of targeting and surveillance techniques, the Foucauldian mechanisms highlighted previously, are likely to result in poorer ethnic-minority communities coming under greater scrutiny. To many minority communities, this is just 'business as usual':

> As a consequence, British black and Asian people feel angry, unsafe and insecure. The 'double whammy' faced by these communities is that they are widely seen by the police and prison services as problematic, suspicious and, sometimes, simply criminal. (Bowling and Phillips, 2002, p. 255)

Against this backdrop, the limited initiatives taken by the Youth Justice Board seem relatively marginal. The development of specialist mentoring schemes, for example, may reflect a genuine attempt to address concerns about the discriminatory impact of youth justice services (see, for example, Leicester Youth Offending Team, 2001). However, the targeting of crime 'hotspots' and those 'at risk of offending' ('the fifty'; Morgan Harris Burrows, 2001) for preventive programmes may intensify the experience of being under scrutiny, and the targeting of areas with relatively high ethnic minority populations for initiatives such as ISSPs might, in itself, have discriminatory consequences.

'It's Different for Girls ...'

For girls and young women, the experience of the youth justice system is, indeed, different. There has been much debate about the reasons for their differential involvement in offending and experience of the justice process, without a substantial measure of agreement. It appears that the involvement of girls and young women in committing offences is lower than that of males, even by their own account, in both nature and intensity. Thus, just over a third of females admit to having committed an offence 'ever', as compared to rather more than half the male population (East and Campbell, 2000); but males are 3 times more likely to commit offences overall, and 5 times more likely to commit 'serious' offences (Graham and Bowling, 1995). In addition, the rate of offending for females appears to reach a peak earlier and subsides more quickly than for males (Home Office, 2001b, p. 101). Overall, females are much less likely to come to the notice of the criminal justice agencies – in 1999, male offenders out-numbered female offenders by the ratio 4:1 (East and Campbell, 2000, p. 20). Despite this, clearly significant numbers of girls and young women do come to the attention of the youth justice system, and the nature of its response is therefore of considerable interest.

While the pattern of offending suggests that girls and young women are more likely to be involved in property offences, such as theft and handling stolen goods, and less likely to be involved in offences of burglary, robbery or criminal damage, the proportion of 'known' violent offences committed by males and females is the same (8%). In addition, over an extended period, the relative level of criminality of girls and young women appears to have increased significantly, with a decline from 7,000 known young male offenders per 100,000 population in 1981 to 5,400 in 1999 contrasted with an increase from 1,300 to 1,400 per 100,000 for females: 'thus, although there remains a substantial decrease in the proportion of offenders among males (23%), there has been an 8% *rise* in the proportion of females found guilty or cautioned over the last 20 years. (East and Campbell, 2000, p. 22). Within that period, however, there have been considerable fluctuations, and it would therefore be unwise to draw dramatic conclusions from these trends. Explanations might be thought to lie in changing patterns of female behaviour, or in changing attitudes to girls and young women (Muncie, 1999; Worrall, 1999; Bowling and Phillips, 2002), but it is also important to be aware of the complexity of interactions between these factors, and others, including the social construction of criminal statistics.

Nevertheless, it is clear that females have consistently remained responsible for a significant proportion of the crimes committed by the young (around 20%). The role of the youth justice system in responding to these offenders must therefore be of interest. It appears that there are substantial differences in the ways in which young males and young females are dealt with by the system. For example, while cautioning rates in general were falling in the 1990s, the differential between the treatment of boys and girls remained. In 1990, for example, 84% of 12–14 year-old boys were cautioned, as compared to 93% of 12–14 year-old girls. By 2000, the most recent year (to date) in which cautions were available, these figures had fallen to 68% and 86% respectively. As a consequence, of course, the proportions of males and females being made subject to convictions and court sentences increased over the same period. Despite this, the pattern revealed by the cautioning figures is repeated, with females being relatively more likely to receive lesser sentences (especially discharges), and less likely to be sent to custody. Once again, however, the trends over time show a narrowing of differentials, with the proportion of females sent to custody doubling over the period 1994–99 (2.5%–5%), while the rate of custodial sentencing for males increased from 10% to 13%. This is at least partly attributable to the availability of a new sentence, the Secure Training Order (STO), which made custody more widely available for girls than had previously been the case. By 1999, 1% of 12–14 year-old girls sentenced by the courts were being made subject to STOs (East and Campbell, 2000).

Worrall (1999) puts these trends in context with her ironic observation that the Conservative government's 1990 White Paper envisaged the abolition of custody for females under the age of 18: 'the 150 or so girls in custody … could be dealt with quite adequately by the "good, demanding and constructive community programmes for juvenile offenders who need intensive supervision"' (Worrall, 1999, p. 29). As she notes, however, this opportunity was not taken, and the increasingly punitive climate of the 1990s swept up young women as readily as young men. Indeed, she argues that the position of girls and young women has actually become worse, because they have been regarded as becoming increasingly criminal and more violent. She cites an intemperate newspaper editorial from 1996 in support of this argument, but little appears to have changed in this respect, with the *Daily Mirror* ('Hell Child', 16 May 2002) proving spectacularly censorious in condemning a 'tearaway girl of 16 with 38 convictions for assaulting police'. Significantly, the newspaper also reported that the young person concerned had received a Secure Training Order at the age of 13, and an 8-month custodial sentence at 14 – little evidence here of custody reducing offending, it would seem.

Worrall argues that this kind of media response to the criminality of girls is part of a pattern, amounting to a 'moral panic' targeted at the consequences of women's liberation. In other words, the apparently increasing criminality of young females is attributed to their rejection of stereotypical gender roles. However, she also argues that there is little evidence of a dramatic increase in the offending rates of girls and young women, a claim borne out by the long-term analysis already quoted. The number of known female offenders declined from 42,000 in 1981 to 35,900 in 1999, while, as we have seen, the *rate* of offending by girls and young women has tended to fluctuate (East and Campbell, 2000, p. 21). Worrall is concerned that this pattern is not reflected in the use of custody, with an increase in its use for girls of 175% between 1992 and 1996, a trend that appears to have persisted since then (Home Office, 2001b; 2002). This may be particularly dramatic evidence of the process of 'bifurcation' in the justice system, whereby minor offences and those less likely to challenge stereotypes (e.g., shoplifting) result in girls being treated more leniently, while more serious offences, which do not conform to gender expectations (e.g. violence), are dealt with relatively more severely.

There is thus evidence of an increasingly and disproportionately harsh regime for the processing and disposal of girls and young women who offend, particularly those who offend more seriously, and again this is exacerbated by the treatment they receive once in custody. As Worrall (1999) observes, girls in prison are likely to have experienced damaging and traumatic episodes at some prior time in their lives (notably, as victims of violence or sexual abuse), and custodial institutions are poorly placed to respond to their consequent needs appropriately (see also Goldson, 2002).

To what extent, then, might we expect the reforms introduced by Labour to change the way in which girls and young women, in particular, are dealt with by the youth justice system? As already noted, the initial impressions are that the reforms have done little to stem the increasing use of custody for young female offenders, and in this respect they appear to be at least as vulnerable as male offenders to a punitive moral climate. For example, in the 12 months from 2001 to 2002 there was a substantial increase in the number of young females in custody, both on remand and after sentence. While the overall number remained relatively small (123 in March 2002, as compared to 92 one year earlier), in percentage terms this is an increase of 34%.

In this context, the failings of the 'new youth justice' might be more those of omission, rather than commission. The relatively small number of girls and young women who are being poorly served by the system may simply have been overlooked. According to the Youth Justice Board 'the ... typical young offender [is] male, white, aged between 14–16, excluded from school and have committed five or more types of offence'

(Youth Justice Board, 2002, p. 2). Targeted interventions, such as the Youth Inclusion Programme, will, by definition, contain only a very small proportion of females 'at risk' of offending, and the programmes offered are unlikely to be designed to cater for their differing needs, an issue which, like ethnicity, is simply not addressed by the YIP evaluation (Morgan Harris Burrows, 2001).

At the other extreme, it is noted by the Chief Inspector of Prisons that in transferring responsibility for the secure estate for those under 18 to the Youth Justice Board in April 2000, female prisoners were overlooked:

> I am ... concerned about young females, including juveniles, for whom the YJB and the Prison Service have not yet made the same arrangements as they have for young males. I was appalled to find 17 year old girls on remand in HMP Holloway with sentenced adult women ...' (HM Chief Inspector of Prisons, 2001, p. 10)

The Youth Justice Board subsequently made a commitment to put things right (Youth Justice Board 2001a). However, these concerns were amplified, when the Chief Inspector's successor visited Eastwood Park Prison. Her report examined:

> ... the treatment and conditions of the 12 under-18s held with 41 18–21 year olds in D wing. They exhibited, in acute form ... chronic problems ... This is an extremely vulnerable and disturbed group of young women: 'It was impossible not to be struck by the profound personality disturbance and mental health problems that many presented and by the inappropriateness of prison, or indeed any other custodial placement, for them'. (HM Chief Inspector of Prisons, 2002, p. 4)

In this sense, at least, the youth justice reforms of the early 2000s passed girls and young women by, leaving them to cope with the consequences of harsh sentences in a hostile climate (see also, Goldson, 2002, for an insight into the personal consequences of this experience).

Notwithstanding all this, there is also some evidence that the restructuring of youth justice has, in some cases, created a service environment where the specific needs of young women can be addressed:

Case Study

Abi is a 17 year old white female living independently. She was referred to the Youth Offending Team in June 2001 after receiving a

Final Warning for an offence of Taking a Vehicle Without Owner's Consent.

At the initial assessment the YOT officer was made aware that Abi had been self-harming (cutting) and had suicidal feelings. An immediate mental health assessment was made by the YOT Primary Mental Health Worker who made a swift referral to the CAMHS [Child and Adolescent Mental Health Service]Young People's Team. Abi was seen by Psychiatrist within 36 hours and later diagnosed with a borderline Personality Disorder.

The primary mental health worker co-coordinated work around coping skills, support networks and cognitive behavioural interventions (interpersonal effectiveness, emotion regulation, distress tolerance). The case manager co-coordinated other interventions (offence focused work, employment and housing) and towards the end of the order Abi was referred to our YJB funded Mentoring Programme.

At the exit review Abi was praised for her co-operation and non-offending ... support networks were identified. She no longer needs the support of the primary mental health worker ... (Prior to the YOT Final Warning scheme, Abi's complex needs would, in all probability have gone unnoticed until she re-offended or self harmed).
(Leicester Youth Offending Team, 2002, p. 95)

On the other hand, the *Daily Mirror's* 'Hell Child' appears to have received little by way of supportive community-based intervention. Perhaps, after all, gender stereotypes do remain a powerful factor in determining the responses of agencies and institutions to the problems of girls and young women who offend.

Ships in the Night: Victims of Crime and Youth Justice

A third key group of stakeholders in the youth justice system are victims of crime by young people. They are particularly significant in a context where government and criminal justice agencies have clearly prioritized the interests of victims, in policy terms at least: 'Victims of crime are a politically popular group, and an increasingly powerful one. Politicians have been quick to take account of these facts, and the balance between offenders and victims has altered correspondingly' (Williams, 2000, p. 176). As we have already observed, these developments have been given substance in both government initiatives, and in implementation measures such as National Standards. The commitment of the White Paper to create 'a system ... which commands the confidence of victims' (Home Office, 1997, p. 29), was translated into a new legislative and policy framework, which required both general and specific interventions to address the concerns of those on the receiving end of youth crime. National Standards would 'ensure that the needs of victims of crime are respected and prioritised' (Youth Justice Board, 2000, p. 2).

Specific measures, such as Reparation Orders and Referral Orders, were put in place to require the offender to make redress to the victim in some way. In addition, a range of other measures could incorporate requirements for the offender to make amends, including Final Warning intervention programmes, Action Plan Orders, and Supervision Orders. This victim orientation would be cemented by the requirement in the preparation of Pre-Sentence Reports for consideration to be given, in every case, to 'what is known about the impact of the offence on any victim, and assessment of the offender's awareness of the consequences to self, family and any victims' (Youth Justice Board, 2000, p. 16). The ASSET form, too, includes a number of references to offence victims, and requires consideration of the victim's perspective. The infusion of the entire range of activities in the youth justice system with this emphasis on victims' interests has resulted in a clear commitment from Youth Offending Teams to intensify their work in this area. Leicester YOT, for example, reports on a number of initiatives undertaken in conjunction with Final Warnings, including 'victim empathy sessions, letters of apology, supervising short periods of reparation [and] 4 Restorative Justice Conferences ... in 2001' (Leicester YOT, 2002, p. 49). Later targets for the Leicester YOT would include the incorporation of 'Restorative Justice Principles' in all Final Warnings, to be reflected in increased involvement of victims and increased victim satisfaction with the outcomes of YOT intervention.

That this is part of a wider development is demonstrated by the Youth Justice Board's account of its activities in funding 46 'totally new restorative justice projects', which are reported to have worked with over 6,800 young people in the period 2000–02, two-thirds of whom were referred as part of a Final Warning intervention programme or a Referral Order. Leaving aside, for the moment, the unhelpful conflation of restorative justice with intervention to help victims, we should perhaps move on to consider whether this 'step-change' in orientation and practices within the youth justice system is really of any great benefit to victims.

The extent of victim involvement itself under the new regime remains limited. In typically bullish fashion, the Youth Justice Board claims that over half (53%) of victims 'agreed to participate' in restorative schemes

(Youth Justice Board, 2002, p. 13). This contrasts rather with the observations of the team evaluating Referral Order pilots, which concluded:

> The involvement of victims and in particular their attendance at panel meetings across the pilot areas has been both lower than was originally anticipated and significantly lower than comparative experiences from restorative justice initiatives around the world. (Newburn et al., 2002, p. 41)

In only 28% of cases where there was 'potential' for victim involvement were victims found to have contributed to the process in any way at all, and victims attended Youth Offender Panel meetings in only 13% of possible cases. They note that 'in the absence of significant victim attendance there are obvious concerns that victims' issue are insufficiently represented' (Newburn et al., 2002, p. 43).

The key issue here, to which we shall return, is that a system whose primary purpose is to process young people who offend will almost inevitably struggle to find appropriate ways of involving other interests, and especially those of offence victims. Rather than address their concerns to this issue, the evaluators seem to have focused more on improving techniques to ensure victim attendance at panel meetings (Newburn et al., 2002, p. 44).

However, for those victims who did get involved, there were positives to be gained from the experience. Their experiences of YOP meetings were mainly good, with some evidence that feelings of 'hurt' and fear were reduced by the end of the meeting. On the other hand, follow-up was not always regarded as positively, with a 'significant' number of victims disappointed not to receive any expression of regret or remorse by the young offender, either at the time or subsequently. These problems, like the low level of direct victim involvement, are seen by the evaluators as largely a technical and administrative problem, rather than indicating any fundamental problem with the Referral Order itself. They base this argument on the enthusiasm for the new order expressed throughout the justice system, from magistrates to youth justice staff, to community panel members and victims (Newburn et al., 2002, p. 62). Their conclusion is upbeat:

> The issue of victim involvement is, in essence, a problem of implementation rather than a problem of principle. Indeed, the majority of the general principles underlying referral orders appear both to be capable of being operationalised in practice and to receive high levels of approval from all the major participants. In a short

period of time referral orders have gone form being an interesting set of proposals to a genuinely robust set of working practices that, notwithstanding some of the tensions identified in this report, look set to have a considerable impact on the youth justice system in England and Wales. (Newburn *et al.*, 2002, p. 63)

This is perhaps a surprising conclusion in the light of what we already know about victim involvement and reparation from past experience. As Haines (2000) observes, despite the general support for measures such as compensation, community service, and other forms of 'making amends' expressed by victims, formal and highly structured mechanisms such as Youth Offender Panels have not been noted for their achievements on behalf of victims in the past. He argues that the evidence, if anything, steers us away from this kind of initiative to those that attempt to be flexible in addressing victims' concerns. Haines suggests that the mismatch between the expectations of victims and the readiness or capacity of young people to make amends will render the panel a particularly difficult setting to resolve this kind of issue. As he puts it, victims' demands for restitution are unlikely to be met readily by young people who simply cannot afford to make amends, which indeed echoes the findings of the YOP evaluation (Newburn *et al.*, 2002, p. 46).

The evaluation of the Northamptonshire Juvenile Liaison Bureaux, carried out in the 1980s, also found a place for reparation, but one where flexibility and negotiation remained at the core of the process: 'the Bureaux ... have come to use reparation only in situations where all parties are able to benefit rather than where it merely responds to social pressures to treat (or punish) delinquent behaviour' (Blagg *et al.*, 1986, p. 135). In this context, the time pressures set by the relevant National Standard add another constraining element, which, in practice, Youth Offending Teams have found it difficult to comply with (Newburn *et al.*, 2002, p. vi). As Williams (2000) comments, the pressures to deal with young offenders increasingly quickly create further obstacles to the principle of putting victims' interests first.

Indeed, Williams (2000) is perhaps the sternest critic of the new arrangements, seeing victim interests as being subsumed under the demands of the broader youth justice reforms, contrasting these with the New Zealand experience, on which the principles of restorative justice in England and Wales are reputedly based:

A youth justice system based on conflict between the prosecution and the defence remains substantially unaffected by the addition of reparation as an extra sentencing option. In New Zealand, the formal criminal justice system is largely by-passed by restorative processes which replace court hearings. In England and Wales, however, these processes are 'bolted on' to an otherwise unchanged retributive sentencing system. (Williams, 2000, p. 189)

According to this analysis, reparation becomes part of the sentencing tariff, representing an imposed forfeit, as opposed to an agreed settlement, where the young offender really 'means' her/his apology. Victims' interests are being used 'cynically', in Williams's view, 'to improve the presentation of punitive criminal justice policies' (Williams, 2000, p. 189). Haines and Drakeford (1998) take the argument further, claiming that 'victim-oriented' restorative measures need to be distinguished from 'offender-oriented' restorative practices, which are more appropriately located within the youth justice system, and focus on reintegrative work with the young offender, as opposed to 'work which is carried out for the benefit of the victim' (Haines and Drakeford, 1998, p. 234). In their view, the emphasis on victims confuses the role of the youth justice system, and, in any case, such approaches cannot be shown to be effective.

Williams, on the other hand, does not reject victim–offender reparation, but argues that it must be relocated at the 'front end' of the justice process. It should be based on a 'fundamental' change of attitudes towards victims, marginalizing courts and penal practices, and it should provide time and space for the development of consensual 'restorative solutions' to the problems created by young people's behaviour (Williams, 2000, p. 190).

In conclusion, then, it cannot be assumed that the youth justice system will deliver outcomes that cannot reasonably be expected of it; nor should we attempt to co-opt the interests of victims in a contrived attempt to achieve the unattainable. It is perhaps worth reminding ourselves that the vast majority of victims are simply not touched by the justice system itself. Something less than half of all crimes are reported to the police, and just over half of these are recorded as crimes by the police (Mirrlees-Black *et al.*, 1998). Of these, 14% resulted in a caution or conviction in 1999–2000 (Home Office, 2001). Assuming that all these crimes have victims, this means that a 'victim' is matched with an 'offender' in no more than 3.5% of cases. As we have also noted here, in a substantial proportion of cases before the Youth Offending Panel, there is no real engagement between offender and victim. If we are to make any claims about the efficacy of the 'new youth justice' in meeting the needs of victims, we must therefore be very modest indeed. Johnstone sums it up very nicely for us:

Restorative justice, which emphasises restitution and other forms of reparation from the offender to the victim, seems therefore to have nothing much to offer the majority of crime victims. It shares this limitation with every other criminal justice intervention. Hence, it might be argued that, if our priority when a crime is committed is really to restore the victim, we should not waste our energy trying to reform the criminal justice system. What is needed is not so much an alternative form of criminal justice, but an alternative to criminal justice. (Johnstone, 2002, p. 78)

Modest Claims are Better than Bragging

Having identified some of the ways in which the interests of both offenders and victims fail to be met by the reformed youth justice system, it will now be helpful to move from the particular to the general. It should perhaps be noted here that the aim is not to discredit the continuing efforts of those committed professionals in youth justice who continue, quite simply, to do a good job in reconciling the interests of young offenders and others with the demands of the justice system itself. One such experienced practitioner, for example, commented to the present author that her interest had always been to address the welfare needs of young people who offend, illustrating this with a specific case, which demonstrated the continuing scope for good practice, even in the context of major reforms which are often experienced as unhelpful (Smith, R., 2002a).

Nevertheless, I think we must be critical of the reform programme, not least because of the dramatic claims made for it (see, for example, Youth Justice Board, 2002). Before addressing the more fundamental question of whether the system is indeed delivering 'youth justice', it will be helpful to reflect on some of the successes claimed in the narrower sense of achieving the stated objectives, by the government and the Youth Justice Board in particular (Home Office, 1997; Youth Justice Board, 2000).

Clearly, the major driving force behind the early changes to youth justice following Labour's election in 1997 was the pledge to halve the time taken to process persistent young offenders between arrest to sentence, from 142 to 71 days. Amid much fanfare, this was reported to have been achieved by August 2001, reaching a figure of 65 days by March 2002 (Youth Justice Board, 2002), despite some regional variations. This could be said to typify the managerialist approach discussed previously (Chapter 4), whereby success is measured in meeting arbitrary targets, in the form of 'outputs' (Everitt and Hardiker, 1996). The extent to which these achievements contribute to more substantial or lasting goals, such as the 'principal aim' of reducing crime, is much harder to determine. On the other hand, there are a number of questions to ask in respect of the 'unintended consequences' of specific measures such as speeding up youth justice procedures. While one evaluation is relatively relaxed about the potential impact on the quality of justice delivered (Ernst and Young, 1999), others appear more equivocal (Holdaway *et al.*, 2001; Shapland *et al.*, 2001). Concerns are expressed, for example, by YOT members who feel that the requirement to meet strict deadlines for the completion of reports is potentially compromising of best practice (Shapland *et al.*, 2001, p. 67), despite the perceived benefits of bringing 'spree' offenders to justice more quickly. The deadlines can also mean that less attention, too, might be given to the needs of victims, as well as offenders, in complex cases (Holdaway *et al.*, 2001, p. 27).

It is also recognized that the reduction of delay in itself might contribute to the creation of persistent young offenders (PYOs), because of the impact of 'splitting' files. The consequence of this in the case of young people who commit more than one offence is that they are more likely to achieve the four separate court proceedings needed to attract the PYO definition (National Standard 6.8.2, Youth Justice Board, 2000, p. 16). Whether this is offset by the reduction in crime expected as a result of reducing re-offending on bail (Home Office, 1997) or by emphasizing 'the link between an offence and its consequences' (Holdaway *et al.*, 2001, p. 27) is by no means clear.

More explicit claims for the crime-reducing impact of the youth justice reforms are made elsewhere (Hine and Celnick, 2001; Jennings, 2002; Youth Justice Board, 2002). It is claimed, for example, that Final Warnings have had a significant impact on reducing the number of further proceedings (Hine and Celnick, 2001), although the Youth Justice Board (Warner, 2001, p. 1) itself is more equivocal.

As we have seen (Chapter 5), the research into reconviction rates following Final Warnings suggests that 'on a like with like basis' the rate of further proceedings is 6% better than might be expected (30% compared to a predicted rate of 36%; Hines and Celnick, 2001, p. 1). The study bases this claim on a comparison between re-offending rates in 1998 under the previous cautioning regime, and those for young offenders made subject to a Final Warning in the pilot youth justice reform areas. In fact, both reconviction and further proceedings rates were higher for those receiving Final Warnings (Hine and Celnick, 2001, p. 16; p. 20), but this is attributed to the combined impact of the end of repeat cautioning and the different characteristics (more males, older age group, more previous formal pro-ceedings) of the Final Warning group. Once these differences are allowed for, Final Warnings can, it is argued, be shown to be more effective in reducing the rate of further proceedings, especially for the 16+ age group. Further proceedings here are used as an indicator of 'programme effectiveness' (Hine and Celnick, 2001, p. 14). However, it is recognized that they are only a 'proxy' for re-offending, since the rate of further proceedings can be influenced by other factors, such as 'police, crown prosecution and court practice', as well as 'clear up and cautioning rates' (Hine and Celnick, 2001, p. 14). Over this period (1998–2001), for example, detection rates were falling, partly as a result of changes in police recording methods, and the proportion of cases discontinued by the Crown Prosecution Service was rising (Home Office, 2001b). Other aspects of the transition from one system of dealing with youth crime to another are not explored, such as the extent to which the informal disposals previously used by the police might have been replaced by Reprimands (see, for example, Evans and Ellis, 1997), which may thus account at least in part for the relatively low numbers in the comparison group with previous recorded offences. Certainly, given the changes in both procedures and recording methods, there must be some doubt that 'like' is really being compared with 'like' in this context. In addition, dubious methodological assumptions, such as the presumption that Final Warnings occur at a later stage in criminal careers than cautions (Hine and Celnick, 2001, p. 5), raise further questions about the comparability of results.

Furthermore, the evaluation found no effect on re-offending rates of intervention programmes put in place to accompany warnings. Indeed, indiscriminate use of such programmes is discouraged:

> Firstly, evaluation of work with adult offenders shows that intervention with offenders with a low risk of reoffending can result in increased reconviction rates ... Secondly, reconviction studies (including this one) show that a large proportion of offenders receiving a first caution do not reoffend, suggesting that intervening too early could be a waste of resources. (Hine and Celnick, 2001, p. 35)

For whatever reason, the Youth Justice Board chose to disregard this evidence, arguing both that the initial impact of Final Warnings was 'variable' (Warner, 2001, p. 1), and that 'research shows that an intervention programme at the Final Warning stage is one of the most effective ways of diverting an individual from criminality' (Youth Justice Board, 2002, p. 10).

Unfortunately, this selective reading of the available evidence (which itself is tentative) has become a feature of the Youth Justice Board's public pronouncements in its early years of operation, and it does nothing to further our understanding of the complexities of the interaction between young people and the youth justice system. Perhaps the most striking example of this tendency is presented by the claim in the Summer of 2002 that 'even before full national roll-out the youth justice reforms in 2000 cut predicted reconviction rates by nearly 15%' (Youth Justice Board Press Release, 9th July 2002).[1] This claim appears to be based on a study (Jennings, 2002) that compares 1997 reconviction rates with those for a cohort of young people dealt with in July 2000. The claimed reduction of 'nearly 15%' is arrived at by deducting the 'raw' reconviction rate for the July 2000 cohort (26.4%) from the 'predicted' rate based on the 1997 sample (30.9%), and calculating this figure as a proportion of the expected rate, in other words, the most dramatic possible construction of the evidence.

Further, and more responsible consideration of the findings presented would have, at best, made a case for modest claims of success, on a number of grounds. First, as the study itself acknowledges, the comparison is skewed by the very substantial 'increase in reprimands and final warnings' which would be expected to produce lower reconviction rates (Jennings, 2002, p. 9). Second, the exclusion of 'pseudo-reconvictions' (further proceedings for offences committed before the first disposal), which is likely to encompass an increasing number of repeat offenders – because of the practice of 'splitting' files (Shapland et al., 2001) – and the simultaneous exclusion of those sentenced to custody (a figure which increased over this period; Home Office, 2001b) are likely to have reduced the relative proportion of further proceedings for the adjusted 2000 sample. Third, as we have noted, procedures and recording methods have changed, which the study itself acknowledges would reduce the 'headline (sic!) improvement rate from 14.6% to between 11 and 12 per cent' (Jennings, 2002, p. 10), without taking into consideration possible changes in the use of informal disposals by the police. Fourth, the study appears to take no account of any external factors that may well have influenced outcomes, especially given the 'gearing effect' of the overall ratio of crimes committed to outcomes in the form of proceedings against individual young offenders. For example, over the period 1997–2000 crime rates were reported as falling on all accepted measures (Home Office, 2001b, p. 27), and it would therefore be difficult to separate out the impact of the youth justice reforms from the impact of other socio-economic factors and wider policy changes. Muncie, indeed, argues that 'changes in law enforcement and in what the law counts as crime preclude much meaningful discussion over whether youth crime is forever rising (or indeed falling)' (Muncie, 1999, p. 17).

The picture is further confused by the evidence of what young people themselves say about their levels of offending. According to one self-report survey, offending levels among young people are rising slightly

---

[1] By 2003, this reduction in reconviction rates was reported to have increased to 22.5% between 1997 and 2001, (Jennings, 2003).

(MORI, 2002, p. 11). A sharp rise is recorded for those identified as particularly 'at risk' of offending, from 60% to 64%. Very small numbers of these offences are known to the police (MORI, 2002, p. 19), with 6% of young people saying that their most recent offence came to official notice, although around a quarter were 'caught' for one offence or another over the previous 12 months. Rather more (47%) say that being caught and punished has little or no deterrent effect than say that it does stop them from re-offending (44%), and, in particular, deterrents appear to be having a declining effect on those who are defined as 'excluded offenders' (excluded from mainstream school, that is). The reported incidence of re-offending after being caught is reported as declining for children in school (50% to 47%) and increasing for those excluded (58% to 62%) from 2001 to 2002.

This evidence, from a large-scale annual survey of young people's reported offending activity, tells a rather different story to that of statistical analyses, it would seem. Patterns of crime among young people are not shifting dramatically, and the impact of official sanctions, which are being used increasingly, is not of itself a particularly powerful influence on desistance from crime, apparently. Indeed, we might conclude rather ironically with the observation that if the evidence from both these sources can be relied on, then the youth justice reforms have been working even more effectively than it might appear, because they have, in fact, dissuaded 'at risk' young people from re-offending, while other unknown causes are generating an increase in offending behaviour among young people in general.

The Nero Effect

At this point, it is important to remind ourselves of other important changes in the treatment of young people by the justice system, which, in the present author's view, have at least an equal claim on our attention. Indeed, the starting point for this is the same reconviction study on which the Youth Justice Board's hyperbolic claim of 15% reductions in re-offending rates is based (Jennings, 2002). Suspicions are aroused by the reported reduction in predicted reconviction rates, from 33.7% in 1997 to 30.9% in 2000 (Jennings, 2002, p. 5). This suggests, even allowing for changes in recording practices, that the cohort of young people dealt with as offenders immediately following the implementation of the reforms was considerably less 'criminal' than its predecessors. Confirmation of this is offered to some extent by the self-report survey, which demonstrates an increasing proportion of young people being caught and dealt with for offences (MORI, 2002, p. 21). The new youth justice system may therefore have contributed to an increasing criminalization of relatively minor offenders. At the same time, it appears, the types of intervention with young offenders themselves appear to have become increasingly intrusive and punitive, with a dramatic rise in the use of Final Warning intervention programmes (52% to 70% from 2000 to 2001/02; Youth Justice Board, 2002, p. 11), despite the lack of evidence for their efficacy.

At the same time, in Foucaultesque fashion, the level and intensity of intervention at all stages of the system also appears to be increasing, with the full implementation of demanding Referral Order contracts and the Intensive Supervision and Surveillance Programme. Young people are accelerated up the 'tariff' by attracting the label 'persistent offender' earlier in their offending careers, and in respect of less serious offences; evidence of their failure to comply with programme requirements is subject to more rigorous breach procedures; and perhaps the inevitable consequence is an increasing use of custody.

In conclusion, then, the available evidence suggests a decline in rates of offending, from 1995 onwards, on all recognized measures (Home Office, 2001b, p. 27). This is not necessarily supported by young people's own accounts (MORI, 2002). While credit for falling crime rates among young people is attributed to the youth justice reforms, the evidence does not appear to support this – the start of the trend towards lower crime rates pre-dated the reforms, and in any case the published evidence used to support these claims is, at best, equivocal or ambiguous (Hine and Celnick, 2001; Jennings, 2002; Loxley *et al.*, 2002).

What the evidence does tell us is that younger, less serious offenders are being drawn into the formal justice system (Jennings, 2002), which is more noteworthy given the longer term decline in the number of young people being processed as offenders – a fall of over 10% between 1998 and 2000, for example (Johnson and colleagues, 2001). Despite this, the balance between those dealt with by relatively less severe means such as cautions (reprimands and warnings since June 2000) and those sentenced by the courts has tipped towards a more punitive approach. In 1997, for example, cautioning represented 48.8% of all disposals, whereas by 2000 (including the first 6 months following implementation of the reforms) it had declined to 42.5% (Johnson and colleagues, 2001). The shift from cautions to Reprimands and Final Warnings did not appear to halt this decline, with a fall in numbers 'given reprimands, final warnings and cautions' from 24,900 in the first quarter of the year 2000 (immediately prior to implementation) to 23,300 in the last quarter, following implementation.

This progressive 'toughening up' of the youth justice system is also evident at subsequent stages. More lenient disposals, such as discharges and fines, were displaced by 'community sentences', while custody rates showed an overall increase (Johnson and colleagues, 2001). An apparent decline in the use of custody for 15–17 year olds in 2000 was offset by an increase in the length of custodial sentences (Johnson and colleagues, 2001, p. 11; Youth Justice Board, 2002, p. 15). As the Youth Justice Board notes, the numbers of young people in custody at any one time have shown a dramatic rise: 'between March 2000 and May 2001, the number of sentenced young offenders in secure establishments rose by 15%' (Youth Justice Board, 2001c, p. 13), and 'the number of young people in custody sentenced and remanded increased in the last year, from 2,753 in April 2001 to 3,034 in April 2002' (Youth Justice Board, 2002, p. 15). At the same time, the Board notes, Intensive Supervision and Surveillance Programmes were made available to nearly 1,500 young people. There can be no question in these circumstances of the ISSP offering a 'credible' alternative to custody.

Despite the vast array of youth justice reforms introduced since 1997, there is little evidence of any significant impact on young people, on the outcomes administered by the courts, or on other key stakeholders such as victims. What evidence is available suggests an intensification of disposals targeted at increasingly minor and less experienced young offenders; while the injustices experienced by particular groups such as young Black people (Bowling and Phillips, 2002), and the shoddy and oppressive treatment administered by custodial institutions continues unabated (HM Chief Inspector of Prisons, 2001; 2002; Bright, 2002; Goldson, 2002).

In some quarters, it might be felt that a greater level of activity and a greater intensity of intervention might simply be indicative of a more responsive and committed approach to youth justice – a sign that the crimes of the young are, indeed, being taken more seriously than in the past (Blair, 2002; Blunkett, 2002). On the other hand, serious questions must be asked about the consequences of this commitment. At the most intensive levels of intervention, as we have observed, there is clearly a diminution of the rights of children and young people, with collateral impacts such as increasing evidence of harmful treatment in custody, and persistent inequality of treatment for particular ethnic groups. At the same time, the propagation of a much broader range of interventions, based on singling out for special treatment young people who offend (or are 'at risk' of offending), is both inefficient in the purely economic sense, and inconsistent with other policy streams intended to promote social integration and a sense of belonging. Far from promoting inclusion, a sense of difference and 'otherness' (Garland, 2001) is cemented in place. The price of a more certain response to youth crime is both too high in human terms and, ultimately, unnecessary.

Chapter 7

Theorizing youth justice

Thinking It Through: the Art of the Possible

Having set out in considerable detail the 'state of play' in youth justice, the task now will be to take a step back and reflect on the possibilities and practicalities of achieving change and moving forward. The preceding overview of recent and contemporary practice suggests that there are very substantial grounds for concern, in that the youth justice system has managed to achieve the dual failures of being both ineffective, even in its own terms, and repressive in its impact. The limited gains that might be identified are hard-won successes, mostly attributable to the strength and imagination of practitioners and managers, and these have been achieved in spite of, rather than because of, the reforms and restructuring of the late 1990s and early 2000s.

If we are to make progress and build on the gains that can be identified, a number of challenges must be overcome. In particular, there is a need for a detailed and meaningful understanding of how and why the youth justice system is constituted in the way that it is, and of the beliefs and assumptions that inform its delivery. What, in short, are the ideological sources of the prevailing obsession with surveillance, containment and punishment? And how can we account for the system dynamics, which determine that these preoccupations will be pursued by means which are prescriptive, micromanaged and target led?

Answering these questions will, in turn, provide us with a platform from which we can begin to consider the question of what we, collectively, want from youth justice. This will involve a consideration of the perspectives of a range of stakeholders, including victims, young people, ethnic minorities and 'the community' (Chapter 8). The aim will be to bring together a theoretical understanding, on the one hand, and the aspirations and experiences of those 'on the ground', on the other, in order to begin to sketch out what is conceivable, practicable, and desirable in the context of youth justice. How might it be possible to achieve a youth justice system that 'does what it says on the tin', that is, delivers justice for young people.

The Practicality of Theory

For many people absorbed in the construction and delivery of youth justice, theory may seem relatively unimportant, or simply irrelevant to what they are doing on a daily basis. So, the first task here is perhaps to justify making the attempt to seek deeper and more abstract under-standings of the context within which justice services are delivered, and in which those responsible struggle to achieve effective practice. Of course, this in itself begs a fundamental question – just what do we mean by effectiveness in youth justice, and how do we know when it is, indeed, 'working'? The establishment of a single aim by the government, the prevention of youth offending, might appear to have resolved this difficulty, but it has not dispensed with the need to understand the assumptions that underpin this clearly expressed objective. The implicit theories that inform everyday strategies and practices are no less theoretical because they are not articulated or subject to critical scrutiny.

To illustrate this point, it might be helpful briefly to consider alternative, if apparently far-fetched, approaches to preventing youth crime which might have been adopted by government, and which would provide a more certain outcome than the strategies in place. First, the law could be revised to decriminalize any and all actions of the young – not so far-fetched perhaps, if we recall that a Labour government came reasonably close to achieving this in 1969. Second, all young people could be made subject to preventive detention. Or, third, the notion of a distinct phase of 'youth' could be dispensed with, leaving an undifferentiated justice system to deal with all crimes and offenders on an equal basis; this too, may not seem quite so far-fetched following the abolition of the rule of *doli incapax* under the Crime and Disorder Act 1998. The fact that none of these courses has been pursued to its logical extreme suggests that the choices actually made by government and those who administer youth justice are based on a series of beliefs and judgements about what is possible, desirable and acceptable; that is, a complex network of theoretical perspectives and value bases are brought to bear on the organization and delivery of penal interventions for young people. Dominelli (1998) makes the point that interventions in social welfare are 'compelled to maintain the link between theory and practice', and this is equally true of youth justice. It is not simply a managerial or technical exercise in delivering prescribed interventions, but rather a product of multifaceted and sometimes conflicting ideas and beliefs. These underlying assumptions must also, therefore, be open to analysis and critical evaluation, especially if we wish to consider the prospects for change and improvement to the delivery of services to deal with youth offending.

In seeking to develop a plausible understanding of how youth justice has emerged in the form it takes, it will be helpful to consider a number of different theoretical 'levels', which correspond effectively to the distinct levels of the justice system itself. This might be seen as distinguishing the 'what' (the definition of the problem), the 'how' (the machinery and processes by which it is addressed), and the 'why' (the underlying rationale).

As already observed, Harris and Webb (1987) explore this kind of distinction quite helpfully, in their analysis of the exercise of power in the context of 'juvenile justice'. They put forward a framework based on three distinct phases of theory and practice, describing these as the 'macro', 'mezzo' and 'micro' levels (see also, Chapter 3). For them, the macro level is represented by the state and its role in determining the shape and orientation of welfare work, which is the source of a series of central contradictions between the aims and purposes prescribed for interventions and the professional culture and principles of welfare 'experts'. They argue that such contradictions lie at the core of many of the difficulties experienced by those responsible for delivering interventions in practice:

> ... motivations and fine feelings are heavily circumscribed by social function, and in the conflict between competing ideologies of state bureaucracy and professional autonomy lies the source of some of the frustrations regularly experienced by the workers themselves. (Harris and Webb, 1987, p. 3)

Harris and Webb's characterization of the mezzo level concentrates on the nature of welfare and justice agencies as mediators in this interchange between state and professional interests. For them, it is important to recognize that it is at this level that interpretation, adaptation, negotiation and even, perhaps, deception bring idealized and centralized demands together with the diverse and challenging realities of delivery in an unpredictable and sometimes intractable environment. This process of seeking accommodation between the idealized goal of social order and the messy and disorganized nature of reality is, in this view, 'in part a reflection of the practicalities of managing people who have already proved to be unmanageable' (Harris and Webb, 1987, p. 102).

At the micro level, where youth justice work is actually carried out, they argue, practice appears to be disparate, disorganized, and simply incomprehensible to those who are its objects, that is, young offenders ('clients'). This is largely a consequence of the attempts at the mezzo and macro levels to apply simplistic models of intervention to complex circumstances. Harris and Webb focus on one aspect of this, 'routine individualisation', a process by which standardized procedures and instruments are applied in specific cases, creating a sense of anomalous and illogical outcomes, such as the indiscriminate use of Supervision Orders, irrespective of offenders' background or the seriousness of the offence. In the empirical study that informed their observations, '58 per cent of "not serious" and 70 per cent of "serious" cases received two-year [supervision] orders, apparently as a routine disposal' (Harris and Webb, 1987, p. 118). Their argument is that these outcomes should be understood within a broader context, such that the 'inherent instability' that characterizes all aspects of youth justice is played out in a series of interactions and compromises, which produce arbitrary and unpredictable outcomes. At the same time, the process ensures that the appearance of order and rationality is maintained, and it is possible to create the conditions such that 'the game itself continues' (Harris and Webb, 1987, p. 3).

While their analysis, in itself, offers some important insights into the internal mechanisms characterizing youth justice, albeit based on empirical evidence from the 1980s, we should also draw from it the value of linking theoretical perspectives situated at different points of a more generalized phenomenon. Thus, I shall follow their lead in pursuing an approach here that considers three critical questions in turn, before trying to sketch out some broader emergent themes. First, it is important to consider the 'micro' issue of the problem of youth – why are young people, as a generation, viewed as problematic? Second, I will focus on the nature of justice, that is, why the problem of disorder should be characterized in the way it is at the 'macro' level of the state and other powerful institutions. And, third and finally, it will be important to revisit the issue of the 'linking' mechanisms, which ensure that youth justice is delivered in the form that it is (see also the account of 'Foucault's Law' in Chapter 3).

Targeting the Young: the Source of All Our Ills?

To begin with, it is necessary to address the question of why societal concerns about disorder and threat appear to be focused to a substantial degree on the behaviour of young people. Given, as we have already observed, that the incidence of criminal behaviour is much more evenly distributed across the age range, and that young people are as likely to be victims as offenders, what are the sources of our specific concerns about the young as perpetrators of crime. Why, in short, are we frightened of young people?

The arbitrary and specific nature of these concerns is further highlighted by the recognition that conceptions of youth are culturally determined. Jenks (1996), for example, argues that 'adolescence' is a peculiarly Western phenomenon, representing the playing-out of the specific social, cultural and economic conditions that persist in such modern, developed societies. Anthropological evidence clearly supports this, with writers such as Benedict (1961) and Erikson (1995) identifying very wide variations in the way that transitions from childhood to adulthood are thought of and managed in different social settings. Such variations suggest that the nature of the experience of adolescence itself is determined by the social context, and by the institutions and beliefs pertaining in any given milieu:

> Undoubtedly each culture ... creates character types marked by its own mixture of defect and excess; and each culture develops rigidities and illusions which protect it against the insight that no ideal, safe, permanent state can emerge from the blueprint it has gropingly evolved. (Erikson, 1995, p. 168)

Adolescence is not, therefore, fixed or constant, and this has prompted some authors to argue on the basis of their findings that it must be considered the product of a broader network of social forces. For commentators such as Willis (1977) and Davies (1986) the experience of being young and growing up is fundamentally influenced by the underlying requirement to socialize the next generation of wage earners, producers and family members. Willis's investigation of what he calls the 'working class counter-school culture' (Willis, 1977, p. 2) is an attempt to identify the means and processes by which 'labour power' is reproduced, and by which young people are socialized into a particular work ethos, rationalizing for themselves their place in the economic system. This is not a straightforward or one-way process, according to him, in that attempts by the state and other social institutions to reproduce the next generation of employees is both contradictory in itself, and is mediated by the experiences, ideas and attitudes of young people. Nevertheless, the purposes of those in power who determine the nature of interventions with young people are clearly identified as being the creation and shaping of a future generation that meets the needs and expectations of the existing social order:

> Youth policies were ... designed to satisfy some powerful sectional (especially class, gender and racial) interests. As the rawest and least valuable recruits to a given social order, the young had to be socialized, schooled, trained and ultimately contained – if necessary [according to a senior civil servant] 'in terms more or less unpalatable' to them. (Davies, 1986, p. 116)

Corrigan (1979), too, in his study of young people 'doing nothing' in Sunderland, links changes in the experience and activities of youth to parallel changes in social structures and the shifting demands of living in a 'capitalist society'. For example, young people are seen as educated to be increasingly 'flexible' in responding to the expectation that they will change jobs and careers regularly over the course of their working lives. Thus, during the 1980s and 1990s, they were increasingly expected to 'equip themselves with the abilities sought after in the fast-food industry and then ... get on their bikes and ... price themselves into work. (Haines and Drakeford, 1998, p. 8).

One element of this 'educative' (see Gramsci, 1971) process is provided by the young people's experience of being policed and processed by the justice system. This can be seen as the implementation of a strategy of containment, whereby young people learn their place in the scheme of things. To them this may have no obvious justification:

> The power of the police is seen as virtually total by the boys ... The police, like the teachers, are a group of people with power that do some very strange and arbitrary things; their power is massive and has to be coped with, if not obeyed. (Corrigan, 1979, p.137)

Furthermore, the control that is exercised is not connected in these youths' perceptions to specific instances of wrongdoing. It is more the case that explicit limits are being set to their behaviour in order to create a sense of the 'natural order' of things, and to enforce conformity. Indeed, there is a broader pattern, which institutionalizes the control process (Cohen , 1985): 'the role of the police and the role of the education system are parallel here, because they are both attempting to change the styles of living of people who … are seen as threatening by ruling groups within society' (Corrigan, 1979, p. 139). According to Jeffs (1997), such developments are not co-incidental. A range of centralized and directive education initiatives, such as home–school contracts, citizenship education, and attendance league tables, serve essentially the same purpose as specific policies to control young offenders, such as 'tagging' and imposing parental liability.

The machinery of criminal justice, then, is but one of the vehicles used to shape the experience and expectations of adolescents, which, in turn, are geared towards creating a spirit of acceptance and compliance with dominant social norms. As Muncie (1999) also observes, it is important to remind ourselves that the roles for which young people are being prepared are also characterized by distinctions of race and gender, with significant implications for young Black males, for example.

It seems to be the case that the preoccupation with controlling the behaviour of young people is at least partly generated by a functionalist concern to see that they are effectively socialized to meet the requirements of dominant (economic) interests. Jeffs (1997), for example, refers to a 'plethora' of government policies covering education, housing, income maintenance and youth crime, which, taken together, '[confirm] the resolve on the part of the government to control those identified as the underclass. In particular, they have exhibited a willingness to adopt increasingly authoritarian policies to control and manage the young poor' (Jeffs, 1997, p. 160). The identified need for control and guidance might stem from an understanding of young people as being 'unfinished', and thus likely to behave in ways inappropriate, or threatening to the status quo (Davies, 1986). Perhaps this is partly why terms such as 'youth' and 'adolescence' can relatively easily, '… conjure up a number of emotive and troubling images. These range from notions of uncontrolled freedom, irresponsibility, vulgarity, rebellion and dangerousness to those of deficiency, neglect, deprivation or immaturity' (Muncie, 1999, p. 3).

However, while concerns about the behaviour and attitudes of the young arise partly because they have not yet been fully prepared for their allotted roles as responsible and productive (or reproductive) members of adult society, it is also the case that the socialization process itself is inconsistent, leading to tensions and contradictions in their experiences. As Willis (1977) has observed, the demands placed on young people by social institutions themselves may not always point in the same direction. MacDonald (1997) argues that their 'survival' strategies compel young people to develop a range of responses to economic pressures and 'chronic insecurity'. Young people can be expected to behave in differing and conflicting ways in order to comply with a complex variety of social expectations; for example, they may be encouraged to take a relatively passive role as 'consumers', but, at the same time be entrepreneurial and proactive as 'producers' of wealth (Smith, R., 2000). This might, in turn, lead to a series of conflicting dynamics within the processes for maintaining or reproducing the existing forms of social organization: 'it is, of course, an absolute requirement for the existing social system that the same standards, ideologies and aspirations are not passed on to all' (Willis, 1977, p.177). This will result in variable, and potentially conflicting, expectations being placed on young people themselves. For example, they might be expected to be dynamic, competitive and ambitious, especially if they are young males, on the one hand, while such attributes as aggression and a spirit of challenge may be discouraged, on the other. They might also be expected to exercise increasing spending power, and hold ever higher aspirations as potential customers, and yet, at the same time, they may confront the constraints of the labour market, as MacDonald (1997, p. 195) puts it, frustrating their hopes for 'sustainable family lives and respectable futures'.

Recognizing these conflicts and constraints can bring us closer to understanding the relationship between the sources of power, and the institutional structures which represent dominant social interests, on the one hand, and the behaviour of the young in response to the 'mixed messages' they receive, on the other.

Frustrated Ambition?

In trying to account for young people's behaviour in this context of conflicting expectations and experiences, it can be helpful to consider the insights offered by a rather older sociological source. The development of a framework for understanding the complexities faced by young people in adjusting or responding to their specific social circumstances was a task specifically addressed by Merton (1957). He concluded that it was possible to offer a 'typology', which enabled one to make sense of the different ways in which individuals adapt to social norms, depending on the influences acting upon them. At the core of this model is the distinction between 'goals' and 'means', which he uses to demonstrate that a range of orientations and attitudes are possible in relation to each of these.

Thus, for example, if an individual shares the dominant cultural goals of a given society, and both possesses and utilizes the institutionalized (socially acceptable) means to achieve these, then that person is demonstrating social conformity. However, a number of other patterns of adaptation are clearly possible, including, notably, 'innovation'. In this mode, the individual shares the dominant goals, but adopts other than institutionalized means to achieve these. For Merton (writing in the United States), this was a predictable response to the fact that

Table 7.1   A Typology of Modes of Individual Adaptation

Modes of Adaptation	Culture Goals	Institutionalized Means
Conformity	+	+
Innovation	+	–
Ritualism	–	+
Retreatism	–	–
Rebellion	±	±

Adapted from: *Social Theory and Social Structure* (Merton, 1957, p. 140)

'contemporary American culture continues to be characterized by a heavy emphasis on wealth as a basic symbol of success, without a corresponding emphasis upon the legitimate avenues on which to march towards this goal' (Merton, 1957, p. 139). The 'innovative' response to this apparent contradiction may well be demonstrated through some form of criminal activity. Merton argues that there is a distinct class bias to such patterns of behaviour, in that 'the lower strata' will have fewer opportunities to achieve success or wealth through the conventional labour market:

> ... specialised areas of vice and crime constitute a 'normal' response to a situation where the cultural emphasis upon pecuniary success has been absorbed, but where there is little access to conventional and legitimate means for becoming successful. (Merton, 1957, p.139)

While this may account for some forms of acquisitive crime (theft, fraud and shoplifting, for example), it appears rather too simplistic to explain all the types and patterns of behaviour which are defined as criminal (see, for example, Soothill *et al.*, 2000). Nevertheless, it is a helpful characterization of the way in which generally accepted social norms and aspirations can, in themselves, prompt rational forms of adaptive behaviour which do not meet the expected standards exemplified by institutional codes, such as the criminal law. The crimes of the young might, at least in part, be understandable as the consequence of rational choices made in a context of unequal and contradictory social pressures and behavioural norms. Craine (1997), for example, uses an ethnographic approach to illustrate the emergence of 'alternative careers' for young people in the illicit economy as a response to 'triple failure'. Young people were found to be constructing viable but unlawful alternatives for themselves in a context where, in formal terms:

They had 'failed' educationally, 'failed' to secure post-school employment, 'failed' to 'get into' working-class adulthood through
employment, even after participation in a succession of government
schemes and special programmes. (Craine, 1997, p. 148)

Behaviour defined as 'criminal' might, therefore, be a by-product of the
conflicting expectations experienced by the young. Nevertheless, we must
accept that this behaviour can also be experienced by others as unpleasant
and unacceptable. As MacDonald (1997) points out, it is a matter of
concern that crimes committed by young people are likely to have an
adverse impact, particularly on their own communities: 'the social and
financial costs of acquisitive and more random and violent criminality ...
cannot be dismissed' (MacDonald, 1997, p. 184).

The Reality of Youth Crime

While it has been recognized that both 'youth' and 'crime and disorder'
are social constructions (Muncie, 1999), it must also be acknowledged that
however defined, some of the behaviour demonstrated by young people
must be seen as problematic, anti-social or simply unpleasant. This
perspective is consistent with the position adopted by the 'left realists' in
criminology, who argue that the problem of youth crime is not simply one
of labelling or the imposition of oppressive forms of social control (Lea
and Young, 1984). The behaviour of young people can be genuinely
damaging, oppressive and frightening to individuals and particular
groups living in neighbourhoods already disadvantaged in other ways:

> ... criminologists have come to realise the essentially contradictory
> nature of crime, economically, socially and politically ... Radical
> criminology ... notes quite urgently that there is a substantial
> element in street crime which is merely the poor taking up the
> individualistic, competitive ethos of capitalism itself ... (Lea and
> Young, 1984, p. 116)

Lea and Young have identified young people, in particular, as a source of
much of the antisocial behaviour that gives rise to fear and hostility. They
have also, controversially, suggested that there may be a racial dimension
to this, in that young Black people might be responsible for a
disproportionate amount of crime, or at least of a certain type of crime, in
effect, 'compounding the oppression' of victims (Pitts, 2001b). Gilroy
(2002, p. 66) has argued by contrast that this must not be allowed to
generate assumptions that 'blacks are a high crime group' (see Chapter 6),

or provide any justification for racist practices in addressing offending behaviour.

The recognition of the role of criminal behaviour in contributing to the disadvantages and suffering of poorer communities, as we have seen (Chapter 3), has had much to do with the refocusing of the Labour Party's thinking on youth crime, and its concern to address directly the behaviour that creates problems for poor communities themselves. There has been a corresponding re-emergence of interest in the 'situated' nature of crime, and in the antecedents of young offending. By contrast, structural accounts do not account for differential outcomes; nor do they offer readily accessible or deliverable solutions. After all, it is observed, not all young people experiencing disadvantage become criminals:

> This more realist approach to the delinquency of young men is a useful antidote to the excessive social constructionism which has pervaded liberal criminology ... It also reiterates the importance of appreciating the way that socially structured aspects of identity – particularly those informed by gender, class and race – help shape the cultural survival strategies of young people. Future research on social exclusion would need ... to investigate more fully the way that some young men, sharing apparently similar social attributes, do not attempt ... delinquent solutions .... (MacDonald, 1997, p. 192)

This refocusing of concern about the crimes of the young, increasingly associated with New Labour, also has considerable pragmatic value. The shift of emphasis in thinking on the social-democratic left has achieved at least two important political objectives: it responds to public concerns to 'do something' about the day-to-day reality of social disorder, and it coincides with 'commonsense' assumptions about the source of the problem, that is 'poor child-rearing practices and weak parental control' (Pitts, 2000, p. 10).

Explaining Youth Crime?

In the light of this, it will also be important to take account of analyses of the offending behaviour of young people that offer an alternative to structural explanations and which identify the causes of their criminal actions, rooted in the circumstances, experiences and characteristics of young people themselves, and their families.

Farrington, for example, has found that there are a number of risk factors associated with offending by young people, including:

- low income and poor housing
- living in 'deteriorated' inner city areas
- a high degree of impulsiveness and hyperactivity
- low intelligence and low school attainment
- poor parental supervision and harsh and erratic discipline
- parental conflict and broken families

(Farrington, 1996)

Similarly, Rutter and his colleagues identify a range of factors associated with 'antisocial behaviour' by young people, including:

- Individual characteristics, such as 'hyperactivity', 'cognitive impairment', 'temperamental features', and 'a distorted style of social information processing'
- Psychosocial factors, such as the nature of parenting, family discord and parental depression
- Population-wide influences, such as the mass media, school ethos and behaviour, and 'area differences'

(Rutter *et al.*, 1998)

Both meta-analyses generate a range of policy options in the views of their authors. Farrington (2002) argues for the development of initiatives directed at securing behavioural change, school improvement, parental education and 'enrichment' programmes for the early years. He also suggests the establishment of wider-ranging 'community-based programmes against crime', on the *Communities that Care* model (France and Crow, 2001). Rutter and colleagues (1998) share his optimism about models of early prevention such as the Perry Pre-School Project, 'parenting enhancement', school-wide interventions and the 'early treatment' of problem behaviour. They caution, however, that 'focusing on high-risk samples will miss a substantial number of offenders' (Rutter *et al.*, 1998, p. 24).

While they are clearly of considerable value, such analyses have also given rise to some methodological confusion, notably over the distinction between 'predictors', 'risk factors' and 'causes' – knowing that there is a relationship between certain indicators and the incidence of offending is a far cry from claiming or even assuming that this represents a causal relationship: 'even the most elaborate predictors of individual offending devised by criminologists have always over-predicted the incidence of crime alarmingly' (Pitts, 2001b, p. 82). The necessary degree of caution is not always evident in the response of 'politicians, policy wonks, "opinion formers" and some youth justice managers and professionals', who draw rather simplistic conclusions about the use of predictive instruments to 'target, and then eradicate, youth crime' (Pitts, 2001b, p. 82). Evidence of this tendency is provided in the work of the government-sponsored Social Exclusion Unit, which singles out a number of characteristics that are given causal status:

> Most juvenile prisoners have experienced a range of social exclusion factors, which may have contributed to their offending behaviour. These include:
> low educational attainment;
> disrupted family backgrounds;
> coming from a black or minority ethnic background;
> behavioural and mental health problems; and
> problems of alcohol and/or drug misuse.
> (Social Exclusion Unit, 2002, para D.6)

Attempts to generate a comprehensive empirical account of the factors associated with youth crime are important, not least because they have formed the basis for much of recent government thinking in this area. Muncie, for example, argues that much of the government's pre-occupation with parenting stems from concerns about the links between the quality of family life and offending by young people (Muncie, 2000). As a consequence, he suggests, policies and intervention strategies are explicitly designed to address these 'presenting' problems:

> New Labour's acceptance that crime runs in certain families and that anti-social behaviour in childhood is a predictor of later criminality has opened the door to a range of legislative initiatives which target 'disorderly' as well as criminal behaviour. (Muncie, 2000, p. 23)

Similarly, the justification for the introduction of specific measures such as Anti-Social Behaviour Orders is provided by the apparent need to impose direct behavioural controls on those who demonstrate the characteristics of 'impulsiveness and hyperactivity'. Behavioural management programmes have also become something of a staple form of intervention across the range of youth justice disposals, being strongly encouraged by the Youth Justice Board (2002). As Muncie also points out, the association of youth crime with 'social' causes, such as poor housing and unemployment, might lead to a broader range of initiatives; however the primary foci of youth justice practice remain the individual and the family:

> Parental training and a range of behavioural and cognitive interventions are considered to be most effective … In such ways the targets of social crime prevention have invariably become individualised and behavioural. Primary attention is given to responding to the symptoms, rather than the causes of young people's disaffection and dislocation. The social contexts of offending are bypassed. (Muncie, 2000, p. 26)

It is suggested by Muncie that New Labour has derived much of its youth crime strategy from just such a position, narrowing the focus of concern to specific groups and individuals who are 'at risk', and concerning itself only with the superficial aspects of the problem; the crusade against street crime in the summer of 2002 and the development of the technology of control, in the form of 'tagging' and 'voice recognition' systems, could be seen as two significant manifestations of this approach.

On the other hand, it is equally the case that the 'factors' which have been linked by detailed empirical studies with the incidence of youth crime are not inconsistent with the kind of structural causes and influences discussed previously. Leonard (1984), for example, suggests that individual personalities are clearly shaped by forces associated with the economy and the state. As he puts it, the individual is 'moulded, inculcated or penetrated by the institutions and activities of the social order and the ideologies which inform and legitimate them' (Leonard, 1984, p. 116). The deviant behaviour of individuals is thus characterized as the product of interactive and dynamic processes. Criminal activities emerge as the outcome of a complex interplay of social forces and personal experiences: 'contradictions within and between the economy, the family and the state, connecting to the highly variable experience of specific individuals, provide space for avoidance, resistance and dissent' (Leonard, 1984, p. 116). Thus, specific criminal acts, which may be reprehensible in themselves, cannot be understood or dealt with solely on the basis of their immediate manifestation. Attempts to deal with the offending of young people by addressing observable influences and patterns of behaviour alone therefore represent, at best, a partial solution. Ironically, as Christie (2000) observes, such forms of 'individualised' response, also effectively 'depersonalise' explanations of youth crime:

> A political decision to eliminate concern for the social background of the defendant involves much more than making those characteristics inappropriate for decisions on pain [punishment]. By the same token, the offender is to a large extent excluded as a person. There is

no point in exploring a social background, childhood, dreams, defeats ... (Christie, 2000, p. 162)

In the present context, this gives rise to further questions about the nature of the formal response to the crimes of the young, and the extent to which it 'misses the point'. In order to understand how 'youth justice' operates we must give further consideration to the way in which institutional systems for dealing with youth offending are constituted, and how these give rise to specific forms of delivery that focus on, and problematize, just one aspect of the phenomenon – that is, the activities of those young people identified as potential or actual offenders.

The Locus of Power: Ideologies and Structures

Much attention has already been given to the exploration and explanation of the sources of power in society, and their relationship to specific beliefs about – and strategies for – dealing with crime and disorder. The exercise of social control is a source of continuing fascination (Garland, 2001). Authors such as Cohen (1985) have explored this area in some detail, and there is widespread agreement that it is an important component of an adequate understanding of youth justice (see, for example, Goldson, 1997; Goldson (ed.), 2000; Muncie *et al.* (eds), 2002). The key questions here relate to the manner in which the specific machinery of the justice system can be linked to more fundamental matters of the exercise of state power and the maintenance of the moral and political order. Clarke (2002), for example, argues that the courts and other state institutions are constituted in such a way as to carry out a range of legitimizing functions, which contribute to sustaining a particular set of social relations. It is their ability to claim legitimacy which provides them with the basis for imposing sanctions on individuals and their families, both in order to control their behaviour directly, and in order to reinforce the system of norms and rules on which they are based. The institutions of the law are thus held to have a kind of self-affirming quality.

As we have already observed, it is likely that the underlying rationale for the operation of the institutions of youth justice lie in pervasive and persistent concerns about the maintenance and subsequent reproduction of social order. For Clarke (2002), the fear of disorder, in general, and of unruly youth, in particular, is almost endemic, being evident in historical accounts of unrest and confrontation for at least 'the past three centuries'. For Pearson (1985), too, there is considerable evidence that modern societies have been beset by a perennial sense of threat, notably from the young, who become caricatured and demonized as a result. Often, as he observes, this kind of characterization of external threats to social order will have racist overtones, too. Cohen's (1972) seminal *Folk Devils and Moral Panics* takes further the argument that part of the reason for our fear of the young is a process of reification, which contributes to an almost constant sense of unease among the population in general about the danger they pose to the very social fabric.

While there is good reason to suppose that the behaviour of the young might, of itself, represent something of a challenge to social expectations, there is also substantial support for the argument that the threat posed by them is mediated and amplified by the manner in which it is defined. In other words, whatever the content of their behaviour, other purposes are being served through its depiction and the responses it engenders. In highlighting the role of the media, for example, in acting on fears about deviant or frightening behaviour, McRobbie and Thornton argue that this is an inevitable part of the process of achieving meaning: 'Social reality is experienced through language, communication and imagery. Social meaning and social difference are irretrievably tied up with representation.' (McRobbie and Thornton, 2002, p. 76). That is to say, the way in which images of disorder among young people are generated and presented is not accidental; rather, it is serving a specific purpose in tying us in to a common understanding of their behaviour.

This proposition, in turn, takes us into the territory of 'hegemony' (Gramsci, 1971) and 'ideology' (Althusser, 1977). The administration of youth justice does not simply reflect the routine delivery of established and agreed norms; it also achieves a distinct function in providing explicit confirmation of the apparently fixed definitions of acceptable and unacceptable behaviour. It is not only a matter of distinguishing between qualities of 'right' and 'wrong', but also that the exercise of judicial power serves to provide the justification for this distinction as it is made in any given social context. We should, in order to seek fuller understanding, be clear and open about the sectional interests at play when these moral distinctions are made.

For Gramsci (1971), for example, the extent to which specific interests can win the authority to determine what is legitimate and what is not is crucial in determining the way in which power is exercised. Legitimacy has to be earned, and the exercise of authority has to gain the consent of citizens in order to secure their active engagement in achieving a measure of social control. The smooth and efficient running of societal institutions depends on, for the most part, a common commitment to the principles and organizational structures on which they are based (we are reminded of the notion of 'policing by consent'; Scarman, 1982).

In fact, the authority to govern is gained in two ways, according to Gramsci: by the achievement of the 'spontaneous' consent of the population, and by the direct invocation of the 'apparatus of state coercive power', in order to 'legally' enforce discipline on those who do not conform. The latter, however, is very much a reserve power, only brought to bear when consent has failed, for some element of the population. It cannot become the norm because it implies the failure of consensual means, and becomes increasingly difficult to sustain. The explicit use of state power is, in fact, of much less value than the day-to-day project of earning and sustaining the consensual compliance of most, if not all, groups in society. In order to achieve this primary objective, the state adopts an 'educative and formative' role (Gramsci, 1971, p. 242). This is a particular characteristic of 'liberal democratic governments [which] make a major attempt to secure public support for state criminalisation and crime control through centralised high profile politics of 'law and order' (Lea, 2002, p. 172).

The 'rule of law' creates an external, objective and apparently neutral standard by which behaviour can be judged, and by which the line between the law-abiding and the criminal can be determined. It is not simply a matter of creating an effective criminal system to control and punish those who transgress the rules; it is also the purpose of the law to carry out this 'educative' function, in setting the terms for a common belief in acceptable standards of behaviour, and generating the only valid criteria by which such judgements can be made.

Althusser (1977) pursues a similar line of argument, suggesting that it is important to distinguish the ideological function of the law from its practical purposes. His helpful, if over-deterministic, characterization of the exercise of social control relies on the concept of 'state apparatuses'. These entities can be subdivided into 'Repressive State Apparatuses' and 'Ideological State Apparatuses', which are directed towards the same end, but differ in the manner of their operation. In the judicial context, some institutions can be thought of as primarily repressive, such as the courts and prisons, while others, including community justice agencies, for example, can be seen to perform a more ideological function, in establishing legitimacy and gaining consent for the rule of law. In this way, 'the law belongs both to the [Repressive] State Apparatus and to the system of ISAs [Ideological State Apparatuses]' (Althusser, 1977, p. 137).

This distinction helps us to understand the way in which legal institutions and judicial processes operate both directly, in controlling certain types of behaviour by force, and indirectly by creating the conditions under which these behaviours are defined as unlawful, and then dealt with as transgressions. The use of the means of repression is supported by the ideological task of establishing a legal definition of what is acceptable and unacceptable.

Althusser also argues that there is a complementary relationship between the ISAs, which support each other in carrying out their unified function of defending dominant interests. This network includes, for example, the educational ISA, the family ISA, the communications ISA and the religious ISA. Developing this argument, Garland argues that the specific forms taken by the justice agencies must be seen as interlinked with other organizations:

> Institutions of crime control and criminal justice have definite conditions of existence. They form part of a network of governance and social ordering that, in modern societies, includes the legal system, the labour market, and welfare state institutions. They refer to, and are supported by, other social institutions and social controls, and are grounded in specific configurations of cultural, political and economic action. (Garland, 2001, p. 5)

In the specific context of youth justice, the way in which such elements coalesce to establish and maintain a system of social control is classically illustrated by Hall and his colleagues (1978). Their extensive study, based on an analysis of the emergence of fears about 'mugging' in the 1970s, shows how perceptions of criminal behaviour can be generated and then intensified by a network of social institutions, including the media, political interests and the judiciary, each intervening in public debates in such a way as to create an overwhelming sense of lawlessness and threat (also, Hearn, 2003). The consequence of this interactive process is shown to be a heightened level of public sensitivity to a particular type of offence, such as street robbery, and a readiness to sanction more authoritarian judicial practices. This is illustrative of a kind of amplificatory spiral which legitimizes and strengthens ideological assumptions about the way in which offending behaviour is defined and dealt with – compounded in the case of mugging by issues of race and racism, which is a recurrent theme, as Garland confirms (2001).

A more contemporary insight into the relationship between the repressive and ideological functions of state apparatuses might be offered by the example of the Youth Justice Board. The Board, as has been observed, clearly operates in a number of ways to inculcate a particular model of intervention in youth justice, based on a series of assumptions about the offending behaviour of young people. The Board is constituted in a way that gives the impression that it is an independent body, apolitical and yet representing a diverse range of relevant interests. It also lays claim to authority based on credentials of expertise, knowledge and relevant experience, which seemingly puts it in a privileged position in leading change and innovation in practice. This authority, in turn, provides the Board with sufficient credibility and clout to be able to determine what is understood as 'good practice', and what principles should underpin interventions in the field of work with young offenders. One model of 'restorative justice' is thus promoted, at the expense of alternative approaches (Haines, 2000).

However, the 'ideological' function of the Board in reconstituting our understanding of appropriate forms of intervention is complemented by its more 'repressive' innovations, such as Intensive Surveillance and Support Programmes and its acquisition of responsibility for much of the juvenile secure estate. The Board's apparent autonomy and its 'professional' credentials will, of course, help to legitimize these interventions; for example, its claims to have improved conditions and services for young people in custody helps to make such disposals more acceptable to those who might otherwise baulk at the use of imprisonment for 12-year olds (Pitts, 2003).

Cohen (1985) is particularly sceptical about this kind of development. The 'humanization' of previously repressive forms of intervention in the name of progress is something of which he is highly suspicious. He argues, instead, that this represents no more than an extension of the networks of control, made possible precisely because of the appearance of reasonableness and concern. He also claims that this 'softly, softly' approach is likely to pervade all aspects of the criminal process:

> ... at the shallow end [of the justice system], the generation of new treatment criteria and the pervasiveness of the social welfare and preventive structures, often ensure an erosion of traditional rights and liberties. In a system of low visibility and accountability, where a high degree of discretion is given to administrative and professional bodies ... there is often less room for such niceties as due process and legal rights. (Cohen, 1985, p. 70)

This observation may have predated the Final Warning and the Referral Order by some 15 years, but the concerns remain the same.

On the other hand, Cohen takes issue with the fact that 'heavy end' and repressive community interventions (such as ISSPs in the present era) are justified largely on the grounds that they are not custody. Thus, at both ends of the spectrum, increased levels of control are imported into the community, while at the same time claiming to represent a more liberal (as well as a more effective) form of intervention. Cohen, again, is scathing:

Meanwhile, there is no problem in finding criminologists, psychologists, social workers and others who will justify all these community alternatives as humane, kindly and even 'therapeutic' … This is the particularly wondrous advantage … of those programmes which use the explicit rationale of behaviourism. (Cohen, 1985, p. 75)

Indeed, the rationale of humanitarian and beneficial behaviour change supports the principle of 'community corrections': 'Deviance … must be "brought back home". Parents, peers, schools, the neighbourhood, even the police should dedicate themselves to keeping the deviant out of the formal system.' (Cohen, 1985, p. 77). This requires 'the primary institutions of society', such as schools, family or neighbourhood to take responsibility for scrutinizing and controlling the behaviour of those young people at risk of offending. However, this kind of strategy is likely to have unintended consequences, as a result of the application of specific 'actuarial justice techniques':

Thus, if the youth is already under the surveillance of the system – even a preventive program serving a non-offending youth from a 'high risk' neighbourhood, but particularly an offender supervised intensively – he or she is far more likely to be caught offending and sanctioned sooner, and more often. (Kempf-Leonard and Peterson, 2002, p. 438)

Cohen's vision seems remarkably prescient, fitting well with the emergence of an explicit political strategy of 'inclusion' in the late 1990s. The language of being 'tough on crime, tough on the causes of crime', of linking 'rights' with 'responsibilities', of promoting 'parental responsibility', and of 'targeting' – in sum, the New Labour vision – fits well with his view of a correctional approach being exported from the justice system into the community.

Cohen further illustrates his argument by reference to the use of the family as a 'correctional resource', which has become a 'site for expert invasion and penetration' (Cohen, 1985, p. 79). Clearly, the Parenting Order introduced by the Crime and Disorder Act 1998 fits closely this kind of strategy. Schools and neighbourhoods are also identified as locations for the development of sophisticated methods of surveillance, supervision and correction – Cohen was perhaps anticipating the large-scale development of Pupil Referral Units, and the increasingly fashionable interest in mentoring schemes (Tarling et al., 2001). Youth Inclusion Programmes (Eccles, 2001) and Summer Splash Schemes (Loxley et al., 2002), both explicitly targeted at 'at risk' young people in areas known as crime 'hot spots', are also more recent examples of the increasingly sophisticated strategy of co-opting communities and neighbourhoods into the project of maintaining social order – even if their effectiveness in this respect remains open to question (Loxley *et al.*, 2002). As well as seeking to improve the efficacy of social control initiatives, these schemes also carry out an important ideological function, focusing concern on particular young people in particular areas, thereby shifting attention away from wider questions of disadvantage or racial inequality, or from structural explanations for crime. Indeed, as Cohen argues, with the move towards a greater emphasis on managerial and technical solutions to the problem of crime, causes become relatively less important – the logic being that 'if we can control crime, we don't really need to understand the causes', the epitome of the 'what works' philosophy of crime control (Cohen, 1985, p. 176). Hence, perhaps, New Labour's relative lack of concern about the 'causes of crime', which it has narrowed down to a range of targeted programmes aimed at specific 'at risk' groups, such as those excluded from school, the children of teenage parents, or drug users (Social Exclusion Unit, 2001), as well as those directly identified as potential young offenders.

In concluding this discussion, then, it may be helpful to reflect on the means by which this sleight of hand is carried out. A particular and 'situated' ideology of crime and disorder is reconstituted by a variety of mechanisms as representing the natural order of things, requiring a specific strategy based on isolating those responsible and dealing with their behaviour. Other (structural and causal) issues are relegated to the margins. However, in reality, the nature of offending behaviour is both socially constructed and, as a consequence, open to debate. This is perhaps a crucial observation for those who feel trapped in a routinized, irrational and vicious cycle of surveillance, processing and regulation of young people to no beneficial end. Having seen how legitimacy may be secured for a particular model of dealing with youth crime, we will now turn to consider the way in which this is realized in the mechanisms of delivery and the routines of everyday practice.

Foucault and the Techniques of Justice

As already noted (Chapter 3), the Crime and Disorder Act 1998 can be read as representing a Foucaultesque strategy for classifying and controlling the problematic behaviour of the young. At this point it may be helpful to consider how this political initiative might be linked to the machinery put in place to give it substance.

The starting point for this discussion will be Foucault's thesis that the modern era (late 18th century onwards) is characterized by a significant shift from forms of punishment based on spectacle and example to an approach based on measures designed to discipline criminals and redirect their behaviour towards compliance with acceptable norms and social conformity. Foucault, in his seminal book *Discipline and Punish,* argues that the last 200 years have witnessed a reduction in 'penal severity' and a 'displacement in the very object of the punitive operation'. Punishment is no longer to be characterized as a direct physical operation inflicting pain and suffering on the body, but as a more insidious activity, acting, in his words 'on the soul'. Notions of correction and treatment have come to be incorporated into penal discourse, with a focus on controlling the activities of those who offend and changing their behaviour.

Foucault associates these changes with a range of other social transformations, such as the development of the legal concept of contract and a 'new economy'. Generalized tactics of punishment were the characteristics of this new order, with '... new principles for regularizing, refocusing, universalizing the act of punishment. Humanize its application. Reduce its economic and political cost by increasing its effectiveness and by multiplying its circuits' (Foucault, 1979, p. 89). The criminal, by breaking her/his contract with the social body, becomes liable to punitive intervention and must accept the rational and measured consequences that this implies. Punishment is therefore seen to be appropriate, reasonable and proportional to the offence committed.

It follows that the machinery of the justice system and its coercive practices must be clearly and precisely specified and applied, rather in the manner of Weber's (1957) 'legal-rational' organization of administrative decisions. According to Foucault, 'the new arsenal of penalties ... must be as unarbitrary as possible' (Foucault, 1979, p. 104), and must be clearly calculable as the consequences of specific criminal acts. This emphasis on efficiency and the routinization of judicial mechanisms suggests certain similarities between the 'scientific' strategies suggested by Foucault and the kind of 'actuarial techniques' which are now held to be permeating the administration of youth justice: '... actuarial justice presents a theoretical model of criminal justice processing in which the pursuit of efficiency and techniques that streamline case processing and offender supervision replace traditional goals of rehabilitation, punishment, deterrence and incapacitation ...' (Kempf-Leonard and Peterson, 2002, p. 432).

Foucault elaborates two further aspects of the technologization of punishment which are of significance: the forms and conduct of disciplinary mechanisms themselves, and the development of professional specialisms for the assessment and management of individual offenders and the implementation of their personalized corrective programmes:

> ... ultimately, what one is trying to restore in this technique of correction is not so much the judicial subject ... but the obedient subject, the individual subjected to habits, rules, orders, an authority that is exercised continually around him and upon him ... (Foucault, 1979, p. 129)

Standardized procedures (such as the ASSET form) are applied to young people reported for offences in such a way as to discount many of the factors which are relevant or important to them. Christie (2000) comments that, in many criminal cases:

> ... the defendant might as well not have been in court ... When such attributes are eliminated, a seemingly 'objective' and impersonal system is created ... in full accord with normal bureaucratic standards, and at the same time extraordinarily well-suited for power-holders. (Christie, 2000, p. 163)

The kind of disciplinary techniques to be applied include specific regimes for ordering and controlling the individual's day-to-day experience, thereby ensuring that conformity can be demonstrably achieved. For example, perhaps mundanely, the 'timetable' is established in order to regulate and monitor compliance. The timetable itself provides a basis for exerting power over the individual, at the same time as specifying activities and sequences of behaviour. Every aspect of the offender's day is structured and planned according to the agenda of control. Christie (2000, p. 127) argues that such developments are predictable for other reasons, too, given wider trends towards the development and commercialization of forms of technological management and surveillance. He offers the contemporary examples of electronic bracelets and voice verification systems as means by which this level of coercive scrutiny can be achieved. The development of such methods of intervention has made possible 'the integration of a temporal, unitary, continuous, cumulative dimension in the exercise of controls and the practice of dominations' (Foucault, 1979, p. 160). This process is reflected in the emergence of 'disciplinary networks', which involve experts in the fields of 'medicine, psychology, education, public assistance (and) social work'. These agents will assume quasi-judicial powers of assessment and programme delivery, so that a wide range of professional interventions in the field of welfare will acquire the characteristics of penal and disciplinary power. As Lea (2002, p. 29) puts it, the development of a wide-ranging coalition of agencies with a crime control function (such as Youth Offending Teams) is part of a process of securing the widest possible 'collaboration in the task of regulating society'.

Donzelot (1979) takes this an important stage further, by associating the development of these techniques and systems of control with changes in the form of official interventions in the family. Donzelot's view is that similar mechanisms can be identified in the processes by which families and individual family members are pathologized and made subject to statutory interventions. This is of particular relevance when we come to consider new measures aimed at "improving" the way in which parents exercise their responsibilities and act to control their children's behaviour. Donzelot believes that this kind of measure represents a shift in the modes of social discipline, so that government *of* the family becomes government *through* the family:

> ... the modern family is not so much an institution as a *mechanism* [his emphasis] ... A wonderful mechanism since it enables the social body to deal with marginality through a near-total dispersion of private rights, and to encourage positive integration. (Donzelot, 1979, p. 94)

In other words, parents themselves are persuaded or coerced into accepting and then exercising the modes of discipline which ensure conformity in younger family members. Pitts argues that strategies of this kind, targeted at families and individuals, are clearly evident in the range of practices put in place by New Labour in its reform programme:

> The 'new' professional practices in the form of cognitive-behavioural treatment, reparation and mediation and mentoring all strive to make good those deficits in the behaviour, beliefs and attitudes of individual offenders and their parents, and to instil in them a new, disciplined, capacity for self-regulation. (Pitts, 2000, p. 10)

The Limits of Functionalism

Foucault's arguments have been subject to criticism on a number of grounds, not least the functionalism which appears to run through them, incorporating visions of monolithic structures and mechanisms of state power and control. Giddens (1991), for example, takes the view that his position is both too functionalist and too general to provide a proper explanation of the variety of social institutions and their inherent tensions and contradictions, as well as of their propensity to change over time. Similar views are also expressed by Ignatieff (1985): 'Foucault's conception of the disciplinary world view, the *savoir* as he calls it, effectively forecloses on the possibility that the *savoir* itself was a site of contradiction, argument and conflict' (Ignatieff, 1985, p. 95).

Garland (1990), however, takes criticism of Foucault rather further, arguing that his thesis is open to question both on historical and sociological grounds. He, too, takes issue with Foucault's 'functionalism', which, he believes, leads to a narrow argument that all aspects of the penal system are determined by the pursuit and exercise of power: 'In this sense, Foucault's conception of power is strangely apolitical. It appears as a kind of empty structure, stripped of any agents, interests or grounding, reduced to a bare technological scaffolding' (Garland, 1990, p. 170). Garland appears to be suggesting that the symbolic purposes and functions of custody and other penal mechanisms are confused with their real and lived impact, which is much more uneven and unpredictable. Conflicts of aims and outcomes are commonplace. The problem for Foucault is that the prison and other apparatuses of control do not always achieve the outcomes prescribed for them. They are actually quite inefficient, and their effectiveness as direct instruments of discipline is limited, as we are repeatedly reminded (see Lyon *et al.*, 2000; Goldson, 2002).

Foucault (1981) himself acknowledges that the relations of power themselves generate opposing currents, which modify and distort patterns of social order. These 'resistances' are found to be:

> ... distributed in irregular fashion: the points, knots, or focuses of resistance are spread over time and space at varying densities, at times mobilizing groups or individuals in a definitive way, inflaming certain points of the body, certain moments in life, certain types of behaviour. (Foucault, 1981, p. 96)

In the context of the judicial system, these counter-currents will manifest themselves in specific modifying effects on the administration of the law in its pure form:

> ... the orientation of the agents involved, their ideologies, their resources or lack of them, the legal limits placed on their powers, the rights of clients and the resistance that they offer, can all moderate the extent to which the sanction's power is actualised. (Garland, 1990, p. 168)

On the one hand, therefore, Foucault's analysis provides a thoroughgoing account of the means and mechanisms by which disciplinary power is exercised and legitimized in pursuit of the objective of controlling young people's behaviour. On the other hand, however, his critics, in common with Harris and Webb (1987), demonstrate that the realities of intervention are, in practice, rather more complex and contradictory than might at first appear to be the case. Christie (2000), too, argues that legal structures should not be seen simply as rational instruments of 'utility'. Rather, law has to elaborate and resolve competing aims, purposes and values. Courts, for example:

> ... cannot function as instrumental tools for management without sacrificing their greatest strengths in the protection of values: spelling them out, evaluating them against each other, and also seeing to it that single-minded goals in some institutional settings are not given undue weight in the totality. (Christie, 2000, p. 198)

Power is, and should be, mediated by practice. This leads to the relatively optimistic conclusion that at the level of practice it is possible to modify, resist, and even transform some of the repressive implications of the contemporary youth justice system, an issue to which we shall return in the final chapter.

Youth Justice: the Value of Theory

This brief excursion into the theoretical terrain surrounding youth, ideology and the machinery of justice has sought to open up some alternative perspectives to those offered by the rather narrow contemporary preoccupation with effective system management. In bringing together characterizations of 'youth' and 'crime', theories of power and legitimacy, and accounts of the mechanisms of control, I have attempted to show that our understandings of these phenomena are not fixed, and that their interactions are of considerable importance in developing an appreciation of what is both necessary and practical in developing a humane, yet still responsive, approach to dealing with the problems of youth offending.

As this chapter illustrates, adolescent transitions are a feature of most societies, but their specific nature and the way in which the behaviour of the young is defined are social constructs. These are typically characterized by contradictory expectations and demands, deriving from the conflicts between socially desirable attributes, on the one hand, and the means available for attaining these, on the other, as Merton (1957) shows. The rapid emergence of mobile-phone theft as a feature of the criminal statistics might be a good example of the actualization of this principle.

In order to manage the transitions of youth, however, dominant interests in society will seek to establish the kind of hegemonic control identified by Gramsci (1971), with the aim of constructing a pattern of beliefs which legitimates a specific form of intervention through the justice system. This is exemplified by the establishment of structures that are able to function repressively, but which still operate ideologically to secure popular consent (Althusser, 1977; Cohen, 1985). Foucault's (1979) analysis amplifies this proprosition by illustrating how the state's control strategy can be depoliticized and reduced to a managerial and technical question of efficient delivery (Clarke *et al.*, 2000). Relevant and significant research findings (Farrington, 1996; Rutter *et al.*, 1998) are decontextualised, and causal explanations are reduced to soundbites such as 'poor parenting' (Muncie, 2000). In this way, the highly problematic nature of youth justice and the injustices perpetrated in its name are subsumed by what appears to be a natural, logical and scientifically rational approach to dealing with the problem behaviour of the young.

However, this apparent uniformity of purposes and function does also contain the seeds of its own demise, not least because of the practical consequences of implementing an increasingly costly 'top heavy' regime for dealing with the infractions of the young, including those which are pre-criminal, and relatively minor offences. By the autumn of 2002, for example, the Treasury was expressing real concern about the spiralling costs of penal sanctions for young people (the *Guardian*, 9 October 2002).

Chapter 8

Expecting miracles?

The Pragmatic and the Practical

Having dallied briefly in the realm of theory and abstraction, it will also be worthwhile to consider the question of youth crime from a quite different perspective, rooted in everyday realities and popular aspirations. While theorizing helps us to understand the meaning and dynamics of the youth justice system, and, indeed, suggests some of the origins of widely held beliefs about young people and crime control, consideration of the way forward needs also to take into account the expectations and demands of those who are 'stakeholders' in the system. On the one hand, this will help us to gain a firm grasp of the range of perspectives that are, legitimately, brought to bear on the matter; on the other, it will provide an important link between our understanding of what is going on and what may be seen as practical, realistic and achievable solutions. In reality, we must recognize that key influences and interest groups will have a powerful constraining effect at all levels of decision-making in relation to youth justice. Indeed, the message of the previous chapter, in the context of hegemony and power, is that these are inevitable factors in determining what is thinkable and what is achievable. Nevertheless, a clearer understanding of the views and aspirations of some of the constituencies believed to have a legitimate interest in the delivery of youth justice will shed more light on these areas, as we move toward a consideration of 'what is to be done?'

The Victim's Perspective

The starting point for this review will be the viewpoint of victims of crime, particularly because victims' interests have steadily progressed up the political, and operational, agenda in recent years. Indeed, concern for victims has become somewhat totemic, albeit tokenistic. As we have already noted (Chapter 6), Williams (2000) observes that victims have become something of a 'political football' themselves, with the issuing of the *Victim's Charter* in 1996 and subsequent moves to strengthen and build on it, even following a change of government. As a result, the 'balance' between offenders and victims appears to have shifted (Williams, 2000, p. 176).

We have already seen evidence of the readiness of policy-makers to respond to these developments in the context of the reforms introduced by New Labour, typified by the introduction of the Referral Order, which effectively mandates youth justice services to involve victims in responding to offences. The expectation here, and elsewhere, is that victims' perspectives will be routinely incorporated into the decision-making process in youth justice: 'YOT managers must be able to demonstrate that ... the wishes of victims in relation to their involvement in restorative justice processes should be respected by YOT staff at all times ... youth offending teams must offer reparation services. This must include, where appropriate, apology, explanation, and direct work by young offenders for the benefit of victims' (Youth Justice Board, 2000, p. 10).

But what does our increasing awareness of victims' views about crime and punishment tell us about dealing with young people who offend? Of course it is important to avoid falling into the trap of stereotyping victims, just as we must not stereotype young people who commit crimes. As the British Crime Survey now regularly reminds us, the risk of becoming a victim of crime is not distributed evenly (Kershaw *et al.*, 2001). Indeed, it is young people themselves, and particularly young men, who are most at risk of violent offences (Kershaw *et al.*, 2001, p. 31). The picture is further complicated by evidence that the experiences of being a victim and a perpetrator of crime appear to overlap quite considerably. MORI's (2002) research into young people's perceptions and behaviour suggests that those who are more likely to offend ('children who are excluded from school') are also more likely to be victims of crime, and, indeed, they are more likely to be victims (82%) than offenders (64%). Interestingly, but worryingly, official statistics are reported not to take account specifically of young people under the age of 16 as victims (*Daily Mirror*, 16 September, 2002). A simplistic opposition of 'offenders' and 'victims' is clearly neither feasible nor helpful.

The tendency to reify the notion of 'victimhood' must, indeed, be avoided, although this is not to suggest that there are not real, damaging and distressing experiences lying behind the concept itself. As Lea and Young (1984) have clearly documented, the impact of crime on areas already disadvantaged for other reasons is likely to have a powerful and demoralizing effect. This, as Rock (2002) points out, represents a substantial shift in awareness compared to even the relatively recent past: 'until the late 1970s, victims were almost wholly neglected in criminology and criminal justice' (Rock, 2002, p. 1). While, as he observes, the growing awareness of the needs of those affected by crime became (and remains) associated with a crude sort of populism, there also emerged a much more thoughtful and reflective strand of analysis:

> We know that our earlier assumptions about the impact, quantity and spread of crime have had to be replaced not only by an appreciation of its deep, persistent, pervasive and often unexpected effects, but also by an awareness of its capacity to confound typifications of who the victim and offender might actually be. (Rock, 2002, p. 11)

He goes on to argue that this demands a more sensitive understanding of 'the victim', what it means to her/him to be the object of an offence, and what s/he then does to come to terms with the experience. It is not simply a matter of following a predetermined script, as is provided readily by some types of media: 'What else do crime series and shows such as *Kilroy* and *Oprah* achieve if not to offer public representations of wounded sentiment?' (Rock, 2002, p. 18).

One implication of these reflections must clearly be that victims' perceptions of the level and nature of offenders' responsibility, and their views about the appropriate means of dealing with offenders are likely to be variable and to be influenced by a wide range of factors not limited to the nature and seriousness of the crimes committed. In addition, the fact that 'corporate victims' are likely both to have their own distinctive perspective, and to be seen differently by those who offend against them, represents a further complicating factor (Young, R., 2002).

These considerations, added to the recognition that very few offenders are 'matched' with victims (see Chapter 6), must lead us to express a good deal of caution about taking strong messages from the experiences of those who become involved in restorative justice processes under the New Labour reforms. While it is helpful to consider how victims perceive their role and treatment in this context, we must always retain a sense of proportion here.

It will, nonetheless, be informative to consider some of the findings from recent initiatives to give victims a more central place in responding to the crimes of the young (Holdaway *et al.*, 2001; Hoyle, 2002; Newburn *et al.*, 2002; Young, 2002). The introduction of the Referral Order, for example, has provided a good opportunity to consider the participation and views of victims at close hand. While it has proved difficult to secure victim involvement (Holdaway *et al.*, 2001), it has been possible to evaluate their responses to participation in Youth Offender Panels in some cases. Victims' motives for attending panel meetings has been shown to be varied, with more emphasis on expression of feelings and having a say in how the offence was dealt with than on ensuring that they would be compensated or that the penalty for the offence is 'appropriate'.

Table 8.1 Victims' motivating factors for attending panel meetings

Motivating factor	Strength of factor			
	Not at All	Not Very	Somewhat	Very
Expression feelings	4%	9%	7%	78%
Offence resolution	22%	4%	28%	43%
Helping the offender	28%	13%	26%	28%
Seeking compensation	33%	13%	15%	35%
Ensuring appropriate penalty	52%	11%	20%	15%

Adapted from: *The Introduction of Referral Orders into the Youth Justice System: Final Report* (Newburn *et al.*, 2002, p. 45)

Thus, it seems, the aspirations of victims who take up the offer to attend panel meetings – a minority – are very much concerned with engaging with the offender, and solving the problems that the offence has caused for them. Hoyle's study of the Thames Valley Restorative Justice Project appears to support this observation: 'I just wanted to get the message across to him that if it happened to him how would he feel, basically, I mean, for him to put himself in my shoes' (crime victim, quoted in Hoyle, 2002, p. 120). Even 'helping the offender' appears to come higher up victims' list of priorities than seeking redress (Newburn *et al.*, 2002, p. 45).

Exploring victims' views in more detail, the researchers found that their generally positive views of the process were somewhat tempered by the limited nature of their involvement and the inability to secure the outcomes they wished, either in the form of compensation or apologies. Victims appeared to want a greater sense of involvement in the entire disposal process, rather than the panel meeting alone. In particular they wanted to know 'if the young person had managed to stay out of trouble. One of the most important factors for many of the victims was "has it worked?" ' (Newburn *et al.*, 2002, p. 47). The researchers conclude that, for those victims who were involved in Youth Offender Panels, the process was generally viewed in very positive terms, and as beneficial. These findings seem to indicate an aspiration on the part of victims towards an approach based on offence resolution, rather than on a straightforwardly punitive agenda. Of course, it must be acknowledged that this was a relatively small, self-selected sample, whose very involvement may have indicated a rather more positive orientation towards mediated solutions than may be shared more widely.

This result is borne out to some extent by other evaluations of the 'new youth justice', which seem to suggest relatively limited victim interest in getting involved in 'restorative justice' initiatives. Holdaway *et al.* (2001) report 'low consent rates' for victims in relation to involvement in Reparation Orders and Action Plan Orders, with only half agreeing to either direct or indirect forms of making amends by the offender. Victims were much more likely to get involved if they were not required to 'opt in' to the process, that is, where they were specifically encouraged to participate, rather than left to decide on their own. Nevertheless, the general conclusion would appear to be that there is limited enthusiasm among victims for more direct engagement with young offenders, and a feeling in some cases that victims' interests are being subsumed under those of the system, or those of young offenders themselves (Holdaway *et al.*, 2001, p. 81).

These observations appear to be supported by other findings, (Davis *et al.*, 1988; Hoyle, 2002). For Hoyle, this is unsurprising, given that crime victims will, inevitably, have their own priorities. She questions the 'often unquestioned assumption that victims want to assume a role in the state response to "their" offender ... most restorative justice schemes find that by no means all victims wish to be fully involved' (Hoyle, 2002, p. 104). This certainly coincides with the present author's experience based in a juvenile diversion project of the 1980s, where the pressure to involve victims did not feel as intense as it appears to have become more recently.

Victims' unwillingness to get involved has a number of sources, including the fear of retaliation and the belief that it is the job of the police and the justice system to deal with the offence – in the same way, perhaps, as a householder might ask a plumber to come round to mend a tap, rather than simply be shown how to do it. For some victims, though, their lack of enthusiasm needs to be set in the context of a more general sense of disenchantment with the justice system: 'I have to say if I was a victim of a similar crime again ... I've got a feeling I would administer my own justice and not involve the police ...' (crime victim, quoted in Hoyle, 2002, p. 125). This, again, acts as a reminder that we should not draw excessively optimistic conclusions from positive accounts of victims' involvement in restorative initiatives. Hoyle concludes that to focus solely on perfecting restorative mechanisms to ensure that victims' concerns are addressed risks overlooking the more important challenge of 'empowering victims generally' (Hoyle, 2002, p. 130). The interests of victims, indeed, can be seen to range much more widely beyond appropriate involvement in youth justice processes to incorporate a more general concern about feeling safe and secure – they, too, would prefer that youth crime was 'prevented' rather than simply dealt with in a more inclusive way after the event.

The Community Perspective: 'There's not enough to do 'round here'

This is perhaps an opportune point to move from the specific concerns of victims of youth crime, who are identifiable as such, to the broader concerns of communities and neighbourhoods who are affected by crime and disorder, much of which is attributed, rightly or wrongly, to young people.

There seems little doubt that concerns about the behaviour of young people are linked with wider fears about deteriorating standards of living, isolation and neighbourhood decay. For a fuller understanding of this apparently self-evident conjuncture, we might consider the previous chapter's discussion of hegemony and socialization. For the moment, however, the focus will be on community perceptions and the belief that 'something must be done' about the problems posed by the young. Hancock's (2001) evaluation of community safety initiatives in two 'disadvantaged' neighbourhoods captures a general sense of communities 'going downhill'. While this may be as much a matter of perception as of material change, it is, of course, perceptions that shape people's attitudes and aspirations:

> There are lots of young people hanging around at weekends ... There is a *lot* of litter. People throw their litter down as they walk past. We have also had problems with broken windows. Buildings have deteriorated ... pride in the area has gone down. (elderly resident of Edgebank, quoted in Hancock, 2001, p. 92)

Indeed, the association of young people with disorder and neighbourhood decline appears to be widespread. The British Crime Survey (Budd and

Sims, 2001) reveals a substantial degree of concern about antisocial behaviour, which appears to be linked in people's minds with 'teenagers hanging around on the streets'; we are reminded again of Corrigan's (1979) observations about young people 'doing nothing' on the streets of Sunderland in the mid-1970s. By 2000, over half of those surveyed thought that young people 'hanging around' was 'very or fairly common', and 32% identified this as a problem. Equally, 31% of respondents thought that this was having a 'negative impact' on the quality of life in their neighbour-hood (Budd and Sims, 2001, p. 2): the single biggest factor mentioned. A fifth of those questioned cited specific examples of 'young people being rude or abusive' to them over the preceding 12 months (Budd and Sims, 2001, p. 4), again the most common example of such behaviour cited. In addition, it should be noted, people in poorer areas, and those from Black and minority ethnic groups, were more likely to report being victimized in this way. Young people thus appear to be widely associated with disorder and a decline in the quality of life. As a consequence, we might expect this to be associated with a fairly punitive orientation towards their offending (and 'anti-social') behaviour.

Further work arising from the British Crime Survey (Mattinson and Mirrlees-Black, 2000) appears to bear this out. The public is reported as substantially overestimating 'juvenile involvement in crime', with 28% of respondents believing that young people were responsible for most crime, whereas, in fact, 89% of 'known offenders' are aged over 18. This may partly be accounted for by different understandings of the term 'young', and by perceptions about those 'crimes' that do not come to official notice. For example, this survey also reports that 40% of respondents thought that 'teenagers hanging around' and damage to property were a problem in their area:

> Respondents are likely to extrapolate from their own local experience when forming a view about the national crime picture. Certainly, those respondents who said teenagers hanging around was a very big problem in their area were significantly more likely to say crime was mainly committed by juvenile offenders. (Mattinson and Mirrlees-Black, 2000, p. 12)

Of course, it is not inevitable that these views will feed straightforwardly into attitudes and beliefs about how to deal with the crimes of the young. However, earlier studies from the British Crime Survey have found both an underestimate of the severity of punishment actually administered (Hough and Mayhew, 1985; Hough and Roberts, 1998), and a corre-sponding demand for greater use of more stringent penalties, particularly custody, for specified offences (Hough and Roberts, 1998). Those who are actually victimized are reported as being slightly more likely to demand harsher sentences (Hough and Roberts, 1998), although these results do not achieve statistical significance. As well as having a distorted perception of sentencing practice, those surveyed are repeatedly observed to hold erroneous views about the trends in juvenile crime (Hough and Roberts, 1998; Mattinson and Mirrlees-Black, 2000), which might also be associated with a belief in the need for more punitive sentences. Given that perceptions of the pattern of youth crime are distorted, 'media portrayals of persistent juvenile offenders and the continuing influence of the James Bulger murder on the public psyche ... are the most likely cause' (Mattinson and Mirrlees-Black, 2000, p. 14). Interestingly, the authors do not speculate on the role of politicians in 'bidding up' the menace represented by young people (see Chapter 3, for example) (which cannot in any way be attributed to the fact that the study is published by the Home Office!).

So, how are these widely held beliefs about the nature of youth crime and current sentencing practices linked with views about the appropriate means of dealing with young people who offend? It is of interest to note that most of those surveyed during the British Crime Survey did not think that the 'juvenile courts' were doing a good job (only 14% of respondents thought they were; Mattinson and Mirrlees-Black, 2000, p. 17), and recent victims held even more negative views in this respect. These judgements appear to be related, in turn, to a belief that the courts that deal with young offenders are 'too lenient' (76% of those surveyed were of this opinion; Mattinson and Mirrlees-Black, 2000, p. 18) – a much more common perception than that adult courts are insufficiently punitive. As the researchers observe, there appears to be a correlation between ignorance of the justice system and a belief that the courts perform poorly and are not harsh enough. There also appears to be a correlation between the perception of 'teenagers hanging around' as a problem and poor opinions of the courts:

> It may be that physical and social disorder is taken as evidence of a crime problem that is not being adequately contained. Or, perhaps, [this] reflects a belief that the police and courts remit does – or ought to – encompass dealing with such issues. (Mattinson and Mirrlees-Black, 2000, p. 23)

With the extension of the availability of Curfew Orders, and the introduction of Child Safety Orders and Anti-Social Behaviour Orders, it could perhaps be argued that their remit has indeed been extended to address this area of concern. Whether or not this will have any impact on public confidence remains to be seen. What is evident to the researchers, however, is that the link between poor knowledge and negative perceptions indicates the value of providing better public information about youth crime and sentencing practices.

The British Crime Survey further explored respondents' views about enhancing courts' powers to deal with the crimes of the young, and found that there was considerable support for making parents more responsible for their children's actions (15%) and greater use of custody (11%). There was support also for other options, such as corporal punishment, tagging or curfews, community work, and restitution. In this respect, it could be argued, the range of sentencing reforms introduced in 2000 did, indeed, reflect widely held public views, although the urge for more punitive sanctions did appear to be offset to some degree by a desire to see more use of restorative or welfare interventions (Mattinson and Mirrlees-Black, 2000, p. 24). As is noted, these findings reinforce earlier evidence, which suggested that 'increased discipline in the home' (36%) and 'tougher sentences' (20%) remain relatively, but not overwhelmingly, popular strategies for preventing as well as responding to delinquency (Hough and Roberts, 1998, p. 33). The fact that 'criminal justice' measures, as solutions to the problem of crime, are favoured by no more than a third of those questioned is used to support the argument for a wider preventive strategy, in the same way that it has been suggested that we need to distinguish between 'youth justice' measures and the issue of reducing 'youth crime':

> Thus although [it has been] established that lenient sentencing is a concern to the British public, four out of five people see the most effective solution to crime as lying outside the criminal justice system, namely in the home, the schools and the workplace. These trends are worth noting as they contradict the view of the public as being exclusively oriented towards punishment. (Hough and Roberts, 1998, p. 34)

This, in turn, suggests a degree of continuity over time, with respondents to the British Crime Survey repeatedly demonstrating a willingness to consider less harsh sentencing options for some offenders, in certain circumstances at least. A readiness to consider non-custodial options for non-violent offenders, for example, was demonstrated as early as 1984 (Hough and Mayhew, 1985, p. 45).

More detailed investigation of public sentencing preferences suggests that 'persistence' is believed to merit increasingly punitive disposals, with

36% of those questioned believing that imprisonment is the most appropriate sentence for a 3-time 15-year-old male shoplifter (Mattinson and Mirrlees-Black, 2000, p. 28). Burglary is seen, in turn, as more serious than shoplifting, and 59% of respondents are reported to believe that imprisonment is the best sentencing option for a 15-year-old male on his third such offence (Mattinson and Mirrlees-Black, 2000, p.29). Violence, in any form, is seen as yet more serious, although in all 3 scenarios, there remains some support for more lenient measures in response to first-time offences, including 'cautions' and 'community sentences'. Victims are reported as somewhat more punitively inclined than the public in general, in relation to the specific offence of burglary (Mattinson and Mirrlees-Black, 2000, p. 33). The researchers who conducted this survey go on to pose some questions for policy development based on their findings – in a sense, trying to represent the expressed concerns of the public at this level. They conclude, again, that better public understanding of youth offending and youth justice is important; that better awareness of the range of non-custodial sentencing options would be helpful; that 'persistence' is seen as a particularly 'aggravating factor'; that concerns about 'disorder' are important in their own right, as well as influencing perceptions of the youth justice system in general; and that moves towards a more restorative approach might, by engaging victims and the community more fully, improve public confidence (Mattinson and Mirrlees-Black, 2000, pp. 45–46). This argument is offered further support by the evidence of a MORI survey conducted for the *Rethinking Crime and Punishment* Initiative (MORI, 2001), which demonstrated substantial support for community-based crime prevention with young people, as well as recognition of the negative impact of custody and a desire to reduce the use of imprisonment.

There is also a notable shift of emphasis when questions about the problems of youth are reframed. Against the general message of concern about young people's behaviour and a preference for harsher sentencing should be set our knowledge of the rather less hostile characterizations of young people when they are considered collectively, as members of a community. In this context, the focus is much more likely to be on the lack of opportunities and facilities for the young, rather than on their offending. Crime prevention initiatives, for example, which focus on involving the community in the task of addressing crime, might well be found to develop positive proposals for improved facilities for young people as a product of this process. Indeed, young people themselves may even become contributors to the task of reducing crime (Crime Concern, 2001, p. 5, for example). Further evidence is available to support the suggestion that a switch of focus away from individual offenders to young people in general engenders a rather different response. The Audit Commission (2002), for example, argues that most people are concerned about crime, especially those who have recently been victimised. Nevertheless, a MORI survey conducted for the same Audit Commission report shows that there is very substantial support for action to improve facilities for young people, as a means to promote community safety and reduce youth crime. This observation seems to provide us with an interesting contrast, between the caricature of an offender who is 'not one of us', and deserves to be treated severely, and a more inclusive notion of a young person as part of the community with legitimate concerns and needs which should be addressed. Lea and Young (1984) provide some support for this dual perception of young people, referring to evidence of complex perceptions within neighbourhoods, which always seem to locate the locus of criminality 'elsewhere', even in areas with a reputation for offending. This apparent contradiction finds further support from Garland (2001), who portrays two 'criminologies', which can be related to these divergent understandings of youth and crime:

> There is a *criminology of the self* that characterizes offenders as normal, rational consumers, just like us; and there is a *criminology of the other*, of the threatening outcast, the fearsome stranger, the excluded and the embittered. One is invoked to routinise crime, to allay disproportionate fears, and to promote preventative action. The other functions to demonise the criminal, to act out popular fears and resentments, and to promote support for state punishment. (Garland, 2001, p. 137)

It is the *criminology of the other* that manifests itself in much public and political debate, in his view, with the result that there is a dominant public perception of offenders who reflect a particular stereotype: 'young minority males, caught up in the underclass world of crime, drugs, broken families and welfare dependency' (Garland, 2001, p. 136). This view, however, appears to mask more complex perceptions and experiences, not least among those who are the subjects of such stereotypes.

Youth Crime, and Black and Minority Ethnic Communities

It will be helpful to explore these concerns a little further by considering the position of those who are from Black and minority ethnic groups. These communities appear to have a particular interest in the issues of youth and crime, for two reasons. They are, on the one hand, more likely than normal to be the victims of crime; and, on the other hand, young Black men, in particular, are disproportionately likely to be processed as offenders by the youth justice system, as already observed (see Chapter 6).

In considering the issue of victimization, the British Crime Survey has repeatedly shown that certain groups are exposed to 'unequal risks' of experiencing crimes against them (for example, Mirrlees-Black et al., 1998; Kershaw et al., 2001). Certain types of crime, such as burglary, vehicle-related theft and violent offences, are found to occur to a greater extent in 'multi-ethnic areas' (Mirrlees-Black et al., 1998), and those people living in inner-city areas also appear to be at a greater risk of repeat victimization, which is likely to affect Black and minority ethnic communities in particular. However, it has been noted that not all minority groups are affected equally, with 'risks of almost all crimes' noted as being greater for people of Pakistani and Bangladeshi origins (Percy, 1998).

In a very specific sense, minority ethnic groups are likely to be dis-proportionately affected by racist crimes. As Bowling and Phillips (2002) demonstrate, such crimes, from harassment to murder, have been evident throughout the history of Black communities in Britain, but that recognition of this, from criminologists and official sources, was slow to follow. For example, records of 'racial incidents' have only been kept since the 1980s. They argue that it has only been since the 1990s that 'concern about racist violence' has been heightened (Bowling and Phillips, 2002, p. 109), particularly as a result of the murder of Stephen Lawrence. The report of the inquiry into his murder concluded that too little attention was paid by official agencies to 'racist incidents' (Macpherson, 1999). Accordingly, records of 'racial incidents' increased from 13,878 in the year ending March 1998 to 47,814 in the year ending March 2000.

Such statistics are, as already noted, at best imprecise indicators of what is actually happening. They may show one or more of at least 3 different processes taking place. They may reflect a greater willingness of police and other agents of the justice system to take such incidents seriously; they may show that the number of racist crimes is, indeed, increasing rapidly; or, they may show a greater degree of confidence in the justice system among people from ethnic minorities, and thus a greater willingness to report incidents. Whatever the reason, the figures suggest at least that there is a very substantial amount of racist crime taking place. In one survey undertaken by one of the authors, around 1 in 5 of all Black and Asian adults in Newham had experienced 'some form of racist victimisation' (Bowling and Phillips, 2002, p. 112). Perceptions about the perpetrators of these offences are similar to those reported earlier in relation to offending in general, with 'young, white males' being seen as primarily responsible (Percy, 1998, p. 1).

As Bowling and Phillips observe, this evidence helps to explain the extent to which minority ethnic communities are more fearful of crime than their white counterparts:

> Although the relationship between fear, crime and victimisation is a complex one, fear of 'ordinary crime' among people from ethnic minority communities is fundamentally shaped by their *fear of racist victimisation*. (Bowling and Phillips, 2002, p. 113)

It is, indeed, the case that people from ethnic minorities are more likely to be fearful of crime (Percy, 1998; Clancy *et al.*, 2001). Percy, for example, reports 40% of ethnic minorities being 'very worried' about burglary compared to 21% of white people (Percy, 1998, p. 29). He concludes:

> Ethnic minorities scored higher than white people on all BCS measures of fear of crime. They perceive themselves to be at greater risk of crime than whites, worry more about falling victim of a crime and feel less safe on the streets or within their own homes at night. To a large extent this is a reflection of their higher risks of victimisation and harassment. (Percy, 1998, p. 1)

Much of this, too, is attributed to young people, who are often identified as the perpetrators: 'Young boys shout out racist chants to me as I leave my house or walk in the street.' (Chinese woman, quoted in Saini, 1997). As the Stephen Lawrence inquiry most forcefully reminds us, Black and minority ethnic communities are often dissatisfied with the official responses to the crimes against them. The inquiry report commented on a pervasive sense of mistrust among ethnic minorities and the police, arguing that:

> ... the atmosphere in which racist incidents and crimes are investigated must be considered since that will condition the actions and responses which may follow. That atmosphere was strongly voiced in the attitude of those who came to our hearings. In the words of David Muir, representing senior Black Church leaders 'the experience of black people over the last 30 years has been that we have been over policed and to a large extent under protected.' (Macpherson, 1999, paragraph 45.7)

Similar feelings are expressed towards the police in local surveys (Saini, 1997), with a widespread view among victims that involving the police would have been pointless. These perceptions are echoed in the overall levels of satisfaction with the police, according to the 2000 British Crime Survey, with 70% of white respondents being 'very/fairly satisfied' as compared to 56% of Pakistani or Bangladeshi respondents. Among victims, similar disparities were also noted (Clancy *et al.*, 2001, p.3). These concerns, according to Bowling and Phillips (2002), are persistent, and can be related to dissatisfaction with the 'overall performance' of the police, based on a number of elements, such as 'showing enough interest' and being polite. Such concerns about the nature of the police response are further supported, it would seem, by more general concerns expressed in local studies about unfair treatment of certain groups. The belief in inconsistency, unfairness and lack of interest among the police seems to permeate minority communities fairly widely (Bowling and Phillips, 2002, p. 136).

However, there appears to be less concern among ethnic minorities about *other* aspects of the justice system. Indeed, they appear to be more confident than white respondents that the system is 'effective in bringing people who commit crimes to justice' and that it 'meets the needs of victims of crime' (Mirrlees-Black, 2001, p. 3). In other words, the concerns of Black and minority ethnic respondents to detailed questions about the justice system appear to be more discriminating than simply reflecting blanket disapproval. The police and prisons are more likely to be seen by these groups as doing a poor 'job' than by white people; however, courts, probation and prosecutors are more likely to be seen by them as doing a 'good' job (Mirrlees-Black, 2001, p. 4). The explanation for these disparities is not clear, but they do suggest that there is some pattern to the views held by ethnic minorities of the justice system, and of its discrete elements. It is likely that the police are particularly the focus of attention because they are the first point of contact between the public and the justice system, and there is no doubt that this contact has been experienced as both inadequate and discriminatory by ethnic minorities, as the report of the Stephen Lawrence inquiry makes clear (Macpherson, 1999, paragraph 45.10). The unfair treatment of young people in this context is at least as significant as the perceived failure to provide an efficient and respectful response to those who are victims of crime, and the solutions identified by minority communities seem to reflect these dual concerns. Unsurprisingly, perhaps, these solutions do not simply focus on technical enhancements to pro-cedures and structures for the delivery of youth justice, but they range much more widely. For Black and minority ethnic communities in particular, the strands of racist crime, victimization and fear, and the unfair treatment of those targeted as offenders, are intertwined, and lead to the conclusion that a broader strategy of (re)building trust and mutual respect is required. The Black Community Safety Project in Leicester has produced one such agenda for change, some elements of which clearly overlap with the aspirations of other stakeholders, including victims and young people (Saini, 1997). Those people surveyed for this project wanted 'more police patrolling the streets', but they also wanted the police to treat them with more respect, and desired that more police officers be recruited from ethnic minorities. They wanted the police to improve the service offered to those affected by crime, and also to work on building a better relationship with young people.

In addition to police-specific improvements, the survey identified a desire to see greater emphasis on community safety and crime prevention, including prevention of racial attacks. These aspirations extended to a desire to see greater attention given to the role of the education system in teaching respect for people and property, and promoting greater 'parental control'. The attention given to changes *within* the youth justice system itself was very limited, being restricted to a wish to see more support for Black people within the court setting (Saini, 1997, p. 40). Britton (2000), too, suggests that from the perspective of Black and minority ethnic communities a holistic approach to reform is needed: 'statutory organisations should place tackling institutionalised racism at the centre of their policy agendas ... statutory organisations should have their policies and daily practice rigorously monitored' (Britton, 2000, p. 108).

Bowling and Phillips (2002) argue that, to be fair, the justice system itself must take account of social variations and structural inequalities; for example, changes should be made in the way that family circumstances are used to determine bail/remand status. They conclude that it is unacceptable to allow the continuation of trends in criminal justice which 'marginalise, criminalise and socially exclude ethnic minority communities in England' (Bowling and Phillips, 2002, p. 260). This is not simply a matter of addressing discrimination in the treatment of offenders and alleged offenders, but also in providing a better and ethnically sensitive service to those communities affected by crime.

For Black and minority ethnic communities, then, simplistic calls for harsher treatment of young offenders are highly problematic, since the 'system' itself is a source of unfairness and discrimination. Solutions must be found not just in the context of processing those reported for offences, but in promoting inclusion and anti-discrimination in general, and in taking an approach which puts the challenging of injustice at its core. The technical and managerial preoccupations of New Labour reforms seem pretty limp by comparison (see, for example, Bowling and Phillips, 2002, p. 258).

'What about Us?' Young People's Views

Another group that is both 'over-policed' and 'under-protected' is that of young people themselves. It is pertinent here to consider how they feel about youth crime, punishment and the administration of youth justice. The perspectives of young people in general, and those who are identified as offenders are of interest, not least because their opinions appear to be more similar to those of the general population than might be expected.

The context in which young people form their views about crime and punishment is one in which they are disproportionately likely to become victims of crime or experience 'anti-social behaviour' (Haines and Drakeford, 1998; Budd and Sims, 2001; Kershaw *et al.*, 2001; MORI, 2002). Like adults, many children report feeling unsafe; for example, as many (42%) feel unsafe 'walking around their local area alone in the dark' as feel safe (MORI, 2002), although those identified as at risk of offending appear somewhat more confident. Levels of concern about the possibility of becoming a victim of crime are high, with 48% reported as fearing theft, 51% worrying about being physically assaulted, and 54% of non-white young people being concerned about the possibility of racism. These fears are not baseless, in that over half of those school children surveyed reported being the victim of crime in the previous 12 months, pre-dominantly of theft (24%), or of threats (27%) or bullying (17%). Of these offences, more than half were attributed to another young person. More of these offences are reported to parents (51%) or friends (41%) than to police (15%) or other authority figures such as teachers (26%) (MORI, 2002). The picture here appears to be one of routine victimization of young people, but at the same time of little reliance on the formal machinery of the justice system to resolve offences – according to MORI (2002, p. 41), 26% of victims 'say they sorted it out themselves' (see also Haines and Drakeford, 1998, p. 22).

Although young people are at least as likely as adults to experience crime, their views on the justice system do differ to some extent. In comparing the views of adult respondents with those of 'juveniles', researchers suggest that the important determining factor for differences of opinion is that of age, rather than being involved in committing offences (Mattinson and Mirrlees-Black, 2000, p. 20). Those aged 12–17 appear considerably less likely to think that the courts are too lenient (29%) than either 18–30 year olds (67%) or adults in general (76%). However, even young people are reported as believing that the youth justice system is too lenient overall. Young offenders (12–17 year olds) appear somewhat more likely than non-offenders to state that the police and courts are 'too tough' (15% as compared to 7%), but even for offenders, at least twice as many believe that the justice system is too soft on those who commit crimes. Young people are thus more likely to hold the perception of the justice system as too punitive than older people, while at the same time, all age categories are weighted towards a belief that the treatment of offenders is too lenient.

Consultations with young people have provided some support for the view that young people do believe in tough punishment: 'if somebody is caught they should be punished severely' (12-year-old boy, quoted in Children and Young Persons Unit, 2001), and 'tougher penalties for young offenders' were also called for by young people surveyed in Greater Manchester when asked their views on 'policing matters' (Greater Manchester Police Authority, 2002). On the other hand, it remains the case that young people are more likely than the adult population in general to believe that the police and courts' treatment of young offenders is 'about right'. The reasons for this are not entirely clear, although it could be that they are more familiar with the actual workings of the system, and do not share the unrealistic beliefs of the adult population. Young people might also be less in favour of punitive measures. In some surveys, young people are reported as being more 'understanding' of those who commit crime: 'Some people in gangs get involved because they could have a bad life at home, and … [they're] pressured into it. That's how people join gangs, they're pressured into it. Having a lot of trouble at home and that' (Quoted in Willow, 1999, p. 52).

There is no evidence that young people take a less serious view of 'delinquent acts' than the population in general (Smith *et al.*, 2001). They are reported as sharing a view of a continuum of criminal behaviours, from minor infringements, such as fare dodging, through 'quite serious' behaviours such as shoplifting and graffiti, to 'very serious' acts such as housebreaking, joy-riding and fire-setting (see also, MORI, 2002). However, those who have engaged in 'less serious' criminal behaviour are less likely than their law-abiding peers to see these as significant transgressions – a sign perhaps of the 'neutralization' process identified by sociologists such as Matza (1964).

A picture seems to be emerging that portrays young people as generally sharing many of the moral judgements of the community in general, expressing similar concerns about personal safety and the fear of crime (see, for example, Greater Manchester Police Authority, 2002), and holding similar views about the need for tighter control and tough punishment. This assessment finds support from wider investigations into the values and beliefs of young people, which have found, for example, that 'young people's values did not differ significantly to those documented for adults' (Thomson *et al.*, 1999, p. 5). Nevertheless, there is evidence that young people feel that their interests are not always represented effectively by the formal justice system, with many offences not reported, as we have seen, and a general sense of 'not being listened to'. Young people in Greater Manchester, for example, are reported as identifying a need for 'more interaction by the police with young people; serious treatment of young people when reporting a crime; treating young people with respect; not being judgemental' (Greater Manchester Police Authority, 2002, p. 1). These apparent conflicts between young people's beliefs and their experiences may account for their rather ambiguous views about authority and the legitimacy of various sources of power (Thomson *et al.*, 1999). As active participants in the social world (Smith, R., 2002c), young people do not simply take existing structures and systems of authority as given; indeed, respect and recognition must be earned:

> Traditional authority figures such as the police, religious leaders and the royal family received very little automatic respect from young people. They explained that respect must be earned, authority won and merit proven ... While young people did not always invest teachers with moral authority, they watched them closely to see if they were worthy of it. (Thomson *et al.*, 1999, p. 6)

Young people are observed to be looking for certain characteristics in those who claim authority, in order to assess the legitimacy of these claims – characteristics such as 'consistency, care, the ability to listen and practical skills' (Thomson *et al.*, 1999, p. 6).

It is perhaps important, here, to distinguish between a considerable degree of consensus about what is seen as appropriate behaviour and the rules by which this is enforced, on the one hand, and the application of these rules in practice, on the other. The evidence of a disparity in this respect is fairly clear. Young people do not feel that their concerns are taken seriously, or that they are treated fairly or consistently: 'Police ... don't make us feel safe and take their time getting to the crime scene' (14-year-old girl), and 'I have had police harassment on the streets for no reason other than being young' (16-year-old male) (quoted by Children and Young People's Unit, 2001). That these concerns are not new is powerfully conveyed to us by Parker: 'I fuckin' hate coppers. They've just tried to do us for robbing some fuckin' sword or something. Murky and me were walking up the hill. Up they screeched, pulls us into the back of the car and start acting hard' (young man, quoted in Parker, 1974, p. 162).

This kind of perception creates some difficulty for the youth justice system in laying claim to legitimacy and the authority to impose interventions. Feelings that the system is unjust, and does not serve them well are intensified for young people who are identified and processed as offenders. While Parker's study identifies the police as the initial source of confrontation and distrust, this resentment of unfairly imposed power is extended to other elements of the justice system, including probation officers and social workers: 'Tank was extremely disillusioned to find that the social worker who had always helped out with his rather chaotic family circumstances had finally recommended him for a period of detention' (Parker, 1974, p. 173).

Moving forward in time, it seems that legitimacy and fair treatment remain significant areas of concern for those processed as young offenders. In terms of system effectiveness alone, it is likely that rates of non-compliance, and even re-offending, might be influenced by their perceptions; but these issues also raise more fundamental questions about what sort of youth justice system we want. An important study carried out with young people (15–21 year olds) in custody sheds some light in these areas (Lyon et al., 2000). These young people talked first about the contextual factors they felt were associated with their involvement in crime:

> They talked about growing up in bad areas, with high levels of crime and drug use; being labelled by education as a 'problem' and subsequently being excluded; they gave explanations for beginning offending; and they were critical of the way they had been treated by the criminal justice system. (Lyon et al., 2000, p. 7)

Their criticisms focused on the police, the courts and other participants in the justice system. Police, for example, were seen as 'taking advantage of their power': '... the majority of young people did not have respect for the police. Nor did they see them as any deterrent against becoming involved in crime' (Lyon et al., 2000, p. 23). These views extended also to courts, where judges were seen as both racist and biased against young women, and sentencers were identified as 'not caring'. Youth justice professionals were seen as indifferent and lazy: 'The probation officer doesn't know what's going on. They should know you – they're your probation officer. They should know that you're going down again – they should know what's happening in your life shouldn't they?' (young man, quoted in Lyon et al., 2000, p. 27). The experience of custody itself was felt to be a poor preparation for a law-abiding life outside. For most, 'prison was a dislocating experience ... It was a "whole other life", not connected to their everyday lives before entering custody, and often not preparing them at all well for release back into the community' (Lyon et al., 2000, p. 29).

Despite their overwhelmingly negative experiences, the young people studied appeared to have a real commitment to avoid offending in the future; and they did have a range of suggestions for improving the justice system, which could address the issues both of effectiveness, and more importantly, legitimacy. They supported ideas for preventing crime by targeting the young and ending social exclusion; they argued for improved peer support programmes, an emphasis on continued access to education, and improved stability and continuity in local authority care.

Within the justice system, the young people questioned argued for tougher treatment of drug dealers, improved relations between the police and young people, and fairer, anti-racist practice at all stages of the judicial process. They were also supportive of ideas such as mentoring, reparation and citizenship education (see, for example, Children's Society, 1992), which they felt might reduce re-offending. In addition, they argued for better and more consistent forms of support to allow them to be reintegrated into the community. Above all, it is reported, young people processed by the justice system wanted to be treated with respect, and it is clear that this is not the case in many areas of practice.

The authors conclude on an upbeat note that:

> Many of the young people's concerns about lack of professionalism are being tackled by the Government's agenda for reform of the youth justice system and the work of the Youth Justice Board ... The young people highlighted the need for complex solutions to complex problems. Their views support the Government's joined-up approach to tackling social inequalities as a way to reduce crime. (Lyon *et al.*, 2000, pp. 80–81)

While the present author is by no means as optimistic about the New Labour reform programme, it remains the case that young people (offenders and non-offenders) appear to share the view that simplistic and one-sided responses to the problems of youth offending are not the answer. Reforms need to be holistic, and to concentrate on the social setting of crime ('the causes') as well as – arguably more than – its specific manifestations. To concentrate on dealing with their behaviour alone, and out of context, is seen by young people as partial, unfair and often simply irrelevant. Despite these concerns, however, there may be some grounds for optimism in the holistic analysis and intervention strategy developed by the Social Exclusion Unit, with its aim of preventing re-offending (Social Exclusion Unit, 2002).

The Answers are Complex

The perceptions and attitudes of those with an interest in the youth justice system, far from throwing up simplistic judgements and simple solutions, present ample evidence that the issue is multifaceted and that it demands careful analysis and sensitive treatment. For example, attitudes appear, at least partly, to be shaped by the fact that the public is not well informed (Mirrlees-Black and Allen, 1998). On the other hand, popular opinion is not uncompromisingly punitive (MORI, 2001). Even among victims, there is some support for alternative approaches, including reparation (Mattinson and Mirrlees-Black, 2000). Young people, including those who offend, appear to share widely held views about 'right' and 'wrong' (MORI, 2002), but they are concerned about the inadequacies and unfairnesses of the justice system itself, feeling that it does not take them seriously, and that it is a source of racism and oppressive practice (Lyon *et al.*, 2000; Bowling and Phillips, 2002; Children and Young Persons Unit, 2002).

Notwithstanding the diversity of perspectives considered, there is a clear consensus that the system as presently constituted 'doesn't work' (Mattinson and Mirrlees-Black, 2000). This perception may account for the evidence of emerging support for alternative approaches, including those encompassed by the notion of 'restorative justice' (Hough and Mayhew, 1985; Mattinson and Mirrlees-Black, 2000), however imprecisely that term might be understood.

Chapter 9

Where do we go from here?

Restating the Problem

The previous chapters have documented and attempted to explain the manifest inadequacies of the youth justice system at the beginning of the 2000s. The task of this concluding chapter will be to offer some suggestions as to how to move on from an unsustainable and fundamentally flawed position. First, though, it will be helpful to summarize the extent and nature of the problem.

Youth justice is located at a particularly uncomfortable conjuncture, where the seemingly perennial question of how to socialize and control our young people is addressed by the machinery of the state and other social institutions, such as faith groups and the media. Ultimately, the failings of the youth justice system can be traced back to the complex dynamics arising from this challenge. Contradictory and counter-productive outcomes arise from a profoundly unstable and conflict-ridden context. As observed previously, the development of the youth justice system can be seen to be rooted in the state's objectives of achieving effective means of control, in support of the broader goal of reproducing the prevailing structure of social relations (Althusser, 1977). The construction of 'youth' as the source of the crime problem contributes to this by achieving some important hegemonic tasks (Gramsci, 1971), by individualizing profoundly social dynamics, and by moving the focus away from those underlying structural factors associated with deviant behaviour. It would be unwise to go so far as to deny that the behaviour of the young is problematic; but the criminalization of this behaviour ensures that its causes and, indeed, its objectives, recede into the background. An effective separation is achieved, between the crime itself and 'the causes of crime'.

It is this false separation that lies at the heart of most of our problems in arriving at a legitimate understanding of youth offending, and consequently the failure to devise and implement appropriate responses. Whether the conceptual separation of the behaviour of the young from its social and structural origins is deliberate, accidental or simply a misjudgement is relatively unimportant. In any case, we are likely to find a complex cocktail of perceptions and beliefs underpinning the judgements and decisions of those involved in the justice system. Althusser's (1977) view that the judicial apparatus is simply a vehicle by which the powerful legitimize and impose their will is over-simplistic, while Foucault's (1979) characterization of the machinery of justice attributes a greater degree of logic and consistency to the system than would be evident to those who work within it. The extent to which Foucault conveys a picture of runaway carriages and headless horsemen, that is, a judicial complex that hurtles forward with no-one in control, might be rather more credible, in the light of the inexorable rise in custody characterizing the late 1990s and early 2000s.

Cohen's (1985) analysis is yet more helpful, in that he manages to capture the sense of criminal justice as contested territory, where participants hold competing views and motives, which, in turn, are played out in the construction and delivery of youth justice itself. He identifies 3 positions which can, to some extent, be identified with different interests in youth justice.

First, there are those who believe that its history can be represented as a form of steady, if uneven, progress. This perspective might be associated with those who believe that the justice system can be improved by the application of increasingly 'scientific' methods of management and practice, which will inevitably ensure that interventions can be appropriately targeted, and that it will be progressively easier to ensure that 'what works' is delivered. Thus, the development of National Standards, the implementation of performance targets, and the adoption of specific tools such as the ASSET form are all part of a process of refinement and advancement of good practice. The use of more intrusive and sophisticated means of control, such as surveillance, tagging and secure containment is not an issue from this perspective, if it leads to a greater ability to contain criminal behaviour. Political transitions, such as the change of government in 1997, are largely irrelevant, since the continuing task for the experts is to improve the machinery for prediction, monitoring and control of those young people who are at risk of offending (or re-offending).

Cohen's second group of opinions, characterized by the phrase 'we blew it', sees change in youth justice as very much a process of action and reaction, whereby each successive era witnesses frantic attempts to put right the mistakes of preceding periods. This perspective fits well with the impression sometimes created of the history of youth justice as a catalogue of continuing debates, with initiatives and counter-initiatives deriving from the relative ascendancy of competing positions. Thus, the 'welfare'-led reforms of the Labour government of the 1960s could be seen as a reaction to the oppressive, class-based regimes that preceded them (represented by Approved Schools and Borstals). These reforms, in themselves, appear to have generated a backlash, represented by an emergent coalition of sentencers and practitioners, leading to the 'back to justice' movement of the late 1970s (Morris et al., 1980; Thorpe et al., 1980). The 'justice model' became the dominant paradigm of the 1980s, but, as we have seen, the reduction in the use of custody that resulted could not be sustained in the light of a further 'backlash', this time prioritizing punishment and control over rights and offence resolution. This radical shift of perspective, and the emergence of a new coalition concerned with 'protecting the community', helped to legitimize the reforms of the late 1990s. This ostensible pattern of radical shifts in policy and practice also, it should be noted, fits nicely with a political context dominated by two political parties. Much of the Labour rhetoric of the late 1990s emphasized the alleged failures of the Conservative governments before 1997. From a rather different perspective, Pitts (2002) also argues that the recent history of juvenile/youth justice can be characterized in the form of paradigm shifts (Kuhn, 1970), with four distinct 'eras' in evidence: welfare, justice, systems management, and correctionalism.

The third position identified by Cohen – 'it's all a con' – is more often associated with those on the Left (practitioners and academic interests) who take the view that developments within the justice system merely reflect attempts to legitimize the exercise of social control by dominant interests, at the expense of minority groups and the socially excluded. Thus, even favourable developments are treated with suspicion. For example, Pratt's (1989) dismissal of juvenile diversion as an exercise of corporatist control represents a wholly cynical view of what might have been seen as a progressive form of practice. Goldson (2000), more recently, has similarly advanced criticisms of the Referral Order on the grounds that it creates an illusory form of 'contract' which is merely a cipher for the denial of children's rights. For those working within youth justice who take this view, the challenge becomes one of developing forms of progressive practice that 'prefigure' a radically different form of intervention (Smith, R., 1989). There are two strands of thought associated with this position – 'radical pessimism' and 'radical optimism' – which have led to a range of practice innovations, including 'radical non-intervention' (Schur, 1973; Rutherford, 1992), as well as more active strategies such as diversion, remand rescue and anti-racist practice initiatives (such as Right Track in Bristol). The weakness of this position lies in the challenge of working within, and according to the rules of, a structure which is seen as fundamentally flawed (Corrigan and Leonard, 1978).

Each of the three perspectives identified by Cohen can be found to influence the management and practice of youth justice, suggesting, in turn, that the composite picture that emerges is likely to constitute a confused and sometimes contradictory pattern. It is the interplay of different interests, and their relative strengths and weaknesses, that result in the particular form of the youth justice system at any one time.

The balance, by the early 2000s, seems to be in favour of those seeking to impose a routinized model of surveillance and control, based on arguments for the superiority of technical and managerial solutions to the problem of youth offending. This appears to have coincided with a broader mood of 'managerialisation' (Clarke *et al.* (eds), 2000), in the context of a belief in the 'infallibility of science' (Beck, 1992). This trend also fits in well with the political objective of delivering, quickly and with certainty, an agenda of radical change to meet popular expectations. Thus, the pressure to produce instant results and guaranteed outcomes coincides with the emerging strands of practice, which emphasize the possibility of 'perfecting' methods of prediction, surveillance, risk management and control – thereby generating the specific characteristics of the youth justice system under the New Labour reform programme. It has been concluded, for example, that 'what is noticeable in this gamut of management restructuring and evaluation is that all aspects of young people's lives are now potentially open to official monitoring and scrutiny' (McLaughlin and Muncie, 2000, p. 180). The fact that these interventions manage to combine the features of oppressiveness and inefficiency is simply a consequence of the fallacious assumptions on which they are based.

The extent to which radical alternatives, in theory and in practice, have failed to provide an effective bulwark against this tide of technocratic solutions is also worthy of note. Complacency, arising from the successes of the 1980s, and co-option by a 'friendly' government after 1997 (McLaughlin and Muncie, 2000) might be two causes; but Pitts (2001b) also argues that the weaknesses of the radical position can be related to its unwillingness to be explicit about the structural factors underlying youth crime – it made more sense, tactically, to collude with government thinking when it was convenient to do so. Thus, for example, court reports were not constructed in a way that addressed the contextual issues that could be related to specific offences, such as poverty and discrimination; arguments against punitive sentences were more likely to be based on individual characteristics and 'mitigating factors'. The underlying rationale of punishment and due process has gone unchallenged in this context. Such a pragmatic approach, in turn, provides a relatively weak base from which to develop principled arguments against populist calls for harsher sentences and tighter control in the interests of protecting communities and promoting the interests of crime victims.

The disastrous consequences of this convergence of populist ideologies, political opportunism and technocratic management styles is evident in the specific outputs of the youth justice system itself. In many ways, the outcomes were predictable. The move towards 'wider, stronger and different nets' (Austin and Krisberg, 2002) was complemented by ensuring that they were also deeper, and more finely meshed. The system became increasingly efficient at processing and punishing young people, developing a fearsome logic of its own (Pratt, 2000). The demonstrable evidence of this is clearest at the apex of the structure, with a dramatic rise in the use of custody becoming firmly entrenched (Simes and Chads, 2002). The government's view that the actions of the courts in creating increased demand for custodial places should be endorsed, and even encouraged, by the building of more secure establishments (Home Office Press Release, 1 May 2002), can be contrasted with the Netherlands and Ireland, for example, where the use of imprisonment for young people is subject to a fixed ceiling (Irish Examiner, 21 August 2002).

This outcome is not just the result of populist measures to increase the availability of custody as a sentencing option (it is worth noting that the abolition of custody for children and young people seemed a realistic possibility as recently as 1990). It is also the case that the machinery of justice has contributed in a number of ways to these trends. Despite a static or falling crime rate (again, contrary to populist mythology fanned by government rhetoric; see, for example, Blunkett, Home Office Press Release, 20 March 2002), the greater resources and a more sophisticated machinery of control have produced increasingly oppressive outcomes. Even before they commit offences, young people are increasingly scrutinized and targeted for interventions – first, through preventive programmes such as Youth Intervention Projects and Summer Splash Schemes, born out of 'fear not need' according to one commentator, and subsequently through the use of Anti-Social Behaviour Orders, Curfew Orders and Child Safety Orders.

As they progress to the commission of offences, more young people are being formally processed; they are being drawn into the justice system younger, for relatively more minor offences; they are experiencing formal and recordable sanctions earlier in their offending careers. The loss of the option of repeat cautions almost certainly guarantees a quicker progression to the court setting, where more demanding and intrusive intervention programmes are imposed at an earlier stage, especially with the loss of discharges as a disposal option. As a result, the opportunities for non-compliance, failure and breach are also increased.

Principles of voluntarism are squeezed out at all points in the process, with the contractual nature of the Referral Order, for example, contrasting dramatically with the negotiated and informal diversionary mechanisms of the 1980s. Failure to comply, or further offences, will speed young people towards the classification of 'persistent young offender', which qualifies them for yet more intrusive forms of surveillance and constraint (regardless of the gravity of their actions). These are supplemented by the imposition of an increasing array of conditions for the granting of bail which, combined with the intensity of the scrutiny to which young people are subject, will almost certainly increase the level of breaches and custodial remands.

The ASSET form represents the ideal mechanism for systematizing an approach based on 'actuarial' principles of risk management (see, for example, Lea, 2002, p. 123). Despite the rather overblown claims for its predictive accuracy (Youth Justice Board, 2002) the form is of little value in identifying needs (Roberts *et al.*, 2001) or assisting in the construction of supportive intervention strategies – welfare is written out of its remit. As youth justice practitioners themselves have repeatedly observed, the ASSET form is highly unbalanced and selective. Indeed, the preoccupation with risk is likely to generate a predisposition to 'seeing the worst in people' and focusing unduly on the possibility of failure. Is it entirely a coincidence that its adoption as a key assessment tool has accompanied a surge in custodial sentencing? Such developments, while observed as a national phenomenon, are not uniform. There are indications of wide variations in the use of custody (Youth Justice Board Press Release, 22 August 2001). This, perhaps, offers a glimmer of hope, suggesting that in some areas there are still 'radical' youth justice practitioners and managers at work, exploiting the opportunities available for minimizing punitive interventions, and perhaps even promoting genuinely inclusive forms of youth justice. That these 'resisters' do not always meet the expectations of policy-makers seems clear, with hints of veiled threats, accompanied by a celebration of the fact that more young people are being 'dealt with' by the justice system (Youth Justice Board Press Release, 19 May 2002).

In the midst of all this, of course, a number of important issues arise. Perhaps most importantly, the increased use of custody runs counter to the core aim espoused for the youth justice system, of preventing youth crime, since custody itself is known to be among the most effective mechanisms for promoting further offending by young people (Goldson and Peters, 2000). In addition, as already noted, a concentration on 'risk of failure' is likely to have a sensitizing effect, creating both a greater predisposition to find evidence of non-compliance, a greater likelihood that it will be recorded officially, and thus a correspondingly greater propensity to respond punitively in the light of such evidence. The lessons of 'labelling theory' (Becker, 1963) have clearly not been learnt. Furthermore, the increased investment in the machinery of youth justice, including expensive secure establishments and cost-intensive community surveillance, will also contribute to a growing obsession with the wrongdoings of the young – creating a further spiral of increased fear and renewed demands for 'quick-fix' solutions. In Autumn 2002 the Youth Justice Board announced the establishment of 'pre-crime panels' for children as young as 8 years old, to be marked out as potential offenders, and thereby to qualify for correctional interventions. Beck's (1992) analysis of the consequences of a preoccupation with the possibility of things going wrong in a 'risk society' appears to be borne out by this kind of development. As he observes, a greater emphasis on the potential for failure will be associated with an 'actuarial' response, based on managing the assessed likelihood of damaging outcomes. This, however, is likely to heighten fears and create a sense of loss of control, as it becomes apparent that there is no way of providing guarantees of security and personal safety. The 'sensitizing' impact of high profile, populist and politicized initiatives to pursue an illusory objective of certainty in crime control contrasts strongly with the low-key, pragmatic and problem-solving strategies adopted in earlier times, such as the 1980s.

The final irony to note here is the contrast between the emphasis, at one level, on policies to promote social inclusion and a sense of belonging and the continual pressure emerging from youth justice initiatives to mark offenders (and even pre-offenders) apart, to exclude them from main-stream activities and to isolate them in specific programmes or regimes. The inclusive nature of programmes such as New Deal and Connexions, which focus on creating a spirit of opportunity and community for groups, including marginalized young people, would appear to be substantially undermined by the impact of parallel programmes that depend for their rationale and very existence on creating a sense of 'the other' (Garland,

2001). The use of techniques that classify young people according to their criminality, and then subject them to specialized forms of treatment, can only intensify the sense of separateness and exclusion they feel, as well as determining the way they are seen by the 'community' in general. This official strategy has even been extended to ostensibly preventive programmes, such as Youth Inclusion Projects and Summer Splash schemes, which are being judged, partly, on the basis of how many 'at risk' young people they actually reach. When, we might ask, do inclusive policies, of themselves, become exclusive?

Looking Forward: an Agenda for Change

In restating some of the manifest problems associated with a populist/managerialist youth justice strategy, it has not been my intention to create the impression that there is nothing that can be done. Rather, it is important to be clear about the size and nature of the task. In many ways the options for change are not new, because the key principles of a liberal and just system have been elaborated often enough (for example, Smith, R., 1989; Scraton and Haydon, 2002). However, with each new era, the task of moving from 'where we are' to 'where we want to be' does change, and the practical questions of implementing a progressive agenda must be addressed rather differently.

First, however, it will be important to set out some of the principles that ought to underpin the delivery of a fair and inclusive youth justice system.

Rights – not justice

At first this might seem a slightly odd distinction to make, but the argument has been developed recently that substantive rights can be contrasted with formal justice in the sense that formal notions of equal treatment can mask a variety of inequalities. Williams (1999), for example, argues that simply setting the 'rights' of victims against those of young offenders creates a false opposition, which is not necessarily a straightforward representation of broader relationships between the offender and her/his community. MORI (2002) reports that young offenders themselves have a demonstrably greater chance of being victimized, and there is clearly a possibility that this in itself may impact on their attitudes and levels of commitment to social norms (Smith, D. et al., 2001). In addition to this blurring of the status of offender and victim, the rights of the idealized victim are also made problematic, in the sense that the young person may not accept unqualified responsibility for an offence, even when the facts of the matter appear relatively clear cut. This, again, is an inevitable consequence of the complex nature of social and personal relationships. For example, young people may well be unwilling to accept the blame for assaults that arise from long-standing local disputes, when these are taken out of context.

Rights, then, are not pure. However, the concept of rights itself clearly has meaning, and the issue becomes one of applying abstract principles in concrete circumstances:

> In established, 'mature' democracies, the conceptualisation, definition and formulation of commonly held and institutionally applied rights would seem straightforward ... Yet rights discourses are complex – reflecting a long history of contestation. Rights can be defensive in nature proclaiming the "right" not to be on the receiving end of the actions of others ... Also, they can be proactive or positive ... providing the right to something ... (Scraton and Haydon, 2002, p. 312)

According to this view, rights are negotiable, and should be related to the specific context and the network of social relations relevant to the matter at hand. It is thus inappropriate to think in terms of a 'justice' system that invokes standardized procedures and fixed penalties to deal with all forms of problematic behaviour, which originate in unique and variable circumstances. Thus, apparently rational and logical sentencing frameworks must be called into question, to the extent that they fail to take account of contextual issues. The advantages offered by a routinized and seemingly even-handed approaches to the identification, processing and punishment of offenders must be set against '... the "loss" to the offender of relevant mitigating circumstances. It is a significant loss, given the consequences inherent in the determining contexts of class, "race", gender, sexuality and age inequalities' (Scraton and Haydon, 2002, p. 315).

Others agree with this argument. Bowling and Phillips (2002), for example, discuss the potential value of building into the decision-making process of the justice system an 'equalizing' function, which adjusts outcomes to take account of factors that impact on specific groups, such as ethnic minorities, disproportionately. Thus, as already noted, the uneven impact of differing family circumstances on bail/remand decisions (and the consequential impact on the likelihood of custodial sentences) should be allowed for in order to avoid 'building in' discriminatory factors into the judicial process (Bowling and Phillips, 2002, p. 260).

It is clear that a sophisticated and sensitive conception of rights is required, which takes account of pre-existing experiences, inequalities and power imbalances. What is needed here is 'substantive' rather than 'formal' justice. The starting point for the incorporation of this principle into the youth justice system is offered by international frameworks such as the UN Convention on the Rights of the Child (Scraton and Haydon, 2002), the Beijing Rules on the Administration of Juvenile Justice (Goldson, 2000), and the European Convention on Human Rights (Walsh, 2002). These should ensure that the administration of justice incorporates an understanding and a recognition of the distinctive position of children, especially those who experience disadvantage or discrimination. It should not be the role of the justice system to compound or intensify the negative and damaging experiences which some children endure, and which may well be associated with their offending behaviour. Substantive justice must ensure that procedures and decisions made are able to take account of these factors.

Problem-solving

While encompassing some of the ideas associated with 'restorative justice' (Strang and Braithwaite (eds), 2001), the principle of problem-solving is drawn somewhat more widely, to include the expectation that any problem potentially associated with an offence should be addressed. Whereas the starting point should be 'putting right the wrong to the extent that it is possible for *both* victim and offender' (Gelsthorpe and Morris, 2002, p. 242), this aim should be incorporated into a wider framework, encapsulated in the phrase 'responsibility, restoration and reintegration'. These objectives point towards a pragmatic and situational approach, based on ideas of social learning, and they call into question punitive modes of intervention. For example, to the extent that problem-solving approaches such as family group conferences (Jackson, 1999) or res-torative panels (Haines, 2000) are subsumed by the formalities of the justice system, then their meaning and impact is likely to be distorted: 'there have been questions about whether restorative justice principles can work when reparation orders are *imposed* on offenders without their consent' (Gelsthorpe and Morris, 2002, p. 247). Rather, to be genuinely constructive, solutions to the problems caused by the offences of young people need to ensure, as far as possible, that 'the key participants in all of this – offenders, victims and their families – actually ... take charge' (Gelsthorpe and Morris, 2002, p. 249). These authors conclude that the contradictory measures and conflicting signals given out by the Crime and Disorder Act 1998 are likely to ensure that restorative principles will be fundamentally compromised without further reform to promote mutually determined arrangements for addressing the offence and putting things right.

A problem-solving approach will also need to take a wider view than just focusing on 'making amends'. As already indicated, the commission of an offence does not simply represent an interaction between free-standing individuals. It is rather, the culmination of a complex series of dynamics, within which are implicated more traditional preoccupations of the youth justice system, such as family background, peer group influences, personal experience, educational needs, and mental health, not to mention situational factors such as racism and poverty. Whether we think in broad structural terms such as this, or in terms of the factors that contextualize the offence, these issues must be seen as relevant, and therefore worthy of attention. The preoccupation with the offender *as an offender* and nothing else, reflected by the use of instruments such as the ASSET form, creates an arbitrary and ultimately unsustainable separation between the young person concerned and his/her social characteristics and needs.

Voluntarism

As the youth justice system has moved progressively towards tightly prescribed and mandatory interventions, characterized by increasingly detailed correctional programmes, so we are losing sight of an important principle at the heart of progressive and inclusive practice, that of engaging the explicit and active commitment of young people in resolving the offences for which they are responsible. It is not, for example, simply a case of whether or not restorative measures can 'work' when they are imposed rather than negotiated; it is also an important defining feature of the character of the youth justice system as a whole. The attraction of imposing immediate and certain solutions cuts across the opportunities available for achieving a sense of reconciliation, whereby the offender genuinely accepts responsibility. As already noted, serious doubts have been raised about the meaning and value of measures that might claim to be restorative in this sense, but which rely on coercing the involvement of the young person. For instance, where 'the courts ... *direct* personal apologies. This may lead to grudging or insolent attitudes being displayed when young offenders meet their victims.' (Gelsthorpe and Morris, 2002, p. 247). The impression gained, and to some extent supported by early research (Holdaway *et al.*, 2001), is one of routinized and demeaning tasks being required of young offenders in the name of making amends, with 'letters of apology being rehearsed by hard-pressed YOT workers anxious to get young people through' (Gelsthorpe and Morris, 2002, p. 248).

Not only is young people's commitment important in relation to making amends, but their consent to the interventions of the justice system more generally is important. It should perhaps be recalled, from the previous chapter, that while most young offenders do not dispute the need for rules and sanctions they are often antagonistic to the manner in which these are applied (Lyon *et al.*, 2000). It may seem, on the face of things, that the consent of young offenders is irrelevant in the context of criminal behaviour that implicitly forfeits the right to be consulted. But then securing compliance without commitment seems of limited value in terms of securing consent or long-term change. It is also important to consider the question of legitimacy, and the extent to which young people might or might not accord this to the justice process. As the previous chapter shows, there is a substantial degree of mistrust shown towards the various agencies responsible for delivering youth justice, not just among those young people who commit crimes, but among the general population of young people – and even more acutely among specific subgroups, including young Black people. The problem here is that the loss of trust, in general, is likely to be exacerbated by a sense that the priority in justice administration is simply coercion. In this respect, to dispense with consent is merely to compound a sense of injustice.

It should perhaps also be borne in mind that some community sentences (Probation Orders, Community Service Orders and Supervision Orders) actually required the consent of the offender before their use until relatively recently. Clearly, consent in these circumstances would appear to be very heavily circumscribed, but it does indicate the readiness of the justice system, to a certain extent, to recognize the need to engage with those responsible for offences, and to seek a form of negotiated justice, that promotes a sense of both personal responsibility and social solidarity. This aspiration remains valid within the context of youth justice. Indeed, these modest achievements of the past could be taken to prefigure a much more ambitious refocusing of the fundamental principles of criminal justice. As Lea points out, given the right social conditions we could expect that:

> … communities could take the law into their own hands again … Relations of trust and solidarity will be enabled to replace those of risk and unpredictability. Social inclusion will enable robust communities to sort out a large proportion of their own disputes. (Lea, 2002, p. 189)

The bottom line is that the proper role for the state, through its stewardship of the youth justice system, is to promote, rather than circumscribe, the achievement of this kind of voluntaristic outcome.

Minimum intervention

There are a considerable number of reasons for adopting the principle of using the least coercive means of intervention possible, not least that it fits the agenda of rights, problem-solving and voluntarism already set out. The UK government, indeed, has signed up to this principle through its adoption of the UN Convention on the Rights of the Child, but it has repeatedly been taken to task for failing to deliver on it (UN Committee on the Rights of the Child, 2002).

On purely pragmatic grounds, alone, it is extraordinarily wasteful to rely on expensive, intensive and ultimately excessive mechanisms of control, in the manner suggested by Foucault (1979), and as I have commented previously (Smith, R., 2001). The relatively high cost of custody as compared to community sentences, for example, is well recognized. As community sentences themselves are progressively 'toughened up', these, too, will become more expensive to maintain, and it would seem to make good economic sense not to use them unless stringent criteria are met. Regrettably, the expansion of available routes into custody, and the dilution of safeguards against its use, resulting from successive legislative changes under both Conservative and Labour governments, have ensured that the thresholds for the use of imprisonment have clearly been lowered, as the statistical evidence demonstrates (Simes and Chads, 2002). Dramatic increases in the use of custody for young people (15–17 year olds) suggest a system out of control, rather than one that is rigorous in setting limits to the use of extreme measures such as the deprivation of liberty.

Not only is the excessive use of measures of containment inefficient, in economic terms, it is also ineffective, even in the limited sense specified by policy-makers, of 'reducing youth crime'. The cumulative nature of the evidence that demonstrates the failure of custody to discourage future offending would appear to be compelling (Muncie, 1999). This is perhaps unsurprising, given that custody represents a severe rupture in the lives of those who are locked up, and that the experience itself is often oppressive and demoralizing (Goldson and Peters, 2000).

Of course, a rather more important consideration than the inefficiency and ineffectiveness of repressive measures such as imprisonment of the young is the damage it causes to them, for which again there is copious evidence (see, for example, Lyon *et al.*, 2000; Goldson, 2002; Howard League, 2002). The most acute injustices of the youth justice system, and its divisive and discriminatory impact, are most comprehensively experienced through the needless and excessive use of custody. There is no excuse for this, and the failure to address it must beg significant questions about the intentions of government and the role of the Youth Justice Board. In fact, rather than learn the lesson that custody does not work, the drive of policymakers has been towards exporting custodial techniques (surveillance, monitoring, behavioural controls) into the community.

Inclusion

The principle that should lie at the core of youth justice practice is one which has been widely promulgated by government in recent times, so in that sense a considerable degree of contiguity might be expected. The notion of inclusion is attractive in itself, as a means towards an increased spirit of social solidarity and mutuality. In this sense, the government's aspirations should be applauded. Garland (2001) provides theoretical support for this as a principle that should underpin justice processes by contrasting it with the kind of 'exclusionary' criminology frequently espoused. As he puts it, those policies that set offenders apart, representing them as 'the other', are likely to have dramatically divisive consequences. They will effectively institutionalize oppressive and discriminatory practices in societies that are unequal. Alternatively, it is suggested, an inclusive strategy seeks to reintegrate young people into their communities, to promote their acceptance, and to ensure that their crimes are dealt with constructively. The emphasis is on looking forward and promoting positive personal and social development.

This distinction leads us to the central contradiction of the New Labour project, which has attempted to have it both ways, adopting a rhetorical position geared towards social inclusion – which is indeed mirrored in some policy areas (Sure Start, for example) – while in other respects adopting policies and practices that mark out and exclude those who represent an apparent threat, or who do not comply with normative expectations. Even within the field of criminal justice, contrasts are evident, with youth crime-prevention measures such as Youth Inclusion Projects operating on (modified) inclusive principles, while at the same time, and possibly with the same young people, Intensive Supervision and Surveillance Programmes and 'tagging' are piloted and then 'rolled out'. In international terms, the 'inclusive' strategy borrowed from France (étés jeunes; Pitts, 2001b) can be contrasted with the 'exclusive' model operating in the United States (electronic monitoring and surveillance). Ultimately, these two positions are incompatible, and the policy conflicts they give rise to must be resolved in favour of a more comprehensively inclusive strategy.

The Way Ahead: the 'Macro' Level

Beyond merely setting out a series of principles which could, and should, inform future developments in youth justice, it will also be important to set out some concrete ways in which these aspirations could be realized, or at least, to suggest some initial steps. In order to do so, I will follow the structure utilized previously, and consider the 'macro', 'mezzo', and 'micro' levels in turn.

The initial focus will be on the political and public level, partly because this is the site of the most powerful 'levers' of change, and partly because without change here, other progressive initiatives, in management and practice, will remain provisional and vulnerable, as we learned in the course of the 1990s backlash.

New coalitions?

In some senses, of course, proposals for global political change are the easiest to make, and the most difficult to achieve. The kind of 'far-fetched' suggestions set out in Chapter 7, such as the decriminalization of the actions of children and young people, run the risk of simply being dismissed as idealism, with no practical relevance. In the same vein, the kind of global transformation advocated by Lea (2002) might also appear to some as purely utopian. He locates the prospects for change in the administration of justice within a more fundamental transformation, arguing that a major restructuring of social relations and a reordering of community life are the necessary prerequisites for the development of a more humanitarian form of judicial intervention, one which will work in the interests of victims and offenders alike:

> There must be a fundamental redistribution of economic and welfare resources to poor communities, both within advanced capitalist countries and on a global scale. This will enable the disconnection from dependence on criminality, violence and the violation of the rights of others like oneself as a survival necessity ... But [despite this] there will be a need for criminal justice agencies to facilitate dispute resolution by providing legal resources, to track people down and bring disputants together and to furnish legal frameworks for handling disputes ...' (Lea, 2002, p. 189)

According to one scenario advanced by Lea, this outcome may be achieved in political terms by the emergence of a broad global coalition of 'social groups, political and voluntary organisations [and] non-

201

governmental organisations' (Lea, 2002, p. 191), which could well include those currently engaged in the delivery of youth justice, with the skills and experience to develop the problem-solving legal framework he envisages. So, in his view, broad transformations at the level of the state must be supported by practical developments at the level of communities and individuals. This is an important linkage to make, although it still begs the question of how does one achieve intermediate reforms that may address more pressing problems within youth justice.

Youth justice and social inclusion

There is, for example, an immediate challenge for policy-makers at the level of government and other statutory bodies, which is to ensure that the conditions for the delivery of youth justice interventions are consistent with the broader aim of ending social exclusion and promoting a more cohesive society. It is clearly important that the specific policies and structures that shape the criminal process do not contradict or undermine these aspirations. To the extent, for example, that 'targeting' potential criminals from the age of 8 sets them apart, and potentially recruits them into a differentiated pathway of specialist interventions, we should be concerned about the contradiction of such a policy with the aim of promoting a spirit of social inclusion. Nor would we expect youth justice policy to sanction or encourage the needless use of custody, on the same grounds.

Capping the use of custody

In terms of a specific policy agenda, there are a number of clear and relatively straightforward measures available to government, which could help to achieve such aims. For example, an unambiguous and absolute limit could be set to the number of secure places available to young people (Children's Society (1988; 1993) has calculated that the total number of places needed for those under the age of 17 throughout England and Wales is no more than 500, for example). To accompany this, there could be explicit stipulations about the minimum age for the acceptable use of custody, in accordance with the recommendations of the UN Committee on the Rights of the Child (2002) – perhaps the age of 16 would be an appropriate minimum.

Minimum intervention and children's rights

Following the logic of minimum intervention, which is strongly endorsed by the UN Committee, as well as the principle of inclusion, we could expect the use of informal means of dealing with offences to be prioritized, and for the minimum age of criminal responsibility to be brought in line with international norms, perhaps to be set at 14. The criticisms offered by the UN Committee are stringent, and would appear to require some form of positive response in this respect: 'the Committee notes with serious concern that the situation of children in conflict with the law has worsened' (United Nations Committee on the Rights of the Child, 2002, p. 15). Pursuing the argument that the UK government should, at the very least, honour its international obligations in this context, it can be argued that proper implementation of the Beijing Rules for the Administration of Juvenile Justice (United Nations, 1995) and the Human Rights Act 1998 would also have important consequences for the delivery of youth justice. These instruments, if incorporated into the decision-making process, would ensure that family life is not disrupted by the imposition of intrusive and punitive orders, for example, by the use of custody where it is not a 'last resort' (UN Committee on the Rights of the Child, 2002). It would also be the case that restrictive and pre-emptive bail conditions, or surveillance practices, would no longer be acceptable to the extent that they impose stringent sanctions on young people in advance of any finding of guilt.

Problem-solving and policy

Apart from ensuring compliance with its international obligations, government could also take legislative action to promote a voluntaristic and problem-solving approach to youth crime. For example, removal of the arbitrary ceilings placed on the use of Reprimands and 'Final' Warnings should enable a more flexible use of pre-court disposals; while, a similar extension of the availability of the Referral Order would assist by modifying the highly restrictive sentencing tariff. By creating greater space for the development of negotiated, more informal, and genuinely 'restorative' outcomes, such relatively small-scale revisions to the legal framework could represent a significant advance. While this kind of development would clearly cut across the micro-managed, individualized, and finely graded approach to youth justice disposals, which has characterized the New Labour reforms, it should not be seen as completely unrealistic. It is worth recalling that a Labour government in 1969 legislated for the removal of most young offenders from the justice system entirely, and the decriminalization of all those under the age of 14. Equally, as already observed, in the 1980s a government-sanctioned (if not initiated) strategy of diversion (Home Office, 1985) and punishment as a 'last resort' (Home Office, 1988) led to very dramatic reductions in the numbers of young people formally processed and subsequently locked up (see Chapter 1). These initiatives were also associated with the emergence of new forms of intervention, which concentrated on resolving the concerns arising from a particular offence, whether these were those of the victim or related to the offender's needs (Smith, R., 1989; Rutherford, 1992). Government is, therefore, in a position to pull some very powerful levers, which could initiate moves towards a youth justice system that is inclusive – thereby bringing it into line with other aspects of national policy, and at the same time allowing for the development of approaches that create a greater sense of order and cohesion within communities.

Of course, such moves depend on finding the political will to move away from the attractions of inflammatory and misleading populist rhetoric, and on recognizing the need for 'joined up' policies for tackling the problems of crime and social order:

> No More Excuses promised that the Crime and Disorder Bill would establish prevention as a statutory aim of the youth justice system ... That is radical and encouraging – as long as preventive policies are not seen as solely the responsibility of the youth justice system and as long as its strategies are genuinely proactive, preventive and not simply reactive in the face of emergent problems of delinquency. Crime prevention has to be a concern of all public policies. (George and Wilding, 1999, p. 194)

Of course, all the available evidence suggests that the youth justice system itself is particularly poorly placed to do much about preventing or reducing crime. Socially inclusive crime prevention policies could, indeed, be much better resourced if the policy decision was taken to shift resources into communities and away from the expensive and ineffective technology for processing young offenders. Reducing the throughput of the system by way of the policy shifts outlined above would, of course, enable this constructive resource shift to take place, in order to promote the kind of developmental and integrative programmes which have been shown to achieve positive outcomes (George and Wilding, 1999, p. 194).

Oiling the Wheels: the 'Mezzo' Level

Naturally, it is not simply a matter of putting the 'right' policies in place, and then rolling them out to achieve the desired outcomes as a matter of course, despite the claims sometimes made by policymakers themselves:

> The Government's reforms of the youth court in England and Wales will help to shape a more effective youth justice system for the next century. The approach combines the principles of restorative justice

with more traditional punitive measures, which must be available to the courts to protect the public. The overall result should be a more streamlined and effective system, with a clearer focus on preventing offending. (Home Office, 1997, p. 34)

The history of youth justice is, in fact, littered with misguided policies, unrealistic expectations, unimplemented aspirations, unintended consequences, and unresolved contradictions, all of which can be traced back, at least partly, to the limitations of the original formulation of policy itself. There is, therefore, a substantial task facing those whose responsibility it is to organize and shape the delivery of effective interventions – those at the 'mezzo' level responsible for systems and strategies, including the Youth Justice Board, local youth crime partnerships, responsible agencies, and the courts and penal institutions. At this level rests the responsibility for interpreting national policy and translating it into operational expectations and guidance. At the same time, an important responsibility for those at the intermediate level is sometimes overlooked, and that is to pass messages in the other direction as well, as Pitts (2002) has reminded us. It is important that those in the middle tier also accept the responsibility of representing the concerns of providers and recipients of interventions, that is, those who offend and those who are affected by youth crime. This role, as a conduit for ideas, evidence, opinions and critical feedback, appears to be underplayed, except perhaps where the message can be taken as affirmative (see Youth Justice Board News as a prime example of such 'selective listening').

The New Youth Justice Board – a change of direction?

Indeed, the requirement for open and constructive dialogue could be taken as a starting point for recasting the role and functions of the Youth Justice Board. The board's role should not be one of 'franchizing and MacDonaldizing' service delivery; it needs to take on more diverse and representative functions (see also Chapter 4), as:

- a 'buffer' between government and the field, which irons out inconsistencies in government policy;
- an 'informed advisor' to government and other policy-makers on best practice, rather than a purveyor of simplistic and untested assumptions;
- a 'champion of rights' of young people and their families as well as victims of crime;

- a consistent 'purveyor of advice' to practitioners, the judiciary and other interests; and

- a 'developer and supporter' of professionalised youth justice practice, rather than simply promoting a 'homogeneous, offence-oriented culture.

(Pitts, 2002)

All this suggests a shift from a managerial perspective, based on securing routine compliance with standardized performance measures, concerned with the appearance of 'success', towards a more developmental role, which endorses and builds on professional innovation, encourages debate and risk-taking, funds critical and constructive research, and acts as a 'knowledgeable friend' to those in the field. Signs of a more independent role for the board may be detected in its tentative expressions of concern about sentencing variations and the over-use of custody (for example, Youth Justice Board Press Release, 22 August 2001). By the latter part of 2002, the Board was expressing concern that short custodial sentences were being used 'too often' (Youth Justice Board Press Release, 5 September 2002), and suggesting that community alternatives should be used wherever possible. By early 2003, the contradictory nature of government policies on social exclusion were also coming within the Board's sights (Community Care, 6–12 February, p. 12).

The courts as opinion formers

Of course, the Youth Justice Board is not the only 'middle range' body with considerable power and influence over practices within youth justice and the treatment of young people who offend. For instance, the impact of judicial decisions was once again demonstrated with the imposition of an 'exemplary' custodial sentence by the Lord Chief Justice, for the theft of a mobile phone in January 2002. The consequence was a rapid sequence of copy-cat sentences imposed by courts around the country (for example, a 16-year old received a 3½ year sentence for mobile-phone robbery, on 8 February 2002 at Sheffield Crown Court). One of the consequences, clearly, is that the specific circumstances of the offenders concerned became subsumed within the wider movement to stamp out a certain form of criminal behaviour. Such sentencing trends are not new, as Hall and his colleagues (1978) have shown.

However, the courts need not simply be a source of pressure for more severe sentencing, and their direct contribution to the more lenient ethos within which 'alternatives to custody' thrived is sometimes overlooked. Rutherford (1992), for example, has documented the role of the local magistracy in promoting, and then supporting, the development of one such initiative in Basingstoke: the Woodlands Centre. This, indeed, is a good example of the ability of local networks of agencies, sentencers and officials to achieve change, even in the face of a prevailing punitive ethos:

> There was growing despair that the juvenile court did not have local alternatives to incarcerative institutions, and a powerful determination to do something about it. The main initiative was taken by Margaret Baring, chairperson of the juvenile court. She and other magistrates, the clerk to the court and other local people wanted a programme which did more than pack young people and canoes into a mini-bus. (Rutherford, 1992, p. 136)

It is perhaps no coincidence that Hampshire became one of the pioneers of the 'custody-free zones', which became a feature of local youth justice systems throughout England and Wales in the 1980s.

A more contemporary example of the progressive use of judicial authority can be found in the Lord Chief Justice's attempt to encourage his sentencing colleagues to consider non-custodial options for first- or second-time domestic burglars (Woolf, 2002) – somewhat ironic in light of the impact of his earlier pronouncement on mobile-phone theft.

Effective coalitions

Progressive developments have also been well-documented in areas such as Northamptonshire, where the achievement of extremely high diversion rates also arose out of a close and committed inter-agency collaboration, incorporating the principles outlined earlier in this chapter (Smith, R., 1989). Interestingly, in this context, the police were one of the prime movers for the initiative. It is almost inevitable that the emphasis on partnership and inter-agency working that permeates (saturates?) the 1998 reforms will give rise to opportunities for similar developments. However, this will also depend on the ability to establish a degree of independence, and meet the core requirements of a shared vision and collective commitment. Poulantzas's (1978) notion of 'relative autonomy' is a helpful theoretical concept here, in that it demonstrates that even within a highly centralized and bureaucratized framework there remains the probability that specific coalitions of interests will arise, with the power to act independently, and set their own terms of reference. The disparity in behaviour demonstrated by diverse sentencing outcomes (Youth Justice Board Press Release, 5 September 2002) might, in part, reflect this tendency.

The power of the inspectors

Other significant actors at the 'mezzo' level are regulatory bodies, including the various inspectorates and performance auditing bodies, whose impact on practice can be significant (for example, Audit Commission, 1996). The work of the Prison Inspectorate has been of particular interest in this respect, with a series of strongly critical reports on the treatment of young people in custody, and a clear underlying desire to see practice changes. The extent to which these criticisms will have a cumulative effect on policy and practice remains to be seen, but they have had some influence in changing behaviour in individual regimes (Travis, 2002).

Further evidence of the potentially valuable role of inspectors was provided by the Joint Chief Inspectors' report, *Safeguarding Children* (2002). This found, for example that:

> ... the welfare needs of young people who commit offences were not being adequately addressed by those services responsible for their welfare. There were no national minimum standards for the work of YOTs, and there was no regular inspection of their work. They were operating largely in isolation from other services in most areas. (Joint Chief Inspectors, 2002, p. 69)

The report concluded that young people in custody were still seriously at risk, and that youth justice services generally were paying insufficient attention to the protection and safeguarding of children's welfare. A more proactive role for Area Child Protection Committees was recommended (see also, Smith, R., 2002d).

Campaigning organizations

It is also important to acknowledge the role of another kind of 'mezzo' organization, that is, the various trades unions, professional bodies and lobby groups who perform an important function in highlighting areas where change may be needed. 'Good practice' can be developed through these networks, as can an awareness of concerns or matters to be addressed. Risk-taking also becomes easier when support systems can be put in place. The role of bodies such as the National Association for Youth Justice might prove to be significant here, for example through formulating and sustaining a clear philosophical base and manifesto for action (National Association for Youth Justice, 2002a; 2002b).

The extent to which these alternative sources of resistance, power and influence might lead to change over time is always unpredictable, but they do provide a focal point for critical thinking and practical opposition to prevailing norms and practices. We need not, perhaps, be so gloomy in our prognosis as left-wing 'functionalists' such as Althusser (1977), who tend to see power only flowing in one direction. George and Wilding (1999), by contrast, argue that 'institution-building' at the local and community level is a central part of any strategy to contribute to the establishment of an inclusive society. Youth justice agencies should see this task as their starting point, restructuring their thinking as well as their practice. Their role is not simply to impose an 'alien' and inconsistent form of control, which does not 'chime' with the beliefs and experiences of those to whom it is applied (see Chapter 8); they should also develop approaches that build on perceptions such as the parallel beliefs that 'young people are a problem' *and* that 'there's nothing for young people to do 'round here', and incorporate them into their intervention strategies:

> The thesis is that the key force in maintaining people in law-abiding ways is bonding with groups or institutions that disapprove of law-disregarding behaviour. It is fear of 'community' disapproval and the potential and actual impact of family and community disapproval that are the key elements in low crime rates. Society, therefore, has to work to re-establish the essential characteristics of such communities. (George and Wilding, 1999, p. 191)

Local agencies and professional interests, therefore, have a key role in generating approaches to dealing with the problem of offending by the young in ways that engage communities (including young people) and attract their commitment and consent. As was proposed in the context of urban disorder and policing in a previous era, the prime requirement is to work to ensure the delivery of 'youth justice by consent' (see Scarman, 1982 cf. 'policing by consent').

The Search for Progressive Practice: the 'Micro' Level

It will be appropriate to conclude with some observations about the possibilities for working to deliver progressive practice within the youth justice system, in accordance with the principles outlined previously. Obviously, it would be possible to expand on these ideas, with the emergence of 'promising' developments such as mentoring, conferencing, and restorative practices, and the apparent re-emergence of interventions focusing on developmental and welfare needs. However, I shall concentrate here on a few areas of significant potential.

209

Informal justice

While it may seem that the opportunities for diversionary measures have been drastically reduced by the Crime and Disorder Act 1998, the value of informal interventions remains unquestionable – given that they represent a non-criminalizing, quick and cheap way of resolving minor infractions. In some areas of the country it appears that informal action remains an acceptable option, and this probably represents another example of the phenomenon of 'justice by geography'. Not only does this strategy ensure that young people's misdemeanours are dealt with outside the statutory framework, but it also creates space for a more genuine engagement with young people, their families and their victims, to reach mutually agreed solutions, without the pressure to contrive a 'happy ending'. In terms of system efficiency, this form of minimum intervention removes a substantial and unnecessary bureaucratic burden from the youth justice agencies, notably the police. This, in turn, it should be noted, would contribute significantly to the aim of reducing delays, purely by removing large numbers of cases from the system – allowing more time to be devoted to other areas of public concern (such as low clear-up rates). The challenge, here, is to overturn the relentless logic (see Chapter 7) which requires that all infractions are recorded, accounted for and processed in order to achieve the aims of routinized discipline and control.

Meaningful restorative practice

Moving on to consider the question of how to deliver effective 'restorative' practice, given that this has become something of a mantra in youth justice, the emphasis must be on the quality of the process rather than on meeting arbitrary and ultimately irrational targets. Interventions based on the principle of 'making good' are most likely to be effective when they have genuine meaning for offender, victim and other interests (Smith, R., 1985), and where the issues to be resolved are mutually agreed and clearly understood. In many cases, these conditions simply cannot be met, for example, where the young person's formal 'guilt' is mediated by a history of mutual hostility between different groupings within the community. This is not to say that broader conflict-resolution strategies might not be of value (perhaps *Romeo and Juliet* could have turned out differently), but that the constraints of the justice system do not easily lend themselves to dealing with ambiguity and unfinished business.

Contrived solutions are also often unsatisfactory for victims, as the initial evaluation of Referral Orders amply demonstrates (Newburn *et al.*, 2001). The position of 'corporate' (private or public sector) victims is also problematic, as is the perspective young people have of such victims.

Thus, for practitioners, the challenge is to think more widely and more creatively about how to achieve 'restoration' within the constraints of tightly prescribed parameters, such of those of Final Warnings, Reparation Orders, or the Referral Order. It seems clear that a consultative approach is important, which relies on both developing a clear understanding of participants' perspective on the offence, and the ideas young people themselves have about how to deal with the problems arising. Experience suggests that they often are remorseful, apologetic and willing to make amends, but that these responses cannot be extorted from them; it is a process of engagement and dialogue, which may, necessarily, take time.

Managing the system and problem-solving

While the introduction of a range of new orders appears to impose tighter constraints on both young people and professionals on the one hand, it also creates new opportunities for 'system management' (Smith, R., 2002a) on the other. The espousal of restorative principles also generates some support for an approach that is less tariff-based than in the past. The principle that sentences should be 'proportionate' (Youth Justice Board, 2000) also offers a rationale for promoting interventions that do not simply lead to increasingly intrusive or oppressive sentences at each successive court appearance. This is clearly a difficult position to sustain in a context in which the gradation of individuals takes such a prominent place in the machinery of youth justice (Foucault, 1979); which is at the same time a central pillar of sentencing policy (Home Office, 2001a; Home Office et al., 2002); and which ensures that young people progress ever more rapidly to the status of 'persistent young offender'. However, the fact that an increasing emphasis on resolving offences is apparent, at least at the level of rhetoric (Youth Justice Board, 2002), does provide some support for alternatives to the narrow, 'actuarial' approach based on principles of risk management, which pervades much of the youth justice system (Kempf-Leonard and Peterson, 2002). This adaptation of a problem-solving perspective would also help us to avoid the fatalistic assumption that the failure of any given intervention must inevitably speed the progression of young people towards the custodial institution.

Refocusing: welfare and rights

A strategy predicated on dealing with the issues underlying the offence also suggests an orientation to assessment, planning and intervention that is not driven by the spurious scientific accuracy offered by actuarial instruments such as the ASSET form (see Roberts et al., 2001). Rather, we should reassert the importance of 'causes', and at the same time reinsert a proper concern with the 'welfare' principles that have been crowded out of the youth justice system (Joint Chief Inspectors, 2002). We should also be driven by principles of 'justice' that take proper account of factors such as social inequality and discrimination. Bowling and Phillips (2002), for example, argue that to be genuinely equitable, interventions in youth justice must incorporate allowances for the institutional racism and disadvantage that results in a disproportionate number of young Black people being locked up. Legislative attempts to incorporate equalizing principles into the justice system (such as 'unit fines' under the Criminal Justice Act 1991) have not been particularly successful, but it remains open to practitioners and provider agencies to incorporate notions of social as well as criminal justice into their work.

In support of this, consideration should be given to bringing 'rights' more explicitly into the practice arena. As young people progress up the scale of disposals, they clearly become subject to progressively more intrusive interventions, not least because the armoury of methods of control has been substantially increased as a result of the New Labour reforms. To the extent that they also increase the risk of net-widening (and net-strengthening; Austin and Krisberg, 2002), clearly agencies and practitioners must be concerned with the legitimacy of such developments. For example, the certainty offered by the imposition of ever more stringent bail conditions, tags or curfews should not be gained at the expense of basic rights, especially at the pre-trial stage, where questions of guilt have yet to be determined. Home visits, for example, are a better, more natural, and less oppressive option than electronic tags, and they are certainly less likely to represent a breach of the UN Convention on the Rights of the Child, or the Human Rights Act 1998. It is in this sort of area of practice that the 'technologies of control' envisaged by Foucault (1979), Cohen (1985) and Garland (2001) threaten to run riot, leading to routinized oppression and, critically, undermining the establishment of effective and sensitive working relationships between young people, their families and youth justice professionals.

Messages from Elsewhere

Briefly, before concluding, it may also be fruitful to reflect on arrangements for the delivery of youth justice elsewhere than in England and Wales. Buckland and Stevens (2001) argue, for instance, that there are 'significant differences' in approach among European countries. These differences are to be found, it seems, at the level of purpose and philosophy, and at the level of practice. Some fundamental variations in orientation can be identified. France is held to be less inclined to use custody than England, and the Netherlands is particularly resistant to the idea of imprisonment (Christie, 2000). Pitts (2001b) explicitly contrasts the 'inclusive' philosophy informing youth crime policy and 'Specialised Prevention' in France, and what he calls the 'politics of blame' that inform New Labour's thinking. Spain and Belgium are identified as being strongly committed to 'welfare approaches' (Buckland and Stevens, 2001, p. 6). Diversion of children towards 'social welfare methods', as opposed to punishment, is held to be the preferred starting point for youth justice interventions in Sweden and Denmark. Interestingly, too, a commitment to 'diversion' appears much more explicit in the elaboration of strategy in Scotland than it is elsewhere in the UK (Scottish Executive, 2002b). A strong emphasis on consensual community-based interventions is apparent:

> We need youth justice teams to listen to the concerns of local communities to tackle youth crime and to work with communities to identify solutions to reduce crime and the fear of crime. All those who work with young people who offend will know that many young people can be diverted from crime if effective programmes are in place to tackle their behaviour.' (Jamieson, 2002).

Under the 'unique' non-criminal children's hearings system it has proved possible to establish a wide range of interventions to deal with youth offending outside the courts (Scottish Executive, 2002a). These schemes are able to involve young people in tackling offending behaviour, addressing the needs of victims, and promoting social inclusion. For example, 'The Compass Scheme in Dundee diverts young people who offend into local community sports and leisure pursuits. Of 148 referred to the scheme since 1999, 81% have stayed out of trouble.' (Scottish Executive, 2002b). Similarly, the Scottish model of intervention has been able to demonstrate a positive sense of engagement with victims. In relation to the SACRO (Scottish Association for the Care and Resettlement of Offenders) Fife Victim Mediation Scheme, 'independent evaluation' found that 'of 87 referred to the project, 62% were not referred to the Reporter[1] again during the following two months', and that 'victims generally felt that traditional approaches neglected them, whereas SACRO allowed them to become directly involved' (Scottish Executive, 2002b).

[1] All offences committed by children in Scotland are referred to the Reporter in the first instance, for a decisions on whether or not to make a referral to a Children's Hearing.

While we must not allow ourselves to become too idealistic about such alternative approaches (for example, the age of criminal responsibility in Scotland, at 8, is not acceptable; see UN Committee on the Rights of the Child, 2002), other countries are also able to demonstrate successful outcomes based on principles of diversion and informal offence resolution (Buckland and Stevens, 2001). These are evident in the experience of the HALT programme in the Netherlands, and the long-established Täter-Opfer Ausgleich projects in Germany. Typically, these schemes operate as alternatives to court hearings rather than as court-ordered interventions, particularly where the higher age of criminal responsibility precludes the possibility of judicial procedures. Evaluations of such initiatives appear to offer evidence of success on a number of conventional criteria, such as reduced re-offending rates, satisfactory programme compliance, victim satisfaction and reductions in the use of formal procedures and punishments (Buckland and Stevens, 2001). While cautionary notes may be sounded about the quality of evaluations carried out, and the transferability of lessons learned across international boundaries ('criminological tourism'), there is support here for the argument that perspectives from other cultures should be seen as both valid and of potential value in informing ideas, policy and practice at home.

Such ideas appear to offer international support for the principles of youth justice espoused in the present volume; however, it remains to be seen in the domestic context whether the political will to change can be found:

> Despite being a universal problem, policies and practices to deal with juvenile delinquency are related to the social, political, historical and cultural context of the countries in which they are located. This is therefore likely to impact upon the extent to which they can be transformed. (Buckland and Stevens, 2001, p. 6)

The suggestions offered here represent by no means an exhaustive list of the creative options for intervention in light of the clear need to 'refocus' youth justice practice. Nevertheless, the aim has been to generate some inspiration for reinventing the kind of strategy that worked so well in the 1980s. It is to be hoped that in the light of this experience we can once again establish the basis for restorative youth justice interventions that avoid punitive, oppressive and criminogenic outcomes as far as possible. It is true to say that this brief period of progressive achievement foundered on the rocks of political expediency and authoritarian populism; but this is a situation where it might very well be a good idea to 'reinvent the wheel'.

References

Abel, R. (1982) 'The Contradictions of Informal Justice' in R. Abel (ed.) *The Politics of Informal Justice*, Vol. 1, Academic Press, London, 267–320

Allan, R. (2001) 'Why ASSET Must Be a Real Asset for Yots', *Youth Justice Board News*, June, 3

Althusser, L. (1977) *Lenin and Philosophy and Other Essays*, NLB, London

Ashton, J. and Grindrod, M. (1999) 'Institutional Troubleshooting: Lessons for Policy and Practice' in B. Goldson (ed.) *Youth Justice: Contemporary Policy and Practice*, Ashgate, Aldershot, 170–90

Audit Commission (1996) *Misspent Youth*, Audit Commission, London

Audit Commission (2002) *Community Safety Partnerships: Learning from Audit, Inspection and Research*, The Stationery Office, London

Austin, J. and Krisberg, B. (2002) 'Wider, Stronger and Different Nets: The Dialectics of Criminal Justice Reform', in J. Muncie, G. Hughes and E. McLaughlin (eds) *Youth Justice: Critical Readings*, Sage, London, 258–74

Bailey, R. and Williams, B. (2000) *Inter-Agency Partnerships in Youth Justice: Implementing the Crime and Disorder Act 1998*, Joint Unit for Social Services Research, University of Sheffield

Barclay, G. and Mhlanga, B. (2000) *Ethnic Differences in Decisions on Young Defendants Dealt With by the Crown Prosecution Service*, Home Office, London

Beck, U. (1992) *Risk Society*, Sage, London

Becker, H. (1963) *The Outsiders*, Free Press, New York

Bell, A., Hodgson, M. and Pragnell, S. (1999) 'Diverting Children and Young People from Crime and the Criminal Justice System', in B. Goldson (ed.) *Youth Justice: Contemporary Police and Practice*, Ashgate, London, 91–109

Benedict, R. (1961) *Patterns of Culture*, Routledge, London

Bentley, M. (2000) 'An English Magistrate's View of Scottish Youth Justice' in

J. Pickford (ed.) *Youth Justice: Theory and Practice*, Cavendish Publishing, London, 189–216

Blagg, H. (1985) 'Reparation and Justice for Juveniles', *British Journal of Criminology*, 25, 267–79

Blagg, H., Derricourt, N., Finch, J. and Thorpe, D. (1986) *The Final Report on the Juvenile Liaison Bureau Corby*, University of Lancaster, Lancaster

Blair, T. (2002) 'Rebalancing of Criminal Justice System' speech, 18 June

Blunkett, D. (2002) 'Statement on Street Crime', March 20

Bottoms, A. (1995) *Intensive Community Supervision of Young Offenders: Outcomes, Process and Cost*, University of Cambridge Institute of Criminology, Cambridge

Bottoms, A., Brown, P., McWilliams, B., McWilliams, W. and Nellis, M. (1990) *Intermediate Treatment and Juvenile Justice*, London, HMSO

Bowling, B. and Phillips, C. (2002) *Racism, Crime and Justice*, Longman, Harlow

Bright, M. (2002) 'Suicide Fear for Teen Victims of Blunkett's Get-Tough Rules', the *Observer*, 7 July, 12

Britton, N. (2000) *Black Justice? Race, Criminal Justice and Identity*, Trentham Books, Stoke-on-Trent

Brown, S. (1998) *Understanding Youth and Crime*, Open University Press, Buckingham

Buckland, G. and Stevens, A. (2001) *Review of Effective Practice with Young Offenders in Mainland Europe*, European Institute of Social Services, Canterbury

Budd, T. and Sims, L. (2001) *Antisocial Behaviour and Disorder: Findings from the 2000 British Crime Survey*, Home Office, London

Charman, J. and Savage, S. (1999) 'The New Politics of Law and Order: Labour, Crime and Justice' in M. Powell (ed.) *New Labour, New Welfare State?*, Policy Press, Bristol, 191–212

Cheetham, J. (1985) 'Juvenile Offenders and Alternatives to Custody in Northamptonshire: The Views of Magistrates and Social Workers', unpublished

Children and Young People's Unit (2001) *Building a Strategy for Children and Young People*, Children and Young People's Unit, London

Children and Young People's Unit (2002) *Children's Fund*, www.cypu.gov.uk/corporate/childrensfund/ontrack.cfm

Children's Society, The (1988) *The Line of Least Resistance*, The Children's Society, London

Children's Society, The (1992) *Education for Citizenship: A Schools' Pack*, The Children's Society, London

Children's Society, The (1993) *A False Sense of Security*, The Children's Society, London

Christie, N. (2000) *Crime Control as Industry*, Routledge, London

Clancy, A., Hough, M., Aust, R. and Kershaw, C. (2001) *Ethnic Minorities' Experience of Crime and Policing: Findings from the 2000 British Crime Survey*, Home Office, London

Clark, T. (2002) 'New Labour's Big Idea: Joined-up Government', *Social Policy & Society*, 12, 107–17

Clarke, J. (2002) 'Whose Justice? The Politics of Juvenile Control' in J. Muncie, G. Hughes and E. McLaughlin (eds) *Youth Justice: Critical Readings*, Sage, London, 284–95

Clarke, J., Gewirtz, S. and McLaughlin, E. (eds) (2000) *New Managerialism, New Welfare?* Sage, London

Cohen, S. (1972) *Folk Devils and Moral Panics*, Paladin, London

Cohen, S. (1985) *Visions of Social Control*, Polity Press, Cambridge

Corrigan, P. (1979) *Schooling the Smash Street Kids*, Macmillan, London

Corrigan, P. and Leonard, P. (1978) *Social Work Practice under Capitalism: A Marxist Approach*, Macmillan, London

Craine, S. (1997) 'The "Black Magic Roundabout": Cyclical Transitions, Social Exclusion and Alternative Careers' in R. MacDonald (ed.) *Youth, the 'Underclass' and Social Exclusion*, Routledge, London, 130–52

Crime Concern (2001) *Reducing Neighbourhood Crime*, Crime Concern, Swindon

Davies, B. (1986) *Threatening Youth*, Open University Press, Milton Keynes

Davis, G., Boucherat, J. and Watson, D. (1988) 'Reparation in the Service of Diversion: The Subordination of a Good Idea', *British Journal of Criminology*, 27, 127–34

Davis, G., Boucherat, J. and Watson, D. (1989) 'Pre-court Decision-making in Juvenile Justice', *British Journal of Criminology*, 29, 219–35

Department of Health (2000) *Framework for the Assessment of Children in Need and Their Families*, The Stationery Office, London

Department of Health and Social Security (1983) 'Further Development of Intermediate Treatment', *Local Authority Circular*, 83 (3), DHSS, London

Dignan, J. (1992) 'Repairing the Damage: Can Reparation Work in the Service of Diversion?', *British Journal of Criminology*, 32, 453–72

Dominelli, L. (1998) 'Anti-oppressive Practice in Context' in R. Adams, L. Dominelli and M. Payne (eds) *Social Work: Themes, Issues and Critical Debates*, Macmillan, Basingstoke, 3–22

Donzelot, J. (1979) *The Policing of Families*, Johns Hopkins University Press, Baltimore

Drakeford, M. and McCarthy, K. (2000) 'Parents, Responsibility and the New Youth Justice' in B. Goldson (ed.) *The New Youth Justice*, Russell House, Lyme Regis, 96–114

Eadie, T. and Canton, R. (2002) 'Practising in a Context of Ambivalence: The Challenge for Youth Justice Workers', *Youth Justice*, 2(1), 14–26

Earle, R. and Newburn, T. (2002) 'Creative Tensions? Young Offenders, Restorative Justice and the Introduction of Referral Orders', *Youth Justice*, 1(3), 3–13

East, K. and Campbell, S. (2000) *Aspects of Crime: Young Offenders 1999*, Home Office, London

Eccles, P. (2001) 'Youth Inclusion – the Programme Most Likely?', discussion paper, University of Huddersfield, Huddersfield

Ernst & Young (1999) *Reducing Delay in the Criminal Justice System: Evaluation of the Pilot Schemes*, Home Office, London

Erikson, E. (1995) *Childhood and Society*, Vintage, London

Esping-Andersen, G. (1990) *The Three Worlds of Welfare Capitalism*, Polity Press, Oxford

Evans, R. and Ellis, R. (1997) *Police Cautioning in the 1990s*, Home Office, London

Everitt, A. and Hardiker, P. (1996) *Evaluating for Good Practice*, Macmillan, London

Farrington, D. (1996) *Understanding and Preventing Youth Crime*, Joseph Rowntree Foundation, York

Farrington, D., Ditchfield, J., Hancock, G., Howard, P., Jolliffe, D., Livingston, M. and Painter, K. (2002) *Evaluation of Two Intensive Regimes for Young Offenders*, Home Office, London

Foucault, M. (1979) *Discipline and Punish*, Peregrine, Harmondsworth

Foucault, M. (1981) *The History of Sexuality*, Vol 1, *The Will to Knowledge*, Pelican, London

Fox Harding, L. (1997) *Perspectives in Child Care Policy*, 2nd edition, Longman, Harlow

France, A. and Crow. I. (2001) *CTC – the story so far*, Joseph Rowntree Foundation, York

Gamble, A. (1988) *The Free Economy and the Strong State*, Macmillan, Basingstoke

Garland, D. (1990) *Punishment and Modern Society*, Clarendon Press, Oxford

Garland, D. (2001) *The Culture of Control*, Oxford University Press, Oxford

Gelsthorpe, L. and Morris, A. (2002) 'Restorative Youth Justice: The Last Vestiges of Welfare?' in J. Muncie, G. Hughes and E. McLaughlin (eds) *Youth Justice: Critical Readings*, Sage, London, 238–53

George, V. and Wilding, P. (1999) *British Society and Social Welfare: Towards a Sustainable Society*, Macmillan, Basingstoke

Giddens, A. (1991) *Modernity and Self-Identity*, Polity, Cambridge

Gilroy, P. (2002) 'Lesser Breeds Without the Law' in J. Muncie, G. Hughes and E. McLaughlin (eds) *Youth Justice: Critical Readings*, Sage, London, 50–67

Goldblatt, P. and Lewis, C. (eds) *Reducing Offending: An Assessment of Research Evidence on Ways of Dealing with Offending Behaviour*, Home Office, London

Goldson, B. (1997) 'Children, Crime, Policy and Practice: Neither Welfare nor Justice' *Children & Society*, 11, 77–88

Goldson, B. (1999) 'Youth (In)Justice: Contemporary Developments in Policy and Practice' in B. Goldson (ed.) *Youth Justice: Contemporary Policy and Practice*, Ashgate, Aldershot, 1–28

Goldson, B. (ed.) (2000) *The New Youth Justice*, Russell House, Lyme Regis

Goldson, B. (2000) 'Wither Diversion? Interventionism and the New Youth Justice' in B. Goldson (ed.) *The New Youth Justice*, Russell House, Lyme Regis, 33–57

Goldson, B. (2002) *Vulnerable Inside*, The Children's Society, London

Goldson, B. and Chigwada-Bailey, R. (1999) '(What) Justice for Black Children and Young People?' in B. Goldson (ed.) *Youth Justice: Contemporary Policy and Practice*, Ashgate, Aldershot, 51–74

Goldson, B. and Peters, E. (2000) *Tough Justice: Responding to Children in Trouble*, The Children's Society, London

Gordon, P. (1983) *White Law: Racism in the Police, Courts and Prisons*, Pluto Press, London

Graham, J. and Bowling, B. (1995) *Young People and Crime*, Home Office, London

Gramsci, A. (1971) *Selections from Prison Notebooks*, Lawrence and Wishart, London

Greater Manchester Police Authority (2002) *Consultation for Best Value: Young People*, www.gmpa.gov.uk/consultation/young_people.htm

Haines, K. (2000) 'Referral Orders and Youth Offender Panels: Restorative Approaches and the New Youth Justice' in B. Goldson (ed.) *The New Youth Justice*, Russell House, Lyme Regis, 58–80

Haines, K. and Drakeford, M. (1998) *Young People and Youth Justice*, Macmillan, London

Hall, S., Critcher, C., Jefferson, T., Clarke, J. and Roberts, B. (1978) *Policing the Crisis: Mugging, the State and Law and Order*, Macmillan, Basingstoke

Hancock, L. (2001) *Community, Crime and Disorder: Safety and Regeneration in Urban Neighbourhoods*, Palgrave, Basingstoke

Harris, R. and Webb, D. (1987) *Welfare, Power & Juvenile Justice*, Tavistock, London

Hearne, B. (2003) Speech to Nacro Annual Conference, Loughborough, April 10

Hine, J. and Celnick, A. (2001) *A One Year Reconviction Study of Final Warnings*, University of Sheffield, Sheffield

Hinks, N. and Sloper, G. (1984) 'How to Divert in Practice' in H. Fox and R. Williams (eds) *Diversion – Corporate Action with Juveniles*, Northamptonshire County Council, Northampton, 30–34

HM Chief Inspector of Prisons (2001) *Annual Report 1999–2000*, The Stationery Office, London

HM Chief Inspector of Prisons (2002) 'Preface' in *Report on an Unannounced Follow-up Inspection of HM Prison Eastwood Park*, HM Inspectorate of Prisons, London, 2–5

Holdaway, S., Davidson, N., Dignan, J., Hammersley, R., Hine, J. and Marsh, P. (2001) *New Strategies to Address Youth Offending: The National Evaluation of the Pilot Youth Offending Teams*, Home Office, London

Home Affairs Committee (1993) *Juvenile Offenders*, HMSO, London

Home Office (1968) *Children in Trouble*, HMSO, London

Home Office (1981) *Young Offenders*, HMSO, London

Home Office (1984) *Cautioning by the Police: A Consultative Document*, Home Office, London

Home Office (1985) 'The Cautioning of Offenders', *Home Office Circular 14/1985*, Home Office, London

Home Office (1988) *Punishment, Custody and the Community*, HMSO, London

Home Office (1990a) 'The Cautioning of Offenders', *Home Office Circular, 59/1990*, Home Office, London

Home Office (1990b) *Crime, Justice and Protecting the Public*, HMSO, London

Home Office (1992) *National Standards for the Supervision of Offenders in the Community*, Home Office, London

Home Office (1994) 'The Cautioning of Offenders' *Home Office Circular 18/94*, Home Office, London

Home Office (1995) *Strengthening Punishment in the Community*, HMSO, London

Home Office (1997a) *Consultation Paper: Tackling Youth Crime*, Home Office, London

Home Office (1997b) *No More Excuses*, Cm 3809, Home Office, London

Home Office (2000) *Crime and Disorder Act 1998 – Community-Based Orders*, Home Office, London

Home Office (2001a) *Criminal Justice: The Way Ahead*, Cm 5074, Home Office, London

Home Office (2001b) *Criminal Statistics England and Wales 2000*, The Stationery Office, London

Home Office (2001c) *Establishing Referral Order Schemes: A Guidance Note for Youth Offending Teams*, Home Office, London

Home Office (2002a) *Criminal Justice and Police Act 2001: Electronic Monitoring of 12–16 Year Olds on Bail and on Remand to Local Authority Accommodation*, Home Office, London

Home Office (2002b) *Criminal Justice and Police Act 2001: Section 130 Guidance – Secure Remands*, Home Office, London

Home Office (2002c) *Race and the Criminal Justice System*, Home Office, London

Home Office (2003) *Respect and Responsibility*, Home Office, London

Home Office, Department of Health, Department for Education and Employment, and Welsh Office (1998) *Establishing Youth Offending Teams*, Home Office, London

Home Office, Lord Chancellor's Department, Attorney General's Office (2002) *Justice for All*, Cm 5563, The Stationery Office, London

Hope, T. (1998) 'Community Crime Prevention' in P. Goldblatt and C. Lewis (eds) *Reducing Offending: An Assessment of Research Evidence on Ways of Dealing with Offending Behaviour*, Home Office, London, 51–62

Hough, M. and Mayhew, P. (1985) *Taking Account of Crime: Key Findings from the 1984 British Crime Survey*, Home Office, London

Hough, M. and Roberts, J. (1998) *Attitudes to Punishment: Findings from the British Crime Survey*, Home Office, London

Hoyle, C. (2002) 'Securing Restorative Justice for 'Non-Participating' Victims' in C. Hoyle and R. Young (eds) *New Visions of Crime Victims*, Hart, Oxford, 97–128

Howard, M. (1995) Speech to Conservative Party Conference

Howard League (2002) *Children in Prison: Provision and Practice at Ashfield*, The Howard League for Penal Reform, London

Hudson, B. (1987) *Justice through Punishment*, Macmillan, Basingstoke

Hudson, B. (1996) *Understanding Justice*, Open University Press, Buckingham

Ignatieff, M. (1985) 'State, Civil Society and Total Institutions: A Critique of recent Social Histories of Punishment' in S. Cohen and A. Scull (eds) *Social Control and the State*, Blackwell, Oxford, 75–105

Jackson, S. (1999) 'Family Group Conferences and Youth Justice: The New Panacea?' in B. Goldson (ed.) *Youth Justice: Contemporary Policy and Practice*, Ashgate, Aldershot, 127–47

Jamieson, C. (2002) 'Youth Justice in Scotland: A Progress Report for All Those Working for Young People', www.scotland.gov.uk/library5/justice/tycs-oo.asp

Jeffs, T. (1997) 'Changing Their Ways: Youth Work and 'Underclass' Theory' in R. MacDonald (ed.) *Youth, the 'Underclass' and Social Exclusion*, Routledge, London, 153–66

Jenks, C. (1996) *Childhood*, Routledge, London

Jennings, D. (2002) *One Year Juvenile Reconviction Rates: July 2000 Cohort*, Home Office, London

Jennings, D. (2003) *One Year Juvenile Reconviction Rates: first quarter of 2001, Cohout*, Home Office, London

Johnson, K. and colleagues (2001) *Cautions, Court Proceedings and Sentencing*, Home Office, London

Johnstone, G. (2002) *Restorative Justice: Ideas, Values, Debates*, Willan, Cullompton

Joint Chief Inspectors (2002), *Safeguarding Children*, Department of Health, London

Jones, D. (2001) 'Questioning New Labour's Youth Justice Strategy: A Review Article', *Youth Justice*, 1(3), 14–26

Kelling, G. (1998) 'The Evolution of Broken Windows' in M. Weatheritt (ed.) *Zero Tolerance Policing*, The Police Foundation, London

Kemp, V., Sorsby, A., Liddle, M. and Merrington. S. (2002) 'Assessing Responses to Youth Offending in Northamptonshire', *Nacro Research Briefing*, 2 September, Nacro, London

Kempf-Leonard, K. and Peterson, E. (2002) 'Expanding the Realms of the New Penology: The Advent of Actuarial Justice for Juveniles' in J. Muncie, G. Hughes and E. McLaughlin (eds) *Youth Justice: Critical Readings*, Sage, London, 431–50

Kershaw, C., Chivite-Matthews, N., Thomas, C. and Aust, R. (2001) *The 2001 British Crime Survey: First Results, England and Wales*, Home Office, London

Kinsey, R., Lea, J. and Young, J. (1986) *Losing the Fight against Crime*, Blackwell, Oxford

Kuhn, T. (1970) *The Structure of Scientific Revolutions*, University of Chicago Press, Chicago

Landau, S. and Nathan, G. (1983) 'Selecting Delinquents for Cautioning in the London Metropolitan Area', *British Journal of Criminology*, 23, 128–49

Lea, J. (2002) *Crime and Modernity*, Sage, London

Lea, J. and Young, J. (1984) *What is to Be Done about Law and Order?*, Penguin, Harmondsworth

Leicester Youth Offending Team (2001) *Leicester Youth Justice Plan 2001–02*, Leicester City Council, Leicester

Leonard, P. (1984) *Personality and Ideology*, Macmillan, London

Loxley, C., Curtin, L. and Brown, R. (2002) *Summer Splash Schemes 2000: Findings from Six Case Studies*, Home Office, London

Lyon, J., Denison, C. and Wilson, A. (2000) *'Tell Them So They Listen': Messages from Young People in Custody*, Home Office, London

MacDonald, R. (1997) 'Youth, Social Exclusion and the New Millenium' in R. MacDonald (ed.) *Youth, the 'Underclass' and Social Exclusion*, Routledge, London, 167–97

McLaughlin, E. and Muncie, J. (2000) 'The Criminal Justice System: New Labour's New Partnerships' in J. Clarke, S. Gewirtz and E. McLaughlin (eds) *New Managerialism, New Welfare?*, Sage, London, 169–85

Macmillan, J. (1998) 'In Whose Interests? Politics and Policy' in S. Brown *Understanding Youth and Crime*, Open University Press, Buckingham, 53–78

Macpherson, W. (1999) *The Stephen Lawrence Inquiry*, Cm 4262–1, The Stationery Office, London

McRobbie, A. and Thornton, S. (2002) 'Rethinking Moral Panic for Multi-mediated Social Worlds' in J. Muncie, G. Hughes and E. McLaughlin (eds) *Youth Justice: Critical Readings*, Sage, London, 68–79

Maguire, M. and Maguire, S. (1997) 'Young people and the labour market' in R. MacDonald (ed.) *Youth, the 'Underclass' and Social Exclusion*, Routledge, 26–38

Mattinson, J. and Mirrlees-Black, C. (2000) *Attitudes to Crime and Criminal Justice: Findings from the 1998 British Crime Survey*, Home Office, London

Matza, D. (1964) *Delinquency and Drift*, Wiley, New York

Merton, R. (1957) *Social Theory and Social Structure*, Free Press, Glencoe

Ministère de la Justice (2001) *La Justice des mineurs*, Ministère de la Justice, Paris

Mirrlees-Black, C. and Allen, J. (1998) *Concern about Crime: Findings from the 1998 British Crime Survey*, Home Office, London

Mirrlees-Black, C., Budd, T., Partridge, S. and Mayhew, P. (1998) *The 1998 British Crime Survey: England and Wales*, Home Office, London

Moore, S. and Smith, R. (2001) *The Pre-Trial Guide*, The Children's Society, London

Morgan Harris Burrows (2001) *Youth Inclusion Programme: Evaluation Overview*, unpublished

MORI (2001) *Rethinking Crime and Punishment Survey*, MORI, London

MORI (2002) *Youth Survey 2002*, Youth Justice Board, London

Morris, A., Giller, H., Geach, H. and Szwed, E. (1980) *Justice for Children*, Macmillan, London

Muncie, J. (1999) *Youth and Crime: A Critical Introduction*, Sage, London

Muncie, J. (2000) 'Pragmatic Realism? Searching for Criminology in the New Youth Justice' in B. Goldson (ed.) *The New Youth Justice*, Russell House, Lyme Regis, 14–34

Muncie, J. (2001) 'Policy Transfers and 'What Works': Some Reflections on Comparative Youth Justice', *Youth Justice*, 1(3), 27–35

Muncie, J. and Hughes, G. (2002) 'Modes of Youth Governance: Political Rationalities, Criminalisation and Resistance' in J. Muncie, G. Hughes and E. McLaughlin (eds) *Youth Justice: Critical Readings*, Sage, London, 1–18

Muncie, J., Hughes, G. and McLaughlin, E. (eds) (2002) *Youth Justice: Critical Readings*, Sage, London

Nacro [National Association for the Care and Resettlement of Offenders] (1987) *Time for Change: A New Framework for Dealing with Juvenile Crime and Offenders*, Nacro, London

Nacro [National Association for the Care and Resettlement of Offenders] (2001) *Lessons from Pilots: A Summary of the National Evaluation of the Pilot Youth Offending Teams*, Nacro, London

National Assembly for Wales (2000) Extending Entitlement, National Assembly for Wales, Cardiff

National Association for Youth Justice (2001) 'Remands to Local Authority Accommodation with a Security Requirement and Placement in the Ex-Secure Training Centres (per S133 Criminal Justice & Police Act 2001) – A Position Statement from the National Association for Youth Justice', NAYJ, Leicester

National Association for Youth Justice (2002a) *Manifesto for Youth Justice*, www.nayj.org.uk/manifesto.html

National Association for Youth Justice (2002b) *Working with Children in Trouble: The Philosophical Base*, www.nayj.org.uk/philosph.htm

National Association for Youth Justice (2003) *Criminal Justice Bill: Initial Appraisal of Youth Justice Aspects*, NAYJ, Leicester

Newburn, T. and Jones, T. (2001) '"Policy Transfer" and Crime Control: Some Reflections on "Zero Tolerance"', Paper to the Annual Meeting of the American Political Science Association, San Francisco, September

Newburn, T., Masters, G., Earle, R., Goldie, S., Crawford, A., Sharpe, K., Netten, A., Hale, C., Uglow, S. and Saunders, R. (2001a) *The Introduction of Referral Orders into the Youth Justice System: First Interim Report*, Home Office, London

Newburn, T., Earle, R., Goldie, S., Campbell, A., Masters, G., Crawford, A., Sharpe, K., Hale, C., Saunders, R., Uglow, S. and Netten, A. (2001b) *The Introduction of Referral Orders into the Youth Justice System: Second Interim Report*, Home Office, London

Newburn, T., Crawford, A., Earle, R., Goldie, S., Hale, C., Hallam, A., Masters, G., Netten, A., Saunders, R., Sharpe, K. and Uglow, S. (2002) *The Introduction of Referral Orders into the Youth Justice System: Final Report*, Home Office, London

Northamptonshire Youth Offending Team (2001) *Northamptonshire Youth Justice Plan 2001–01*, Northamptonshire County Council, Northampton

PA Consulting (2002) *Reducing Delays*, www.reducing-delays.org

Parker, H. (1974) *A View from the Boys*, David & Charles, Newton Abbott

Patten, J. (1988) Speech to conference, 'Juvenile Justice – Diversion from Custody', London, 18 March

Pearson, G. (1983) *Hooligan: A History of Respectable Fears*, Macmillan, Basingstoke

Percy, A. (1998) *Ethnicity and Victimisation: Findings from the 1996 British Crime Survey*, Home Office, London

Percy-Smith, J. (2000) 'Introduction: The Contours of Social Exclusion' in J. Percy-Smith (ed.) *Policy Responses to Social Exclusion*, Open University Press, Milton Keynes, 1–21

Pickford, J. (2000) 'Introduction: A New Youth Justice for a New Century' in J. Pickford (ed.) *Youth Justice: Theory and Practice*, Cavendish, London, xxi–lx

Pitts, J. (1988) *The Politics of Juvenile Crime*, Sage, London

Pitts, J. (1999) *Working with Young Offenders*, 2nd edition, Macmillan, Basingstoke

Pitts, J. (2000) 'The New Youth Justice and the Politics of Electoral Anxiety' in B. Goldson (ed.) *The New Youth Justice*, Russell House, Lyme Regis, 1–13

Pitts, J. (2001a) 'Korrectional Karaoke: New Labour and the Zombification of Youth Justice', *Youth Justice*, 1(2), 3–16

Pitts, J. (2001b) *The New Politics of Youth Crime*, Palgrave, Basingstoke

Pitts, J. (2002) 'Amnesia and Discontinuity', Speech to National Association of Youth Justice Conference, Milton Keynes, 14 June

Pitts, J. (2003) Speech to Nacro Annual Conference, Loughborough, April 10

Poulantzas, N. (1978) *Political Power and Social Classes*, Verso, London

Pragnell, S. (2001) 'Report to Northamptonshire Youth Offending Team Steering Group', unpublished

Pratt, J. (1989) 'Corporatism: The Third Model of Juvenile Justice', *British Journal of Criminology*, 29, 236–54

Pratt, J. (2000) 'The Return of the Wheelbarrow Men; or, The Arrival of Postmodern Penality?', *British Journal of Criminology*, 40, 127–45

Pratt, J. (2002) 'Corporatism: The Third Model of Juvenile Justice' in J. Muncie, G. Hughes and E. McLaughlin (eds) *Youth Justice: Critical Readings*, Sage, London, 404–12

Reynolds, F. (1985) 'Juvenile Offending in Northamptonshire 1982–3', unpublished

Roberts, C., Baker, K., Merrington, S. and Jones, S. (2001) *Validity and Reliability of ASSET: Interim Report to the Youth Justice Board*, Centre for Criminological Research, Oxford

Rock, P. (2002) 'On Becoming a Victim' in C. Hoyle and R. Young (eds) *New Visions of Crime Victims*, Hart, Oxford, 1–21

Rutherford, A. (1992) *Growing Out of Crime: The New Era*, Waterside Press, Winchester

Rutherford, A. (1996) *Transforming Criminal Policy*, Waterside Press, Winchester

Rutter, M., Giller, H. and Hagell, A. (1998) *Antisocial Behaviour by Young People*, Fields Press, Manchester

Salford Youth Offending Team (2001) *Salford Youth Justice Plan 2001–02*, Salford City Council, Salford

Saini, A. (1997) *'So What's the Point of Telling Anyone?'*, De Montfort University, Leicester

Scarman, L. (1982) *The Scarman Report*, Penguin, Harmondsworth

Schur, E. (1973) *Radical Non-Intervention*, Prentice-Hall, Englewood Cliffs, New Jersey

Scottish Executive (2002a) 'Tackling Youth Crime in Scotland', www.scotland.gov.uk/library5/justice/tycs-00.asp

Scottish Executive (2002b) 'Executive's Youth Crime Review', www.scotland.gov.uk/pages/news/extras/00008300.aspx

Scraton, P. and Haydon, D. (2002) 'Challenging the Criminalisation of Children and Young People: Securing a Rights-based Agenda' in J. Muncie, G. Hughes and E. McLaughlin (eds) *Youth Justice: Critical Readings*, Sage, London, 311–28

Shapland, J., Johnstone, J., Sorsby, A., Stubbing, T., Jackson, J., Hibbert, J. and Howes, M. (2001) *Evaluation of Statutory Time Limit Pilot Schemes in the Youth Court*, University of Sheffield, Sheffield

Simes, J. and Chads, K. (2002) *Prison Population Brief England and Wales: May 2002*, Home Office, London

Smith, D. (1999) 'Social Work with Young People in Trouble: Memory and Prospect' in B. Goldson (ed.) *Youth Justice: Contemporary Policy and Practice*, Ashgate, Aldershot, 148–69

Smith, D. (2000) 'Corporatism and the New Youth Justice' in B. Goldson (ed.) *The New Youth Justice*, Russell House, Lyme Regis, 129–43

Smith, D., McVie, S., Woodward, R., Shute, J., Flint, J. and McAra, L. (2001) *The Edinburgh Study of Youth Transitions and Crime: Key Findings at Ages 12 and 13*, University of Edinburgh, Edinburgh

Smith, R. (1985) 'The Catch-all Term of Reparation', *Community Care*, 25 July, 8

Smith, R. (1987) 'The Practice of Diversion', *Youth and Policy*, 19, 10–14

Smith, R. (1989) *Diversion in Practice*, MPhil thesis, University of Leicester, Leicester

Smith, R. (1995) 'Margaret Thatcher: Soft on Crime', unpublished

Smith, R. (2000) 'Order and Disorder: the Contradictions of Childhood', *Children & Society*, 14, 3–10

Smith, R. (2001) 'Foucault's Law: The Crime and Disorder Act 1998', *Youth Justice* 1(2), 17–29

Smith, R. (2002a) 'Evaluation of Northampton Youth Offending Team, unpublished

Smith, R. (2002b) 'Relearning Old Lessons: Diversion and Restorative Justice', paper to Effective Restorative Justice Conference, De Montfort University, Leicester, 20 March

Smith, R. (2002c) 'Globalisation, Individualisation and Childhood: The Challenge for Social Work', paper to Congress of the International Association of Schools of Social Work, Montpellier, 16 July

Smith, R. (2002d) 'The Wrong End of the Telescope: Child Protection or Child Safety?', *Journal of Social Welfare and Family Law*, 24(3), 247–61

Social Exclusion Unit (1998) *Bringing Britain Together: A National Strategy for Neighbourhood Renewal*, The Stationery Office, London

Social Exclusion Unit (1999a) *Bridging the Gap*, The Stationery Office, London

Social Exclusion Unit (1999b) *Teenage Pregnancy*, The Stationery Office, London

Social Exclusion Unit (2000) *The Social Exclusion Unit Leaflet*, Cabinet Office, London

Social Exclusion Unit (2001) *Preventing Social Exclusion*, The Stationery Office, London

Social Exclusion Unit (2002) *Reducing Re-offending by Ex-Prisoners*, The Stationery Office, London

Soothill, K., Francis, B. and Fligelstone, R. (2002) *Patterns of Offending Behaviour: A New Approach*, Home Office, London

Stevens, M. and Crook, J. (1986) 'What the Devil is Intermediate Treatment?', *Social Work Today*, 18(2), 10–11

Strang, H. and Braithwaite, J. (eds) (2001) *Restorative Justice and Civil Society*, Cambridge University Press, Cambridge

Straw, J. (1995) 'Straw and Order', *New Statesman*, 15 September

Straw, J. and Michael, A. (1996) *Tackling the Causes of Crime: Labour's Proposals to Prevent Crime and Criminality*, Labour Party, London

Sure Start (2000) *What is Sure Start?*, Sure Start, London

Tarling, R., Burrows, J., and Clarke, A. (2001) *Dalston Youth Project Part II (11–14): An Evaluation*, Home Office, London

Taylor, I. (1981) *Law and Order: Arguments for Socialism*, Macmillan, London

Thompson, R., Holland, J., Henderson, S., McGrellis, S. and Sharpe, S. (1999) *Youth Values: A Study of Identity, Diversity and Social Change*, South Bank University, London

Thornton, D., Curran, C., Grayson, D. and Holloway, V. (1984) *Tougher Regimes in Detention Centres*, HMSO, London

Thorpe, D. (1984) 'Does the Northamptonshire Model Work? – Some Preliminary Results' in H. Fox and R. Williams (eds) *Diversion – Corporate Action with Juveniles*, Northamptonshire County Council, Northampton, 40–42

Thorpe, D., Smith, D., Green, C. and Paley, J. (1980) *Out of Care*, Allen and Unwin, London

Travis, A. (2002) 'Youth Jail Taken off the Critical List', the *Guardian*, 15 October

United Nations (1985) *The United Nations Standard Minimum Rules for the Administration of Juvenile Justice (Beijing Rules)*, United Nations, Geneva

United Nations (1989) *Convention on the Rights of the Child*, United Nations, Geneva

United Nations Committee on the Rights of the Child (2002) *Concluding Observations of the Committee on the Rights of the Child: United Kingdom of Great Britain and Northern Ireland*, Geneva

Walsh, C. (2002) 'No More Hanging Around', *Youth Justice*, 2(2), 70–81

Warner, N. (2001) 'Foreword' in Youth Justice Board *The Preliminary Report on the Operation of the New Youth Justice System*, Youth Justice Board, London

Weber, M. (1957) *The Theory of Social and Economic Organisation*, The Free Press, Glencoe

White, M. (2002) 'Anti-crime Plan for Urban Youth Under Threat', the *Guardian*, 16 August

Whyte, B. (2000) 'Youth Justice in Scotland' in J. Pickford (ed.) *Youth Justice: Theory and Practice*, Cavendish, London, 169–88

Williams, B. (1997) *Working with Victims of Crime: Policies, Politics and Practice*, Jessica Kingsley, London

Williams, B. (2000) 'Victims of Crime and the New Youth Justice' in B. Goldson (ed.) *The New Youth Justice*, Russell House, Lyme Regis, 176–92

Willis, P. (1977) *Learning to Labour*, Saxon House, Farnborough

Willow, C. (1999) *It's Not Fair*, The Children's Society, London

Woolf, Lord (2002) *Letter to Circuit Judges and Chairmen of Magistrates' Benches*, 23 December

Worrall, A. (1999) 'Troubled or Troublesome? Justice for Girls and Young Women' in B. Goldson (ed.) *Youth Justice: Contemporary Policy and Practice*, Ashgate, Aldershot, 28–50

Young, R. (2002) 'Testing the Limits of Restorative Justice: The Case of Corporate Victims' in C. Hoyle and R. Young (eds) *New Visions of Crime Victims*, Hart, Oxford, 133–71

Youth Justice Board (1999) *Speeding up Youth Justice*, Youth Justice Board, London

Youth Justice Board (2000) *National Standards for Youth Justice*, Youth Justice Board, London

Youth Justice Board (2001a) *Youth Justice Board for England and Wales Corporate Plan 2001–02 to 2003–04 and Business Plan 2001–02*, Youth Justice Board, London

Youth Justice Board (2001b) *Youth Justice Board Review 2000/2001: Delivering Change*, Youth Justice Board, London

Youth Justice Board (2001c) *The Preliminary Report on the Operation of the New Youth Justice System*, Youth Justice Board, London

Youth Justice Board (2002) *Youth Justice Board Review 2001/02: Building on Success*, Youth Justice Board, London

Youth Justice Board (undated) *ASSET Assessment Profile*, Youth Justice Board, London

Index